TAKING BACK
THE
BOARDROOM

Thriving as a 21st-Century Director

2nd Edition

TAKING BACK
THE
BOARDROOM

Thriving as a 21st-Century Director

2nd Edition

PHILLIP H. PHAN

Rensselaer Polytechnic Institute, USA

Imperial College Press

Published by

Imperial College Press
57 Shelton Street
Covent Garden
London WC2H 9HE

Distributed by

World Scientific Publishing Co. Pte. Ltd.
5 Toh Tuck Link, Singapore 596224
USA office: 27 Warren Street, Suite 401-402, Hackensack, NJ 07601
UK office: 57 Shelton Street, Covent Garden, London WC2H 9HE

British Library Cataloguing-in-Publication Data
A catalogue record for this book is available from the British Library.

TAKING BACK THE BOARDROOM
Thriving as a 21st-Century Director — 2nd Edition

ISBN-13 978-1-86094-836-7
ISBN-10 1-86094-836-7

Typeset by Stallion Press
Email: enquiries@stallionpress.com

Printed in Singapore by World Scientific Printers (S) Pte Ltd

One key element in improving economic efficiency is corporate governance, which involves a set of relationships between a company's management, its board, its shareholders and other stakeholders. Corporate governance also provides the structure through which the objectives of the company are set, and the means of attaining those objectives and monitoring performance are determined. Good corporate governance should provide proper incentives for the board and management to pursue objectives that are in the interests of the company and shareholders and should facilitate effective monitoring, thereby encouraging firms to use resources more efficiently.

OECD DIRECTORATE FOR FINANCIAL,
FISCAL AND ENTERPRISE AFFAIRS
Ad Hoc Task Force on Corporate Governance

Preface

Since the writing of the first edition of this book, the corporate world has experienced the implosion of the Internet boom with losses exceeded US$1 trillion in market values, the fraud-driven collapse of Enron, Worldcom, and Adelphia, a massive investigation on stock option backdating practices engulfing more than 350 corporations including many in the Fortune 500, the collapse of the Thai government triggered by the business dealings of the former prime minister, and ongoing revelations of ethical lapses in such media conglomerates as Hollinger, and technology giants as Siemens. Mismanagement at large corporations like EADS (parent of Airbus), General Motors, DaimlerChrysler, and United Airlines have destroyed billions of dollars in shareholder value. At the same time these corporate disasters were occurring, new legislation, notably the Sarbanes-Oxley Act of 2002, has been introduced, passive institutional investors like mutual funds have become activist, the takeover market, fueled by billions of dollars in private equity, has deepened, and governments worldwide have intensified pressures on corporations to behave better.

At the center of this maelstrom is the corporate director, who sits at the apex of the corporation to monitor the decisions that affect employees, customers, suppliers, shareholders and the community, and continues to be the least understood person in the modern public corporation. This contradiction has resulted from a lack of knowledge among directors on what they should be doing in the boardroom, and how they should fulfill their legal and moral responsibilities; now made more confusing by the plethora of new legal liabilities since the collapse of Enron and the strategic complexities from global competition. The buck stops with the director and so he must understand his responsibilities and the means to discharge them. The increasing pressures for corporate performance and shareholder value maximization mean that the days of the inactive board, dominated by a company's managers are over.

The sea change in the boardrooms of the largest corporations calls for directors to account for their actions on issues as diverse as economic performance to social responsibility. Since the passage of Sarbanes-Oxley (2002), the courts are less sympathetic to the excuse that directors were ignorant of operational lapses and are now more willing to impose higher penalties for non-compliance and violations. Such international organizations as the World Bank, Organization for Economic Co-operation and Development (OECD), the Asian Development Bank (ADB), and global investors as Fidelity and the California Public Employees Retirement System (CalPERS) have set their sights on influencing the direction of corporate governance standards and practices worldwide.

For corporations based in the emerging economies of the Asia-Pacific, awareness of the trends and practiced in the modern corporate boardroom is crucial to competing globally; they must move quickly to conform and even lead in this important area. Corporations in the advanced economies of the European Union (EU) and the United States are increasingly forced to do business in institutional and cultural contexts that challenge their long-held beliefs about appropriate governance practices. This practice-oriented book is aimed at providing the theoretical foundations for 21st century directors and would-be directors to understand key responsibilities, hone managerial skills and improve knowledge on current best practices in the boardroom. Improving practice will protect directors from the statutory and moral liabilities that come with the job, allowing them to achieve even more in their capacity as leaders of their companies.

Introduction

Taking Back the Boardroom: A Director's Call to Arms

Reading this book will not make you a better as a director. Thriving as a better director is a personal decision you have to make. Rather, it will increase your awareness of what it takes to be a better director and to convince you that it is worth the trouble to invest yourself into becoming one.

In the first part of this book, we attempt to understand the philosophical and moral foundations for directing. This is essential to a director during a time of great change and uncertainty. The demands on directors come from the government, society, shareholders, employees and other stakeholders. Often, these demands conflict, and a director has to know how to prioritize and deal with them. Without an internally consistent framework to understand your duties as a director, you will easily become lost, confused and exposed to legal liabilities. First, one has to understand the agency theory view of corporate governance from a law and economics perspective. This view of corporate governance drives the roles and responsibilities of directors from which flow their moral and fiduciary liabilities. Next, one has to know how the chairperson (in the board and in individual committees) contributes to the effective functioning of the board. We will focus on the chairperson's role in setting the agenda, providing vision and leadership, and managing the meeting process so that effective decisions can be taken. The power relationships between the chairperson and the board and management, and how they drive the role of the chairperson are also explored.

In the next part of this book, we examine the issue of boardroom ethics and social responsibility. It has been stated repeatedly that good governance implies transparency and accountability. However, while transparency and accountability are necessary conditions for good corporate governance, they are far from being sufficient. It has become increasingly clear that for directors to perform their jobs well, they need to have a well-placed personal sense of ethics, which translates into the collective ethics of the board. The Asian Crisis of 1997 and the stock option backdating scandal of 2007 have one thing in common: poor ethical conduct by the management of companies and poor oversight by their boards of directors. In this section, we ask how directors should think about ethics, given the diversity in backgrounds, experience, personal beliefs and philosophies that one might encounter in the boardroom. In particular, when dealing with different cultures and country practices, how should the question of ethics figure in our decision making in the boardroom? We need to explore these questions because until we can clarify how our values drive the way we think about business issues we are incapable of good governance.

Finally, we examine the nuts and bolts of how a board of directors should be organized. It has often been said that the board has power *de jure* but not power *de facto*. Although the legal system of governance has imbued the board to act with sovereignty in matters of the business of the firm, it has often been prevented from doing so by a power structure that favors either management or the controlling shareholder or both. This section will review the proper role of management and board of directors under agency theory. To exercise power *de facto*, the board has to *organize* itself. The amount of information, the lack of time and resources, and the imbalance between the control of information by management and the board is such that unless the board is able to obtain and use information effectively, it will always be at a disadvantage to management. The typical way a board is organized is via the committee structure. Thus, this section will discuss the committee structure extensively, including the roles of individual directors in specific committees, the function of the committee, and the relationship of the committee to the board and to management as a whole. Contrary to popular belief, board organization is not only for large boards but also beneficial to smaller boards. Even if individual directors have to assume multiple board responsibilities formal organization ensures that issues are not missed and information is not ignored. Organization places the responsibility for decision taking squarely in the hands of the directors and sends an unequivocal message to management and other stakeholders that the board is in the driver's seat.

The last section of the book focuses on special situations in which directors may find themselves. These situations are driven by changes in the capital and legal structure of the firm. Directors may find themselves in the midst of change in the capital structure, for example a private company undertaking an Initial Public Offering (IPO) or a public company undertaking a going-private transaction. These changes will naturally bring about changes in the responsibilities and liability exposures of directors. Other directors may find themselves in family owned or privately controlled firms, such as venture capital financed start-ups. The roles, responsibilities, and duties of directors in such firms, in which there is no public shareholder, are discussed in this section.

Finally, the cases and illustrations used in this book are used to illustrate the managerial issues discussed in the chapters and are not designed to criticize specific decisions taken by the management of the organizations. Cases are useful because they provide a context, without which it would be difficult to talk specifically about issues. The cases also add human interest and serve to illustrate that the problems you face as a director, which you may think are unique, are in fact commonly shared.

CONTENTS

Chapter 1

Taking Back the Boardroom: Understanding your Duties as a Director

Directors are like the parsley on fish — decorative but useless.

Irving Olds, former Chairman,
United States Steel, April 1992

This chapter discusses the economic theory of the firm and the agency theoretic foundations for the organization of the boardroom. Appreciation for these fundamentals is critical for a director's understanding of his duties and obligations in the boardroom. I will first deal with the concept of residual claims, which will give directors a perspective on how to deal with competing claims when they arise in the boardroom. I will then discuss the question of control and the various mechanisms of control over management that are available to shareholders. The need and role of the board, as representatives of shareholders, is discussed and debated. The translations of the board's legal responsibilities into director's duties are also discussed, with particular attention to the economic and philosophical rationale for these duties.

How the Firm is Defined and Why is that Important for Directors

There are three broad definitions of the firm that come from economics, law, and sociology. From the perspective of economics, the firm is a production function. Simply put, it is the embodiment of a technological (broadly defined) transformation of inputs (capital, raw materials, human effort, and talent, etc.) into outputs (goods and services) for which there is an imputed value (price) in the market-place. This 'production function' can exist in many contexts and forms. For example, one could broadly define a strategic alliance as a production function, in which there is no physical manifestation of an organization as long as it embodies a technology that transforms inputs into outputs for a price. Yet, it is not technically a firm, unless it has a specific legal form. Here, it has to be stressed that the legal definitions of the firm should be treated separately from the economic definitions of the firm. While the former has implications for the fidu-ciary and statutory duties of directors, the latter has important impli-cations for the *moral* duty of directors.

If the firm is a production function, then it stands to reason that the *raison d'être* of the firm is the transformation of input to output. There can be no other. A firm that produces goods and services for which the imputed value is less than the cost of production is one that is not fulfilling the purpose of its existence. Hence, this conceptualiza-tion of the firm takes as its ultimate measure of success the *efficient* transformation of inputs into outputs.

Given that the firm is a creation of the law, its survival depends on its legitimacy conferred by society. As long as society regards the firm as the primary means of wealth creation the maximization of efficiency is the only way the firm can retain that legitimacy. Therefore, in this view of the firm, the moral duty of a director is to ensure the maximally efficient use of the firm's resource.

The second definition of the firm views the firm as a nexus of contracts. This definition embodies the legal manifestation of the firm, which acknowledges that all firms exist in contemplation of the Law. The firm is where the exchange of wages for human effort, capital for return, and technology for money take place. Under this definition, the firm is reducible to a set of contracts so that the main purpose of organization is the assurance of the integrity and dis-charge of these contracts. One way to fulfill this purpose is for managers of the firm to expend the resources to write complete contingent claims contracts, defined as contracts that cover all pos-sible contingencies to an agreement in all possible future states of the world. However, it is often uneconomical, perhaps even impos-sible, to specify complete contracts because the information to create such instruments required may not always be available or may be very costly to obtain. Therefore, it must be possible for parties to *re-contract*, defined as the re-specification of contractual terms given changes in the original conditions of the contract. In order for re-contracting to be possible, there must be an adjudicator that guarantees the integrity of the re-contracting process such that contracting parties are not exposed to the risks of holdup. This *contracting governance* mechanism is the board of directors. In this view of the firm, the law imposes statutory and fiduciary liabilities on directors in recognition of their duties to protect the firm's implicit and explicit contracts and to protect the re-contracting process when necessary.

The third definition of the firm is that of a social organization. There is increasing realization that a firm is a place where people meet to exchange specific information for the purpose of engaging in production. However, given the human dimension of the 'firm', non-economic considerations have become important to the firm's effective functioning. The reality of the merger between home and work has now manifested itself in such organizational innovations as telecommuting, paternal leave, and workplace day care. Sociologists recognize the firm as a community of individuals who collectively create an ethos, which provides the context for production. The idea of the social organization goes beyond the simple idea of a nexus of contracts because contracts assume definable outcomes, delimited time periods, specific geographic boundaries, and calculable payoffs. As a social organization, the firm has a character and a conscience, leading the way to view directors' duties from a moral dimension. In addition, the firm as a social organization also implies that it can only succeed when the stakeholders that comprise this organization are recognized and their claims are met. This last view of the organization has been less popular among those who think about corporate governance in Common Law jurisdictions. However, in countries like Japan and Germany, it is the central view of the firm, leading to a stakeholder approach to corporate governance, where the primary duties of the director is the arbitration of the competing claims of stakeholders to the wealth created by the firm.

In this book, we define the firm *primarily* as a production function, so that its purpose is the efficient transformation of inputs to outputs for a price, secondly as a nexus of contracts and lastly as a social organization. This is because unlike definitions that can be applied to other forms of organization such as the government, charity or social club, the firm's role as a production function is unique in human society. Thus, the duties of directors can be similarly prioritized according to these definitions. In order to fulfill these purposes, the firm employs technology, contracts with the providers of capital and labor, and identifies market opportunities in which the value of the output can be realized to its maximum.

How does the Firm Perform its Productive Function?

In order to engage in production, the firm must make decisions on how it will allocate its resources. The decision process can then be divided into four components. Decision initiation is the process of planning the allocation of resources. This often takes the form of a business or strategic plan or budget. After a plan is formulated, it has to be checked for consistency with the firm's stated mission, which is the process of decision ratification. Ratification ensures that the stated objectives of the firm's mission are reflected in the investment decisions proposed by management. Thus, a firm that is supposed to be in banking should not become distracted as real estate investors unless this business allows the firm to be a better bank. Implementation describes the entire process involved in translating the plan into action. This is an ongoing process and often, directors ignore the limitations that prior implementations of the plan can have on future possibilities contemplated by the plan. Finally, the entire production function has to be monitored. That is, someone has to ensure that actual results are consistent with planned results and deviations are investigated and corrected.

The processes of initiation and implementation are collectively known as decision management. Decision management falls within the preserve of the top management team. These powers are delegated to management by the board of directors by virtue of the specialized knowledge possessed by the management. The processes of ratification and monitoring are collectively known as decision control. Decision control falls within the purview of the board. The board retains these powers for itself because it is ultimately liable for the decisions taken by top management. Thus, the separation of management and control, which is taken up in more detailed later ensures that specialized knowledge can be applied to the greatest benefit while accountability is maintained.

The Relationship Between Managers and Shareholders

In 1934, Adolph Berle and Gardiner Means articulated an important phenomenon that they observed in the evolution of the modern corporation. They noticed that with the growth of the firm came an increasing need for capital to engage in production. The rise of technology in production ensured great benefits from economies of scale. Thus, those firms that could command the most capital (investments) were more able to compete effectively against those who lacked similar capacity. As the need for more capital increased, the ability for an owner-manager to supply all of the monetary requirements of the firm decreased. This meant that capital had to be accumulated from an increasingly large number of individual investors, leading to dispersion in the concentration of ownership (i.e., more people holding smaller amounts of shares in the firm). The dispersion of ownership led to a condition in which owners of the shares become atomistic and anonymous, thus less able to co-ordinate among themselves to monitor the actions of the management. As a result, the relative discretion of managers over the disposition of the firm's resources increased, making them the *de facto* owners. However, these 'owners' were different from those who truly owned shares in the corporation. The true owners were exposed to the risks inherent in the businesses of the corporations in which they had shares. Thus, they were concerned with the efficient deployment of the firm's assets. These 'manager-owners' were not exposed to such risks since the costs of the decisions they made were borne by the true owners. Therefore, these managers could make self-serving business decisions with impunity. Many of these decisions hurt the shareholder.

What sorts of decisions benefit the management but can hurt the shareholder? More than 35 years of empirical study on how managers are compensated has resulted in a single conclusion. Management pay is directly related to the size of the firm but never with profitability. We know from similarly well-established empirical research that firm size, regardless of how it is measured (sales, numbers of employees, assets, etc.) is not always positively related to productive efficiency. In fact, every time there has been an economic crisis, such as the 1997 Asian Currency Crisis or the post-9/11 airline industry crisis, we witness the massive downsizing of giant corporations due to the fact that they often have excess capacity, idle assets, and bloated payrolls that create costs without corresponding productive output. The result is the oft-observed phenomenon that managers, because they are free to allocate resources in any way they see fit, tend to accumulate assets beyond their efficient scale, so they can justify ever increasing levels of compensation and perquisites, with asset size as the justification.

Shareholders only gain when the residual value of the firm, defined as the net of cash flows after positive economic value future investments have been made, is maximized. Beyond some efficient scale of production, given by available technology, the size of the firm's assets matter little to the shareholder. Hence, for the shareholder, because efficiency, and not size, translates into wealth gains, the manager's decision to keep accumulating assets (i.e., grow the firm) can ultimately prove very costly. It is how the firm's productive capacity is employed, and whether it generates a net positive profit that determines the residual value. If the residual is small, the owners keep little. If the residual is large, the owners benefit accordingly.

Thus, the crux of the corporate governance problem can be summarized as the continuing struggle between those who manage the capital assets of the corporation and those who are exposed to the underlying risks of mismanagement (i.e., the owners of these assets). More pointedly, whoever controls how the residual is allocated ultimately wins the struggle. It has been the contention of corporate governance thinkers, particularly those in the Anglo-American legal tradition that owners of the capital have been losing in the struggle to the managers of the capital, because of the formers' inability to coordinate their actions to bring pressure to bear on management. This struggle is known as the agency problem, and defines the continuing relationship between managers and shareholders to this day.

The agency problem

In the agency theory of corporate governance, those who manage the firm's resources act as agents of the shareholders — owners of those resources. A standard agency relationship is governed by contracts. These contracts specify the terms of performance and duties of the contracting party. They may also specify the processes by which performance is to be achieved. Contracts are generally well-defined in terms of timing, scope, and redress for non-performance. However, agency contracts between the shareholder and manager are very costly to write and enforce. Firstly, the managers have the skills and knowledge not possessed by the shareholders. This information asymmetry inevitably leads to the misspecification of performance standards for the managers. Secondly, monitoring is difficult because shareholders are not able to observe everything that a manager does. Thirdly, even when problems are detected, redress is difficult because co-ordinating the actions of all the shareholders, who may be widely dispersed, is very costly. For example, the record of successes in shareholder proxy battles has been dismal. Even shareholders with significantly large blocks of shares have had little success in replacing a poorly performing management team through the proxy battle.

Information inefficiencies faced by shareholders also lead to a decline in transparency and a loss of accountability. When a shareholder cannot accurately determine the point at which the managers stop maximizing the efficiency of the firm, it is not able to take specific action to halt the erosion in the value of the stock. Even when it becomes apparent that the management is not doing its job, all the shareholder can do is to vote with its feet by selling the stock. By this time, however, the value of the shares would have already declined, and the owner would have lost money in the investment. Further, selling stock is not an effective way of directly dealing with managerial excess unless there is a run on the stock of a company, which is unlikely in most situations. Selling stock is merely a way to avoid more losses.

A different but related issue to the expropriation of shareholder wealth is observed in emerging or small economies such as China, India, Canada, northern Europe, and South America where ownership is concentrated in the hands of controlling shareholders such as the government, family members, and entrepreneurs. Here, minority shareholders face an even thornier problem. The combination of informational inefficiencies and the inability to co-ordinate effectively can potentially lead to the expropriation of the minority shareholder's wealth *by the controlling shareholder*, leading to what is now known as the 'principal–principal' problem. Because a majority shareholder does not own all of a company's stock capital, it does not bear all of the costs resulting from poor decisions. A proportionate share is borne by other minority shareholders. However, because the controlling shareholder holds sway over the voting stock, it can often force the board of directors to approve inordinately risky decisions, which may generate extraordinary returns in the short run but at the expense of the other bearers of risk, the minority shareholders. During the 1980s and early 1990s, families and individuals controlled many of the banks and financial institutions in Thailand and Indonesia. Several of these banks were publicly listed corporations, but with a minority of their equity stock in the market. During the Asian Crisis of 1997, many of these banks became insolvent, in great part due to the general poor quality of their loans, and to the unsecured loans made to companies owned by their controlling shareholders. The minority shareholders, who had no power over these decisions, ended up paying part of the bill and lost all of their investments. Again, those who control the use of the flow of resources control the use of the residuals stemming from their use. What are the solutions to this problem?

Managing the agency problem

Broadly, there are two categories of solutions for managing the agency problem. In the case of the large, public corporation with dispersed share ownership, the board of directors represents shareholders who cannot exert influence on management. This is known as an internal mechanism of control. It relies on the expertise and goodwill of corporate watchdogs to protect the interests of shareholders by ensuring that managers abide by the principles of efficiency maximization. The other is external mechanisms of controls. Here, the behavior of managers is indirectly constrained by the workings of competitive markets for product, labor, and capital that punish the company when it systematically deviates from efficiency maximization.

The notion of the separation of ownership and control is the centerpiece of Professors Fama's and Jensen's (1976) seminal article on agency theory and the theory of the firm, in which they stated that such a separation is critical to the efficient functioning of the corporate governance system, because it led to the specialization of risk bearing and managerial expertise. Managers cannot fully diversify their human capital risks from exposure to a firm's systematic risk, defined as risks resulting from non-controllable industry related factors, such as seasonality and technological change. Therefore, managers need to be indemnified against such risks, or they will not take the job of managing companies with high levels of systematic risks. Indemnification usually comes in the form of sufficient basic non-contingent (or fixed) compensation. If managers are not indemnified and they take such jobs, they are likely to make decisions to minimize systematic risks, such as diversifying corporate assets into unrelated businesses, in which they may have little or no managerial expertise, to smooth out the variance in cash flows, a major contributor to risk. The Korean conglomerates or *chaebols* are well known for such 'smoothing' strategies. Hyundai, a family-owned conglomerate, has businesses in numerous industrial sectors ranging from banking to automobile manufacturing, home building, and electronics. In the late 1980s, many of the US conglomerates began a wave of *deconglomerization* that lasted well into the 21st century. Parts of corporations were sold to other companies for which these parts represented core businesses or technologies and were therefore more valuable. Yet others were taken private in transactions known as the leveraged buyout. Yet others were spun-off as free standing public companies through the Initial Public Offering process. Such decisions resulted from the desire to focus on core competences in the corporations' most important businesses to maximize returns on capital invested.

Owners, on the other hand, can easily diversify their systematic risks by holding on to a portfolio of stocks in unrelated companies. However, they cannot diversify their unsystematic risks, defined as the risks specific to the company, such as those associated with poor management, antiquated technology, and bloated organization. Hence, because they cannot engage in the active management of every company they own, shareowners need to rely on the expertise provided by the professional manager. This system of ownership and control allows the owner to specialize in risk bearing through the diversification of stocks, and the manager can specialize in the deployment of productive resources through his expertise.

In a large and complex firm where the means of production are spread throughout the firm, the knowledge that renders a production technology useful is held in the brains of many people. Therefore, individual employees' claims to the wealth created by the firm are settled via employment contracts and paid out in the form of salaries. The residual, which shows up as cash flows net of obligations and reinvestments belongs to the shareholders (risk bearers) and is usually disbursed in the form of dividends or stock buybacks. In order to ensure that the residual is protected and paid out, rather than squandered on non-value creating ('empire building') projects, the shareholders appoint a board of directors to represent their interests. The board protects the interest of the shareholders by ratifying managerial investment decisions, and acts as a liaison to convey shareholder preferences to management.

The external control of the firm

The management of a firm is also disciplined by market-based mechanisms that rely on the operation of an external market for the supply and demand of managerial talent, corporate assets, and goods and services. The business of Business is to transform labor, minerals, and technology, into saleable goods and services. In doing this, Business adds value to otherwise unusable raw materials. Those who do this at the lowest cost or can add the most value to raw inputs get to do it again (and again). Those who cannot are put out of the game. This competitive process occurs continually, so that when management misreads the market and produces the wrong product for sale or sells at the wrong price, resources are misallocated and shareholder value is destroyed. An example of such mismanagement is the failure of executives in the US automobile industry starting from the 1970s to read the signs broadcasted by the marketplace. They missed watershed customer demands for fuel efficiency, price, and reliability in automobiles; instead choosing to focus only on product design. As a result, billions of dollars of shareholder wealth has been destroyed, and thousands of jobs lost. A typical passenger car made and sold by the Big 3 (Ford, General Motors and DaimlerChrysler's United States division) loses an average of $1,500 (2007 dollars) at retail. Contrast this to the Japanese automakers, most notably Toyota and Honda that turn a profit on every sale. In 2007, the Big 3 planned more than 30% cuts in the US production capacity while Japanese automakers planned to double US capacity. Simply put, it is virtually impossible for firms to succeed when they try to make a product that customers do not want to buy.

The second type of external control is the market for managerial labor. Given that every firm has only one CEO and a small group of top executives, the market for top level managerial labor in any economy is relatively small, and therefore efficient. The performance of a CEO today determines his employability and command over salary tomorrow. Thus, in the long run a CEO that consistently performs poorly will soon lose the ability to become employed in the same position or at the same salary.

The third type of external control is exercised through market competition for the control of corporate assets. When firms fail to operate in a manner that maximizes efficiency, competition in product and factor markets forces the firm to take reduced margins as a way to compensate for lower quality. If these signals are ignored, and management fails to turn the situation around, the market for corporate control initializes a hostile tender offer or takeover. This may result in change of ownership, the board acting against an existing management team, or a stockholder initiative proxy battle for seats on the board. In 2005, Kirk Kerkorian, well known billionaire activist investor, acquired more than 5% of the stock of General Motors through his investment firm, Tracinda Corporation. The shares of GM jumped when he successfully placed a director on the board to represent the interests of financial investors such as Tracinda. As a result the GM board began a program of restructuring in which product lines were trimmed, plants were closed and workers laid off, in an attempt to make the company profitable. The restructuring continues today, albeit at a slower place when Mr. Kerkorian, impatient with the pace of change, sold all his shares for a small profit.

A more likely scenario is when entrepreneurs in the form of private equity funds are willing to offer large premiums over market prices to gain control of the shares of an under-performing company, because they believe that they can utilize the assets of the corporation much more effectively than the existing management. The very large size of some of the premiums (sometimes in excess of 60% during the 1980s in the US) over share prices that have been offered in takeover situations is clear evidence that firm performance often deteriorates to very low levels before existing management and directors recognize, let alone do anything, about the problems.

Historically, the management of large enterprises seldom feared the possibility of a hostile takeover in Europe and Asia as the illusion of stability due to size masked the significance of such threats. Case studies, such as the record breaking US$25 billion takeover of RJR-Nabisco, and examples from industries as diverse as real estate to retail to airlines teach us that such threats were seldom salient to management when there had been no history of such activities in the industry or the firm. Furthermore, in many parts of the world, including Canada, the pervasiveness of controlling shareholders effectively prevented potential acquirers from obtaining majority stakes in many of these companies. However, these companies' inefficiencies eventually catch up with them in the era of globalized competition, and financial crises. The activities of Mr. Kerkorian and private equity funds, such as Kohlberg, Kravis, Roberts & Co., Blackstone, Clayton Dubilier,

Texas Pacific Group and others, who control hundreds of billions of dollars in buyout capital, have served noticed to corporate board-rooms around the world that no company is too big to be taken over, and no company is too small to be noticed.

In the US, it was not until the advent of the leveraged buyout (LBO) in the 1980s that boards and managers began to realize that they could lose the iron hold they enjoyed over their companies. Nowadays, most boards in the US operate on the premise that their companies are potential takeover targets. In the 1990s, the LBO movement spread to Europe, following the entry of American capital to finance the wave of mergers in telecommunications, airlines, utilities, and manufacturing. With this have come American-style corporate governance and its implications for boardroom behavior and share-holder activism. In Asia, with the entry of foreign institutional capital from the US and Europe to exploit growth opportunities, the pressure for more shareholder-friendly corporate governance is also increasing. Nowadays, a proactive board will often put in place a regular program of share buybacks or special dividends in order to boost the stock price to reduce the threat of takeover. Such strategies are particularly useful for companies that compete in stable, matured businesses where cash flows are predictable and plentiful.

While there has been much written, for and against, the conse-quences of unfriendly takeovers, empirical research by Michael Jensen of the Harvard School, Stephen Kaplan of the University of Chicago and others generally suggest that when control is taken from an exist-ing group, the result of a change in ownership is usually an increase in value for the shareholders and a more efficient operation of the enterprise. The summary evidence strongly suggests that the market for corporate control, when it operates properly leads to a more effec-tive use of resources within the firm.

External control or the board of directors: which is better?

Effective as markets always are in forcing efficient allocation of resources in the economy, they often are very slow to enforce a rem-edy. In very large organizations, such as General Motors or IBM, the possibility that management misuse of resources escapes immediate notice is significant. Large organizations are often able to bury their errors by using up slack resources, naturally accumulated during periods of growth. Additionally, expenditures in diversification, capital expansion, and corporate empire building are easy to justify and make when the firm does not need the public financial markets for help. Finally, dealing with the daily pressures of running a giant corporation often means that executives manage by exception. Indeed, problems are often not discovered and assessed until the loss of market-share, declining earnings and a sharp drop in the market value of shares is so acute that even the most obtuse of directors realize that something must be done.

The empirical research on takeovers has exclusively dealt with the returns to takeovers, not the returns to the *threat of takeovers*. The theory espoused by Michael Jensen of the Harvard Business School is based on the threat of takeovers as a disciplining mechanism. It is this threat, and not the takeover itself, that prevents managers from making self-serving decisions that hurt the shareholders. The takeover is merely a corrective device, which serves to reverse some of the mistakes made by the management. This distinction is important because such market-based mechanisms operate in crude ways. Takeovers are blunt instruments at best; they often come too late because market signals are noisy and can be unreliable, and the eventual corrective measures are often very severe and disruptive to a firm's normal operations. Furthermore, the takeover market has generated a substantial amount of unpopular political fallout, causing an anti-takeover sentiment among legislators in America, which may serve to increase the illusion of invulnerability among firms that have not yet had to face the threat. If the purpose of corporate governance is to maximize the efficient use of resources, then market mechanisms fall short, because they do not prevent or curtail managerial error, but only act to correct it when it becomes too severe, after the losses have already been incurred. At the very least, it disrupts a firm's normal operations and the costs of a takeover often force shareholders to pay heavily for the privilege of exercising their rights of control over the management.

There is no doubt that managers cannot escape from external market mechanisms in the long run. Such mechanisms eventually work to correct the misuse of resources to make firms more competitive. But they are expensive and far from perfect for achieving the desired results. Often, they only correct failings when they have become incredibly severe and after the costs of these failures have already been incurred.

A superior way of assuring efficiency is through the effective governance of the enterprise by the board of directors. Rather than relying on the markets for control to bring efficiency, shareholders should rely on, and expect, effective boards to assure that their firms are operated in an optimally competitive fashion. There are many reasons why this is true but probably the most important is that information is always more complete and reliable within the firm than outside it. Strategic plans are often not revealed in their entirety to market analysts and institutional investors. The probability of success of a research and development (R&D) effort can only be roughly estimated from the outside, whereas scientists working in the firm will have a better grasp of the odds. Finally, many R&D efforts are closely guarded secrets, especially when the payoffs are as great as in, for example, the pharmaceutical industry.

Recognizing this, most stock markets now have in place laws against the trading of company stocks on insider information. In emerging economies, the enforcement of such laws are beginning to be taken seriously by the regulators as they compete for the listing of company stock in their domestic markets. The practical implication of why insider trading laws exist is that financial markets are only able to make judgments about the enterprise as a whole whereas the governing body of an organization can judge individual components of the business. This means that the board and ultimately, management, can take corrective action on those areas of the firm that are not performing, before the market detects the problems. Clearly good management can detect signs of corporate trouble early, address it, and thereby prevent small problems from becoming major ones, which may have to be dealt with through harsher corrective actions, such as executive dismissals, or in battles for control. Furthermore, because internal information is superior, the range of actions that can be taken is much greater. These actions themselves are finer grained and more discriminating.

In sum, the advantages of a well-functioning board render the monitoring and controlling of the enterprise far less costly for the shareholders, which means they get a higher return for their investments. Shareholders do not need to bear the cost of bankers' and lawyers' fees in a takeover battle. They do not need to pay for the costs of temporary inefficiencies caused by the disruption of routine activities in the enterprise, and finally, they do not need to deal with the costs of negative publicity, adverse reactions of suppliers and customers against uncertainty caused by the takeover, and the costs of government intervention. Thus, it is economically more efficient to have effective boards than effective takeover markets. To have effective boards, boardrooms need effective directors.

The Duties of the Director

So, who are the directors? Where do they come from and what are their roles? Directors have been variously defined as the top echelon of the corporation, the 'controlling mind' of the corporation, and the 'conscience' of the corporation (Gillies, 1992). Within a board, there are two categories of directors. Executive directors or inside directors, as they are known in the US, are those who hold an executive position in the company, such as Chief Executive Officer, Chief Financial Officer, or Chief Operating Officer, in addition to holding a board position. Non-executive or outside directors are those who hold a directorship, but are not involved in the day to day running of the company. Depending on jurisdiction, such as civil law countries, executive, and non-executive directors may have different status under the law. However, in most common law countries, they have the same liability exposures and, therefore, are conferred the same status. Within the general category of non-executives, a controlling shareholder, or significant shareholder may appoint some directors. Known as nominees these directors may also be in the employ of the controlling shareholder. Being in the employ of a third party while acting as a fiduciary for another can lead to potential conflicts of interest — a problem I will discuss later in the book. In Asia and Europe, some boards are known to have alternate directors, to take the places of the primary directors in meetings when they cannot be there. Under Common and Civil Law, there is no distinction between directors and alternates, as long as they are in the position of directing the affairs of the corporation. Therefore, although an alternate appears to have less power and authority, he does not have less liability.

Directors are in place to adjudicate the strategic plans of the corporation, ensure that resources are allocated with the view to maximizing the economic value of the corporation, and protect the interests of all shareholders. Thus, they are given full rights to hire and fire management, declare dividends, acquire, and dispose the corporation's assets, and if need be sell or wind up the corporation. Commensurate with these rights are moral and legal duties, from which flow liabilities.

Directors are bound by categories of duties. The first duty, which is a direct result of the agency theory of corporate governance, is the duty of loyalty. The second duty is related to the first, and this is the duty of care. The twin duties of loyalty and care define the duties of a fiduciary. In addition, society may impose additional duties to the directors, for example to protect the environment, human rights, gender rights, etc. These are known as statutory duties. In the Common Law, a director has unlimited liabilities with respect to the assets of the corporation. Thus, a director can be held personally liable for the recovery of taxes, back pay, or criminal action resulting from the company's activities.

However, in recognition of the weight of such liabilities, the law provides for specific ways a director can discharge his duties. Thus, if a director can show due diligence in making a business decision, even when the outcome is negative, the law will generally consider the director to have discharged his duties appropriately. For example, the Delaware Incorporation Act provides relief to directors who can show that they were not intentionally negligent or criminally motivated when failing to discharge their duties. Such relief is popularly known as the Business Judgment Rule, which is a legal stance that the Delaware Chancery Court has taken in which it deems itself incapable of assessing the *business* decisions of directors and, therefore, can only make judgment on the proper discharge of the directors' fiduciary and statutory duties. By keeping sacrosanct the 'corporate veil', the Delaware Chancery adheres to the long held tradition of 'caveat emptor' — investors have the right to be protected from fraud and misappropriation but not from the inherent risks of investing.

A duty of loyalty demands that a fiduciary shall not engage in practices that directly or indirectly harms the interests of his principal. In legal terms, the duty of loyalty test addresses issues of conflicts of interests, and self-dealing. This precludes fiduciaries from enriching himself at the expense of the principal. Declaring management bonuses and stock options with low or no performance hurdles is an example of self-enrichment. The annual debates over Chief Executive Officer (CEO) compensation in the United States and Britain are indicative of the controversy surrounding the performance of boards in this area. The duty of loyalty also implies that a fiduciary is in a monogamous relationship with the principle. Thus, whenever a person owes fiduciary duties to two parties that transact with each other, he is in a potential conflict of interest. For example, in 1990s case involving Air Canada and Canadian Airlines, two executives from PWA Corporation, the parent of Canadian Airlines, were found to have breached their fiduciary duties because of their positions as nominee directors on Gemini Corporation, a provider of Central Reservations Systems (CRS) for the airline. In this case, PWA was negotiating a merger with American Airlines that would have effectively closed down Gemini. The two executives who knew of the impending move did not inform the board of Gemini. If the nominee directors had informed Gemini, PWA could have taken them to court for violating their fiduciary but because they did not do so, were found guilty of breach of fiduciary to Gemini. Such conflicts are no-win situations for the director. He must either resign from the board before the event or be indemnified by the nominating principal.

The second duty a fiduciary owes is the duty of care. The duty of care is a more stringent test of performance, because it does not only enjoin the fiduciary from self-dealing and adverse action but also demands that it acts in ways to protect and enhance the principal's position. Therefore, it is not good enough for a board to behave legally, but it should also act beyond the minimum standards of performance to make the very best decisions it is able.

A well-established body of thought, known as the shareholder sovereignty or shareholder capitalism, developed in the late 1990s in the United States is based on this concept of the duty of care. Generally, a fiduciary is defined as a trustee of the company so that in the same manner of a trusteeship, his powers and responsibilities are complete and wide-ranging. The notion of trusteeship, however, can lead to a great deal of ambiguity, because it is unclear to whom the director is responsible for the firm's assets and under whose strictures should the disposition of these assets be made. Hence, in the US, legal scholars and economic theorists have advanced the concept of agency to define and narrow the director's powers and responsibilities (Fama and Jensen, 1976). An agent has a clear duty to represent the interests of the firm's shareholders. Agency theory, as espoused by Jensen and Meckling (1976), places the responsibility for the protection of the shareholders' wealth squarely on the shoulders of the directors.

Discharging the duty of care is critical to the survival of the corporation, because if shareholders no longer have confidence that the board is acting in their best interests, they will no longer invest, with the consequence that capital cannot be accumulated and production will cease. The criticality of confidence is starkly illustrated by the precipitous collapse of stock markets around the world through the 1990s and 2000s whenever investors lost confidence in management to deal with the global exigencies of currency risk, political instability, and energy prices.

Most jurisdictions impose additional duties on directors. These stem from various community and country-specific laws dealing with taxation, environmental protection, labor rights, community citizenship, accounting disclosure, and business practices. In many parts of the world, domestic and international companies are exposed to compliance risks associated with employment health and safety legislation, tax laws, public company listing requirements, financial security legislation, national security and defense acts, and anti-corruption laws. In the US, for example, directors can be sent to jail under the Corrupt Practices Act, if their companies are found have engage in the bribery of foreign government officials. The directors of Lockheed Corporation were found criminally liable for bribing Japanese officials in a scandal that rocked the defense industry in the 1980s. In Europe (notably Germany), environmental and labor health and safety legislation also impose criminal penalties on directors of corporations found guilty of violations.

Discharging your duties as a director

In considering the number and depth of risks to which directors are exposed, it might be reasonable to ask if any director can hope to fully discharge his duties even with the best of intentions. The key to discharging ones duties in the boardroom is to be attentive to the information that flows from the executive. Such information can be strategic (relating to market and competitive position), financial (relating to risk exposures and capital structure), operational (relating to compliance with statutory obligations), and external (relating to shareholder relations, and social responsibility). The director must be seen to be actively dealing with such information by actively seeking it before and during board meetings, evaluating the information during board and committee meetings by asking questions, and acting on the information by actively engaging the management in their decision making and being present to vote on resolutions.

The director is to actively communicate his thoughts regarding the company with the board and its chair. If a director feels that things are not right or that some practices by the company are questionable, he/she has a duty to raise objections and have them reflected in the Minutes of the meeting. This is important, because the Minutes represent the thoughts and intentions of the board, and are often the first place that a court will look to assess a director's attention to his duty. In addition, directors may also keep personal notes during board meetings, including his thoughts at the time the decisions were made. Such notes can be entered into evidence as corroborating evidence.

The director should also expect and comply with formal processes for dealing with contingencies, such as takeover bids, unexpected financial losses, and the loss of important executives. He should be seen to be competent, particularly within his sphere of expertise. Although directors are often treated as a group, a director with a known expertise in a particular area will be called to account at a higher standard of performance. For example, if the case is about a company's breach of duty in the area of financial management, then directors who are financial experts will be asked tougher questions on their performance. The key principle governing such standards of performance is the duty of care. All directors are required to exercise the duty of care, commensurate with his area of expertise and sphere of influence. Thus to discharge his duties, a director must be actively involved in the monitoring of management, and the taking of decisions that lie within the domain of his expertise and general duties as a director.

The Non-Executive Director: Key to Board Independence

The most important role that a director can play on the board is that of monitoring and rewarding the management. The non-executive director is best positioned to play this role simply, because there is a natural conflict of interest when an executive director is called upon to evaluate his Chief Executive. The non-executive director can more easily maintain an arms-length relationship with the CEO, and therefore, act with a greater degree of independent thought. In fact, the effectiveness of the individual director depends on his ability to act independently, which in turn contributes to board effectiveness.

The effective board is an independent board. It operates transparently — a state of affairs in which the decision-making *processes* of the board are easily understood by outside parties. This does not mean that every decision of the board has to be subject to public scrutiny. What it does imply is that over time an intelligent observer can detect the logic behind a board's decisions, and conclude that the logic is internally consistent with the business goals of the corporation.

An effective board is also one that takes full responsibility for its own actions and those of the firm's officers. However, unless the board is independent of the influence of management or the majority shareholder, it cannot make this claim because its decisions would be prejudiced.

$64 million question: So what IS director independence?

Having reviewed the research on corporate governance and consulted with numerous boards on this question, I have concluded that director independence is not solely an issue of boardroom structure or process. Having the right structures *and* processes are important, but it is also critical that directors possess the right personalities and values to *act* independently. Independence consists of the feeling of freedom to express personal views in the boardroom and the freedom from undue influence by the top management team or a controlling shareholder. The feeling of freedom coupled with a willingness to express personal views is particularly critical, because the boardroom is typically small, between 6 and 14 people. In such situations, the probability for a strong willed individual, such as the CEO, to impose himself on the group is high, and this probability is increased when the board meets infrequently and has to rely on management for information before taking decisions.

The willingness to express personal views depends on a director's personality and character of will. In addition, the Chairman must also create a boardroom culture that promotes the feeling of freedom. The role of the Chair is to mentor directors and encourage active participation in boardroom discussions. He does this to mitigate the devastating effects of 'groupthink'. Groupthink is phenomenon in which individuals in a group feel too intimidated, either because of ignorance or lack of preparation, to exercise independent thought, choosing instead to follow presumed group norms. The Nazi regime in post-Weimar Germany, the intelligentsia during the Suharto regime in Indonesia, and the political center during the Tiananmen Massacre in China are all stark examples of groupthink gone awry. A similar situation can often be seen in the boardroom of a company facing a takeover, bankruptcy, or morally challenging decision. The independence of the board is compromised when individual directors refuse to exercise their legal right to voice concern. Therefore, an effective board must have directors who can think independently because they possess the right knowledge, skills and attitudes toward their fiduciary duties.

Board independence is also achieved through the use of appropriate processes and structures in the boardroom. A worldwide movement has risen to deal with this issue through the development and promulgation of codes of best practices. In these codes, two of which are illustrated in the Appendix (the original Cadbury Code and the OECD Code) independence is defined as boards with effective committee structures, well-defined and formal processes with feedback loops, and performance standards oriented toward maximizing shareholder value.

In spite of the external controls imposed on the firm by the marketplace, there should be no question on the central role that directors play in the governance of today's corporations. This role has heretofore been neglected because directors, as a group, have remained largely invisible, preferring to do their work in the background. This has changed dramatically in recent years, largely due to the early 1990s recession in the US, the Asian Crisis in the late 1990s, the Internet bubble collapse in the early 2000s, the advent of cross-border mega mergers (e.g., Daimler-Benz of Germany and Chrysler of the US), and the rise of aggressive private equity investors more recently. In addition, pressures from international institutional investors who only care about making their quarterly profitability targets have increased sharply. Global capital markets that demand an unprecedented degree of transparency in corporate reporting have fueled these pressures. At the same time, there has also arisen a high degree of social activism by community based non-government organizations (NGOs). Additionally, the political elite of Asian economies struggling with recession has sharpened its calls for more restrictions on the activities of global corporations, so that they have to respond socially to the national welfare concerns of these countries.

Taken together, the only way a board of directors can deal with these opposing demands is for it to act independently of managerial and political influence. The struggle between profit and welfare is the struggle of the board to maximize the shareholder value, and yet be socially responsive. At one level, these demands seem irresolutely conflicted. However, the reality of managing in today's environment, as illustrated by the following case study, requires directors to manage the contradictions and to excel in doing so.

Sarbanes-Oxley Act of 2002

In 2002, the US Congress passed the most sweeping set of changes to corporate law since the 1934 Securities and Exchange Act. Called the Sarbanes-Oxley Act of 2002, this 66-page legislation impacts all US corporations and their worldwide operations, and all foreign corporations doing business in the United States. The legislation is divided into 6 Titles, two of which, Titles 3 and 4 have direct impact on how boards and directors conduct their business in the boardroom.

A major purpose of the 2002 Sarbanes-Oxley Act was to impose ethical standards, and were seen to have been too laxed in the corporations caught in the scandals that rocked corporate America. In the Act, loans or other extensions of credit to a director or executive officer are prohibited with only very minor exceptions. This prohibition continues to be controversial, because it prohibits not only just the abusive loans to executives that have received adverse press coverage but also legitimate loans and extensions of credit that have been used as part of compensatory arrangements. For example, relocation loans seem to be prohibited. However, it is clear that the practice of making loans to executives to purchase shares in order to avoid taxable income was no longer permitted.

Personal accountability

One of the most sweeping changes to securities laws in the world imposed by the Act is the requirement that the CEO and CFO are required to certify the company's annual and quarterly reports

(Forms 10-K and 10-Q) filed with the SEC. Popularly known as Section 404 (the section in the Act in which the provisions occur), the new certification requires each officer to affirm that he has reviewed the report, and to his knowledge, the report is not misleading and that the financial statements fairly present the company's financial condition and results of operations, that the officer is responsible for establishing internal controls, which ensure that material information is made known to the officer and has evaluated and disclosed the effectiveness of the controls, the officer has disclosed to the independent auditor and audit committee all significant deficiencies in the internal controls and any fraud.

In a separate section of the Act, imposing statutory liabilities, CEOs and CFOs are required to certify the company's periodic reports containing financial statements filed with the SEC, with severe criminal penalties imposed for false certifications. This provision differs from Section 404 in that it requires a statement that the periodic reports fully comply with the SEC reporting requirements, in addition that it fairly presents certification required by SEC rule.

If there is a restatement of financial statements due to material non-compliance as a result of misconduct, the CEO and CFO will have to forfeit any bonus, equity-based compensation or profits realized from the sale of stock during the 12 months following issuance of the non-complying financial statements. The restatement does not necessarily have to be due to an officer's misconduct to trigger a forfeit.

Directors and executive officers may not purchase, sell or otherwise transfer stock of the company received in connection with service as a director or employment as an executive officer during pension blackout periods that prohibit purchases, sales or other transfers of the stock by at least half of the plan participants for at least three consecutive business days, with limited exceptions. The company can bring suit to recover any profit realized in violation of this prohibition.

The legislation includes a sense of the United States Senate provision that corporate federal tax returns should be signed by the CEOs. The authority of the SEC bars a person's serving as a director or officer of a public company is expanded. Substantial increases in other criminal and civil sanctions for violations of the securities laws are imposed. This includes a new crime of securities fraud involving public companies with a maximum penalty of 25 years. Statutes of limitations for securities fraud are also extended, and debts resulting from violation of securities fraud laws are not dischargeable in bankruptcy.

Enhanced disclosure

Officers, directors, and shareholders with at least 10% ownership of a company's stock will have to file Section 16 reports of changes in beneficial ownership of equity securities within two business days of the change rather than within 10 days after the end of the month in which the change occurred as now required. The reports are to be made public by the SEC and on a company's website within one day. In new SEC rules resulting from Sarbanes-Oxley 2002, all material correcting adjustments identified by the independent auditor must be reflected in the financial statements. Annual reports are to contain a management report on the company's internal controls with an assessment of their effectiveness, which is to be attested to by the independent auditor. Companies are required to disclose whether it has adopted a code of ethics for senior financial officers, as well as disclose any changes or waivers to the code.

The following report from the National Association of Corporate Directors lays out three of the most salient issues facing corporate directors in US listed firms today. As you read the discussion, try to understand the reasons for the changes described, and think about whether your company faces the same type of pressures. If so, determine whether your company is prepared to deal with these changes and whether your board has the resources, in terms of expertise, finances, and time to address them in a substantive way. If not, think about how you, as a director, are going to address the challenges facing your company or others that you are familiar with.

Looking Back, Looking Forward[1]

A Report on The Council of Institutional Investors — National Association of Corporate Directors (CII-NACD) Task Force.

There are many issues of concern about effective governance today; after discussion of a wide range of important governance topics, task force members decided to focus on the following three pressing issues, in hopes of raising awareness of common concerns and working together to build consensus around best practices:

(1) proposals to switch from plurality voting to majority voting for directors;
(2) the merits of Section 404 of Sarbanes-Oxley (2002); and
(3) executive compensation (disclosures and amounts).

Task force members are well aware of the damage that weak corporate governance can have on shareowner value. Mark Anson, chief executive of Hermes Pensions Management and BT Pension Scheme, offered a cogent discussion of that risk at the July 2006 meeting of the International Corporate Governance Network. Anson cited the equity risk premium (ERP) — the additional return that investors must earn to hold stocks over bonds — as a measure of investor risk aversion in the stock market. A high ERP implies lower stock market valuations. The ERP peaked in 2002 at the height of the corporate accounting scandals. The upshot, according to Anson: An egregious lack of good corporate governance destroyed investor confidence, raised the ERP, and eroded stock market values.

---

[1] This case was prepared for teaching purposes and does not purport to illustrate the effective or ineffective resolution of specific managerial situations. Used with permission. Source: http://www.nacdonline.org/images/CII-NACD%20Task%20Force%20 Report-Reforms-Final.pdf

Boards, on their own or in response to scandal-cleanup reforms, have become more independent of management and more active. In 2003, only 34% of companies had boards composed of 75% or more independent directors; in 2006, 43% of companies had boards with a supermajority of outside directors. Lead directors, a rarity in Corporate America a few years ago, are increasingly common. Some 37% of boards have lead directors now vs. 10% in 2003. And directors are working harder for shareowners. Directors logged an average of 209 total hours on board duties in 2005, up from 156 in 2003.

While it is difficult to measure the precise impact that stronger boards and post-Enron reform laws and regulations have had in shoring up investor confidence and stock prices, evidence abounds that the wholesale changes in practices and rules have been beneficial. Among the signposts:

- Data compiled by Audit Analytics shows that 15.9% of companies that had to comply with Section 404 in 2004 reported at least one material weakness in internal control, but through August 14, 2006, only 7.4% of companies that had to comply for the second time in 2005 reported at least one material weakness.
- Department of Justice statistics for 2005 show a decline in the number of defendants charged with corporate fraud and a decline in the number of corporate fraud investigations opened. Many think the drop partly reflects the success the government has had in changing the climate on Wall Street and in Corporate America through high profile convictions over the past three years. Other reasons include a shift in resources toward terrorism investigations.
- Securities class action filings have declined sharply. According to a Cornerstone Research study, filings were 45% lower in the first half of 2006 than they were in the same period in 2005. This continues a trend observed in 2005. If filings continue at the current rate, filings for the current year will be 31% lower than in '05 and 36% lower than the average annual rate in 1996-2005. Cornerstone cited the improvements in corporate governance following Enron's implosion and the Sarbanes-Oxley Act (2002) as key factors in the decline in litigation activity. Other reasons include the resolution of

many lawsuits associated with the boom and bust of the late '90s, and a decline in United States stock market volatility.

Still, there is a fair way to go toward reassuring investors that all is well. Some 74% of American investors believe corporate boards are "only somewhat effective" or "not at all effective" in overseeing the companies they govern, according to an April 2005 poll by the National Association of Investors. The same survey also found that 63% of shareowners thought that financial and accounting regulations governing public companies were too lenient.

A 2006 Wall Street Journal Online/Harris Interactive poll also revealed that investor confidence has not fully recovered. Slightly over a third, or 35%, of American investors polled "completely or somewhat disagree" that boards of directors are effective in overseeing the companies they govern. Additionally, only 32% believe that the Sarbanes-Oxley Act (2002) has been effective in improving transparency of financial information of public companies. However, about half, or 49%, "completely or somewhat agree" that they can trust companies to provide complete and accurate financial information on which investment decisions may be based. When asked if the Sarbanes-Oxley Act (2002) had been effective in improving boards of directors' ability to manage executive compensation, only 21% of the respondents indicated it had been "effective" or "very effective."

In the past two years, some of the most avidly discussed corporate governance issues have been majority voting, the merits of Section 404, and executive compensation. A brief recap of each, and the rationale for the task force's interest, follows.

Majority Voting for Directors

In 2004, the Securities and Exchange Commission (SEC) explored the idea of lowering the barriers that discourage shareowners from nominating their own board candidates, through direct access to the proxy. Institutional investors widely supported the idea as a way to shake up unresponsive boards. But opposition from business groups and mixed views among Commissioners led the agency to shelve the initiative.

Many activist investors soon embraced the notion that a director should have to win a majority of shareowner votes to be elected to the board. This represents a major shift from the plurality voting standard that is the norm — and formally the default standard — among United States public companies. In elections that use plurality voting, only votes "for" a candidate matter. Other votes are considered "withhold" votes, not "against" votes, and have no consequence. The upshot is that under the plurality system, a director can get elected without receiving a majority of votes; indeed, he or she only needs one "for" vote to be re-elected.

Institutional investors widely favor majority voting, because it offers them a meaningful vote and a way to hold directors accountable for their performance as fiduciaries. Enthusiasm is growing among boards, too. Shareowner proposals advocating adoption of a majority vote standard dominated the 2006 proxy season. But concerns about technical details and unintended consequences persist.

Section 404

The high costs of assessing the strength of internal financial controls, as required under Section 404, fueled a business backlash against Sarbanes-Oxley (2002). Companies that have had to comply with these rules say costs are far higher than expected — particularly among smaller mid-cap companies. The smallest companies (defined as those with market capitalization under $75 million) received a temporary reprieve, but many fear that costs and paperwork burdens will overwhelm them when the grace period comes to an end.

Still, surveys indicate that directors and shareowners alike perceive an improved "tone at the top" and heightened managerial accountability as a result of Section 404. Investors report that they have greater trust in directors and in the information coming from the board. But they fear that a rollback — or broad exemptions for small companies, which comprise 80% of United States public companies — would usher in a return to the lax controls that paved the way for the torrent of financial scandals of the past few years. Shareowners' ability to trust corporate financial reports depends on their faith in internal controls. Directors, while appreciating the benefits of Section 404, are concerned about high initial compliance costs. Increased "director accountability" and "investor confidence" may make up for these costs, they say, but it is hard to quantify the benefits. Some directors also report that board meetings at times are dominated by "box checking" imposed by Sarbanes-Oxley (2002), leaving insufficient time to focus on strategy and key business risks.

Executive Compensation

Media reports of skyrocketing CEO pay have heightened concerns over this issue for the public in general and the investing public in particular. Shareowners believe that over-the-top compensation at underperforming companies is a prime indicator that a board is not in control of management. Directors are concerned that those who serve on compensation committees are particularly vulnerable to being voted off boards where shareholders believe compensation to be excessive.

Directors and shareowners have a common interest in stemming the growth of compensation and in strengthening the way it is set. The SEC's sweeping new pay disclosure rules, which the Commission approved on July 26, 2006, will not only make it easier for shareowners to see how much top executives are paid; they could also lead boards to make performance hurdles more robust and transparent.

Thinking Points

1. Based on the discussion in this chapter and the preceding reading, why do you think these issues are of special concern to directors in the United States? If you are a non-United States director, do you think such issues will become important to you as well?

2. In later chapters we will deal directly with board composition and management. However, in light of the previous discussions, do you agree that boards should go to a majority vote standard for director elections? What are the risks of doing so?

3. As a director who is not an accountant or lawyer, what do you think is the most straightforward way to discharge your liabilities under Section 404 of the Sarbanes-Oxley Act (2002)?

4. Some have criticized American-style corporate governance for its devastating impact on employee morale. In particular is the continuing debate over executive compensation in an era of downsizing, outsourcing, and de-conglomerization. As a director, in what ways can you begin to think about addressing this explosive issue?

Chapter 2

Taking Back the Boardroom: The Chairperson's Special Role

The chairman's role in securing good corporate governance is crucial. Chairmen are primarily responsible for the working of the board, for its balance of membership subject to board and shareholders' approval, for ensuring that all relevant issues are on the agenda, and for ensuring that all directors, executive and non-executive alike, are enabled and encouraged to play their full part in its activities. Chairmen should be able to stand sufficiently back from the day-to-day running of the business to ensure that their boards are in full control of the company's affairs and alert to their obligations to their shareholders.

Sir Adrian Cadbury, Cadbury Code, 1992, Section 4.7

Perhaps the most important person on the board of directors is the Chairperson. Paradoxically, while the law does not recognize the special place of the Chair by imposing greater liability than an ordinary member of the board, in practice the Chair wields a great deal of influence and power. The formal and informal powers that accrue to the Chair come from his position as head of the corporation and subsequent control over the meeting agenda. Further, as spokesperson for the corporation, the Chair can sway public opinion and thus increase or decrease the legitimacy of the corporation and its officers. As the public persona of the corporation, the chair is naturally imbued with authority, and is thus conferred great levels of informal power.

Chapter 2 covers the duties and responsibilities of the Chair. The relationships between the Chief Executive Officer and the Chair with the Board are then explored. I will also discuss some principles of meeting management and how a Chairperson of the Board or of a committee can apply those principles to run meetings effectively.

33

Finally, I will talk about some leadership principles that will allow the Chair to elicit the best efforts from the board's members.

The Role of the Chairman of the Board

The role of the Chair is to lead the board of directors and the company. Chairpersons are very much involved in setting the strategic direction and organizational structure of the company. By considering what a Chair might do when turning around a poorly-run firm, we get a clearer picture of the roles that he plays. As a company grows large and mature, it can become bureaucratic, competitively unresponsive and culturally apathetic. Here, the Chair can revitalize the corporation by formulating a clear vision that is supported by a set of strong basic values, policies, and strategic priorities. To do so, he must be proactive in managing the appointment of directors that understand the importance of corporate governance, and are willing to take responsibility for their decisions. He must also lead in the appointment of a Chief Executive that is capable of innovative solutions to implement the strategic vision set by the board.

In contrast to the Chairperson, the role of the Chief Executive Officer is to lead the top management team and act as their advocate. The top management team is responsible for implementing the board's vision for the company by creating the strategic plan, ratifying the functional plans proposed by middle management, overseeing the execution of those plans, and assessing the company's performance. The CEO's primary role is to grow the firm while the Chair's role is to ensure that the firm operates at the highest level of efficiency. The two goals are not always congruent, particularly for a firm in a matured industry. Sometimes, maintaining the highest level of efficiency may require shrinking the firm. Put another way, the Chair advocates the shareholder's position while the CEO advocates the management's, so that in this nexus of healthy tension lies the best solution for maximizing shareholder wealth and maintaining the security of the firm's future.

At the heart of the Chairperson's role lies his duty to balance the interests of the management and the board. This role, however, does not suggest that the Chairperson is a referee: a passive enforcer of the rules of the game that have already been pre-determined. In today's fast moving global competitive environment, the rules of the game are constantly changing. In order to win, companies are writing their own rules, breaking with tradition and redefining the marketplace to their advantage. In the area of corporate governance, such innovative companies as General Electric, Campbell's Soup, Intel, 3M, Sony, Toyota, and ARCO are taking aggressive action to define the best practices for their industries. By doing so, they hope to gain the attention of investors who will reward management with patient money and long-term support.

Good corporate governance is about *building trust* between the investor and company management. Therefore, an effective Chairperson is one who understands the needs of shareholders and management and is able to balance, though not compromise, these needs to achieve an optimal outcome for both. The Chair must be an astute politician who understands the advantages of exercising power, and must be willing to exploit the political process to provide substance to the company's vision. This requires an effective Chair to possess a high degree of personal integrity and moral character. In the pervious generation, such Chairpersons as Jack Welch of GE, Bill Gates of Microsoft, and Andy Grove of Intel have left their mark, not only as competent corporate technocrats, but also as visionary leaders who have changed the course of industry with their astute use of power. In the next generation, the challenges impose by the forces of globalization, the Internet, environmentalism, and nationalism are requiring a new crop of Chairpersons to reinvent the way top management perceive and exploit opportunities, while simultaneously dealing with an increasingly well informed and activist investor community.

The Three Responsibilities of the Chair

There are three broad areas of responsibilities in which the Chair takes leadership roles. First, the Chair acts as a liaison between the management and the board, and between the company and its external stakeholders. This is a key strategic position from which the Chair's eagle-eyed view of the company's environment confers upon him a unique position to manage the expectations of the firm's stakeholders. As a liaison, the Chair actively negotiates the conflicting claims of the stakeholder groups so that the objectives of the firm and its shareholders can simultaneously be met.

Second, the Chair has a primary responsibility for setting the agenda and to manage the board meetings. This is a critical role because in order to make effective decisions, board members require relevant and timely information. Their contributions also have to be orchestrated in such a way as to provide positive solutions. A potential pitfall in having a board of independent thinkers is that board discussions can degenerate into ego-centered free-for-all arguments. However, the alternative, which is a rubber stamping board, simply cannot be contemplated in today's corporate governance environment.

Finally, the Chair is the prime instigator of director and management development initiatives. He guides the policies and sets the cultural agenda for director recruitment, evaluation and compensation. He is also responsible for overseeing the development of the board as a whole. Finally, he is ultimately responsible for the development of the CEO and acts as his mentor.

Liaison responsibility

The liaison role of the Chair involves managing the communications and information dissemination processes between the corporation and the stakeholders. Therefore, he has actively listen to the concerns of the firm's stakeholders to address their needs before these turn into liabilities for the firm. In an environment of shareholder activism and institutional power, the corporation that fails to manage shareholder expectations and to effectively communicate its intentions will find itself exposed to threats of takeover, government scrutiny, and shareholder lawsuits. The example of Heinz at the end of this chapter illustrates the forces that can align themselves against a Chair, if he is not perceived to be serving the interests of the company.

The key to an effective liaison role is for the Chair to work closely with the company's public relations function. At the board level, shareholder relations and information disclosure is often seen only as a staff function mandated by the stock exchange listing rules and the public relations function is viewed only as a disaster recovery tool. However, effective Chairmen know that the strategic disclosure of information can create goodwill with stakeholders, resulting in better access to resources and more patient capital. The saga of Microsoft's battles with the United States Department of Justice and European Competition Commission should be a lesson for all transnational corporations. In the US, businesses see big government as a necessary evil and many have carried this attitude overseas. In addition, recent government-linked economic fiascoes in Russia, Thailand, Brazil, and Indonesia have done little to dispel these notions. However, businesses that take this attitude run the risk of dissipating their resources and strategic attention in defending against lawsuits and onerous government regulation, damaging the firm's credibility with its stakeholder groups.

Responsibility for the agenda

The second important role the Chair plays is to set the agenda and manage the board meetings. Setting the agenda is a strategic activity in the boardroom because the agenda determines what issues are aired by the whole board. A Chair who is unscrupulous can often manipulate the board by including or excluding items that suit his political agenda. This does not serve the interests of the corporation. Instead, the Chair should open up the agenda-setting process. He should consult with the chairs of each board committee for agenda items. Then, he should solicit for the pre-meeting material so that board members can come prepared, having read the background material, to discuss the items.

The agenda should link each meeting with a stage of the firm's strategic and audit cycle. Given that a typical board meets four to six times a year for an average of about four hours each time, the board must focus on the issues affecting the strategic direction and performance of the firm. By structuring the meetings to coincide with the natural cycles of a firm's business, the board can include managerial reports and recommendations that come as a natural result of the operations of the firm. Thus, the board is able to obtain the most up to date and relevant information without expending additional resources to do so.

Since the law holds the entire board responsible for its decisions, it is important for the Chairperson to ensure that every member is given the full opportunity to participate in board discussions. He must take a proactive stance in encouraging participation while moderating the presence of those individuals who may dominate the board with their personalities.

Finally, the Chair has to review the ongoing performance of the Chief Executive Officer, important strategic issues, which can be addressed during the board meetings, can be discovered. Since the board's function is not only to monitor and discipline the management but also offer advice, members should be tapped for their collective wisdom and experience to assist the management. Thus, a good Chairman will design an agenda to give time for the board to consider strategic issues and to reflect on the direction that the firm is going.

Responsibility for management and board development

The final role played by the Chairperson of the Board is a developmental one. Specifically, the Chair is responsible for overseeing the development of individual directors and the board as a whole, and for the development of the top management team, and in particular, the CEO. Developmental issues like CEO compensation and board nomination are usually handled by committees populated by non-executive directors, but the Chair plays an important role in coordinating these efforts due to his eagle-eyed view of the corporation, its needs and direction.

The Chairperson is responsible for the development of the board. He, together with the nomination and compensation committees, has to decide on the competencies and experiences required to build and maintain a strong and independent board. To do so, the Chair has to understand the strategic thrust of the corporation and to translate this into the specific roles that individual directors can play in support. He is also responsible for overseeing the director appointment process and often takes an active role in orientating new directors on the board.

Although he should not be the only source of director appointments, the Chair is responsible for maintaining the integrity of the board's culture and therefore plays an active role in suggesting new directors.

In addition to his responsibility for board development, the Chairperson has an active and critical role to play as a mentor to the CEO. This is why corporate governance experts are not keen on the idea of one individual holding both Chair and CEO positions.[2] When the position of the Chair is separate from that of the CEO, the lines of authority are clearer. As a mentor to the CEO, the Chair has to set the performance standards by which the CEO will be judged, work with him on career development, and consider board recommendations on the appropriate compensation package. By doing so, the Chair also reinforces the values of the organization and is able to act as a sounding board for the CEO's ideas before they are formally presented to the board. The Chair is uniquely positioned for this because he has the pulse of the board's stakeholders and thus can give constructive feedback to the CEO.

Part of management development is succession planning. Here, the Chairman is responsible for ensuring that the CEO actively grooms his successor. This is a sensitive job because the Chair does not want to create unhealthy tension in the management team. He has to balance the interests of the corporation, which is to ensure a stable transition during succession, and the feelings of top management, which is to maintain the confidence of the incumbent CEO. The succession process begins with identifying a group of possible successors from within and from outside the corporation. Their job performances are closely monitored after which a handful of potential successors are picked for further grooming. The Chair has to depersonalize the process by setting objective goals and actively monitoring the planning

---

[2] In the US, it is more common for one person to hold the CEO and Chair positions. In this situation, it is vitally important that the Chair creates a board structure that empowers the non-executives to play active roles. This may require the board to create a position of lead non-executive director. Such a structure will confer more powers to the non-executive chairs of the standing committees so that the board can act independently of the management. The Sarbanes-Oxley Act of 2002 deals directly with this issue in Section 4 (see the Appendix).

and implementation of the CEO's succession plan. In the same way that the Chair has to plan for the CEO's succession, he also has to plan for his own by identifying and grooming a successor. He does this with the help of the nomination committee of the board. See the case study on Coca Cola's transition at the end of this chapter for an example of a well-executed succession plan.

Managing meetings: how to herd lions without being bitten

The activity with the greatest impact on the performance of the company is the board meeting. Here is where the board makes strategic decisions and ratifies the allocation of resources and is one of the most important activities over which the Chairman has direct influence. Effective meetings challenge individual board members to contribute their best and send a strong message to top management that the board is competent, cannot be co-opted and is serious about good management.

What are the positive steps that a Chair can take to achieve effective meetings? First, he must decide what kind of a meeting it will be. There are two types of meetings, both of which involve decision-making. The first type of meeting is informational in nature. Here, board members are briefed by the management on various aspects of the firm's operations, and are asked to endorse the management's proposals. In such meetings, the Chairman must be sensitive to the way management proposals are considered. Usually, the management would have discussed their proposal with the relevant board committee. Therefore, it is tempting to bring such proposals to the board as fait accompli, which is a dangerous and counterproductive approach, because it can create a cynical culture in the boardroom and hamstring future decision-making processes. Instead, the Chair must adopt an active listening posture, defined as seeking to understand the motivations behind the members' statements, when fielding contributions and questions on the proposal. To do this well, the Chairman must be sensitive to his power position. A disparaging remark or untoward criticism from him can quickly sour the tone and kill the discussion in the boardroom. While the Chair has to encourage each member to contribute, he must also not allow the discussion to digress and meander, meaning that he has to actively monitor the flow of information exchange and to make sure it is relevant to the issue at hand.

In an informational meeting, the first step is to state the problem and to invite the contribution of experts, which is usually the management. Each board member is given the opportunity to comment by asking for clarification or rendering an opinion. Action items, to be completed before the next meeting, must be created when it is determined that more information is needed. The Chair, with the help of the company secretary, should compile the ideas that surface from the initial discussion. Then a roundtable discussion is held to discuss the list in greater depth, ensuring that each idea receives a formal and considered airing by the whole board. When the issues raised by the list are fully explored, each member is asked to restate the proposal in his own words to ensure that everyone has a common understanding of the proposal. The board then arrives at a consensus when the proposal has been restated to the satisfaction of the entire board. This approach ensures that the best thinking from each member is obtained with the added benefit that it inherently builds commitment through consensus.

During the meeting, the Chair should continually inform members where they are on the agenda and to keep the deliverables uppermost in everyone's minds. If an expert is used, the Chair should keep his eye on his body language to ascertain whether the general direction of the discussion is correct. The Chair should be willing to actively steer the discussion and to shut down lines of inquiry that appear to lead no where, without smothering the energy and willingness to contribute.

The second type of meeting typically encountered in the boardroom is the problem solving variety. Here, the board is presented with a set of problems (e.g., an asset allocation decision, a takeover threat, an unplanned management succession event, or the myriad strategic problems that can confront the corporation) on which it will have to make a decision. Generally, the same procedures used for an informational meeting apply to problem-solving meetings, but with additional steps designed to elicit creative thinking.

After the board has agreed upon how the proposal or problem can be restated to reflect everyone's contributions, the Chair then creates a 'vacation' from the problem. A vacation is simply a way of refocusing, though not defocusing, the thoughts of the board onto a related but different topic. Vacations allow the mind to subconsciously organize the previous discussion so that linkages between bits of seemingly unconnected points of the data can be made. To illustrate: say the board is deciding on how to deal with a public relations problem, and has exhausted all the traditional options. To take a vacation, the Chair initiates a discussion on how cars are marketed, which concludes with a list of ideas and images on the topic. Coming back from the vacation, the Chairman then takes the board into the final round of discussion by asking members to make some connections between how cars are sold and the public relations scandal the company is trying to address. This list of connections is discussed with the most innovative solution voted on by the entire board.

The above process requires time, and cool heads. However, problems at the board level tend to be severe and thus the Chair has an extra responsibility to manage the discussion, first by setting the right tone and then by focusing everyone's thoughts on the relevant issues. In such situations, while sense of urgency should be maintained it should never be allowed to deteriorate into panic, which can easily happen when members do not fully understand how the problem can impact their personal liabilities. Thus, the corporate lawyer should be present to field such questions before the problem-solving session begins.

Finally, the Chair should always strive to leave members feeling positive about a board meeting so they that can look forward to the next meeting. This requires the Chair to maintain a high energy level in the boardroom, which they can do with a variety of tools, including humor to break monotony and argument deadlocks, challenge by posing difficult and thoughtful questions, and surprises, such as the taking of "vacations", to vary the pace of the meeting.

There are four stumbling blocks to effective meetings. Firstly, a meeting in which the attendees are treated casually and unprofessionally is dysfunctional. Instead, the tone of each meeting should be goal-oriented, which is achieved by setting agendas that have clear outcomes along with well-defined deliverables and action plans. To achieve this, members should be given the agenda and pre-meeting reading materials well in advance; typically 2 weeks for a regular board meeting.

Together with treating each member professionally, the Chair must never allow a board member to be put on the defensive; particularly when someone is making a contribution during a brainstorming or roundtable session. To prevent defensiveness, the Chair should never require a justification for an idea at the outset of the meeting. He should make it clear that conflicting points of view are acceptable, and even desirable for the board as the best solutions are those that can resolve the conflicting points of view. During discussions, the Chair must enforce a positive contribution policy as it is very easy to raise objections. He must not allow the immediate dismissal of an idea that initially appears to lack substance. Instead such ideas should be tabled for further examination because obscure ideas may become the solution with further elaboration from other board members. Finally, the Chair should never allow a member to be pinned down in an argument by another member. Such behaviors inevitably discourage future bold contributions.

Secondly, meetings that present options and solutions as *fait accompli* usually discourage creativity, positive attitudes, and decisive decision-making. It is very important for members to feel that their contributions are meaningful to the board as a whole. It is also very important to act on members' suggestions within a short time of the meeting, as this will send a clear message that their contributions are taken seriously. The Chairman of the board is thus responsible for ensuring that members' suggestions are noted in the agenda, and that further action is reported in a timely manner to the entire board before the next meeting.

The Chairman must do all he can to protect the office of the Chair and the integrity of the board by being conscious of his actions, words and non-verbal cues. He should not use the meetings as venues for demonstrating his superiority or feeding his ego. Most importantly, he must not play off one member of the board against another just to 'look good'.

Thirdly, meetings in which the Chairperson inappropriately exercises his power to influence the outcome of the decisions are doomed to failure. This is easily done because the Chairman controls the agenda and decides who is recognized and at what point in the discussions. When members sense that the meetings are 'rigged', they will lose interest, become cynical, and stop contributing. Instead, they are likely to engage in political behaviors to advance their personal interests, often at the expense of the firm.

The Chairman must always adhere to the principle of not competing with board members during the meeting. By noting each director's contribution, the Chair can assemble the wisdom of the board and use this to push the board's thinking beyond the obvious and to challenge individual board members to give their best by enhancing their understanding of the issues and encouraging further thought. This does not mean that a Chair should act as a passive collator of information. However, he has to be sensitive to the fact that when he offers opinions, it will carry more weight than the others in the boardroom. This can have the effect of bringing the discussion to a more sophisticated level of thought or shut it down completely. The Conrad Black case at the end of Chapter 3 illustrates how the latter can happen when the Chair of the board is intent on eliminating all dissent, even when the board is populated by blue-chip directors.

Finally, the Chair must realize that there will be a natural resistance to new ideas in any process of change. A meeting is less effective when such resistance is not given an airing and dealt with honestly. Members will leave the meeting harboring resentment and thus not give full support to the initiatives taken. Given that corporations now exist in an environment of constant change, the Chair must be ever vigilant to identify the sources of resistance and to deal with them when they arise.

Who can Chair?

There is a great demand on the integrity of individuals who play the role of the Chair and research has shown that effective Chairmen share some common characteristics. First, they tend to be people with strong personal convictions. Such leaders as Warren Buffet, Samuel Walton, Bill Gates, and Andy Grove have simple, yet powerful dictums. They understand their place in history and are clear about their mission in life. This clarity of purpose and conviction translates into well defined and clearly articulated vision statements that are easily understood by the board, the management and the stakeholders. The best leaders also share an unusual intellectual capacity to absorb and process complex information. For example, although Lou Gerstner did not have a technical background when he joined IBM, he quickly grasped the implications of the company's technological competencies, and created a turnaround strategy that revitalized IBM into the technological and marketing powerhouse of today.

Successful Chairmen have deep experience managing in a variety of industrial contexts and economic situations. Unlike American managers who had to deal with economic upheaval and corporate restructuring beginning in the late 1980s, emerging economy managers that have only experienced double digit growth in the latter half of the 20th century have not had to face the test of a deep and extended recession. For example, the Asian Crisis of 1997, which lasted barely 18 months, took a heavy toll on companies in the region, indicating the shallowness of the talent pool among Asian top managers. In the 21st century, the job of Chair has dramatically toughened. Therefore, corporations must populate their boards with Chairpersons are who have tasted failure and have turned this experience into positive lessons for winning in personal and corporate life. Successful Chairpersons share an uncommon ability to use the political process to create a sense of shared values and common destiny. They are skilled in dealing with multiple and sometime conflicting constituencies to build consensus and understanding.

A Summary of the Chair's Priorities

For a Chairperson to be effective, he must prioritize the use of his time. The first set of priorities has to be in the area of board leadership. Here, his first priority is the 'care and feeding' of the board, which includes director selection and development. Next, he has to ensure that the strategic decision process has full board participation, ensuring that all the directors are given the opportunity to ratify the plan. The Chairman has to ensure that the firm's strategies are vision-driven — not simply a result of managerial convenience. The third priority for the Chair is to develop the management's talent. To do so, the Chair must consciously manage the succession process and to proactively mentor the CEO in his career development. Finally, the Chairman has to guard the cultural values of the corporation and ensure that it is self-renewing. To do so, the Chair has to create a learning and innovation-driven culture in the corporation. Such values are often encapsulated in the corporate values statement, and it is the preserve of the Chairman to guard the integrity and continued relevance of such statements and to ensure that it is communicated and practiced throughout the organization.

The following case studies illustrate two types of Chairmen. The first discusses the chairmanship of Anthony O'Reilly of Heinz. The second case is an excerpt from a biography of Roberto Goizueta who was the previous Chairman of Coca-Cola. They both run companies that compete in very tough environments. Compare their styles, job duties and performance. Which of the two Chairmen, do you think, comes closest to the principles set forth in this chapter? On the basis of these reports, if you were an investor, would you buy one stock of Coca-Cola or of Heinz? Why? Would it matter?

The CEO and the Board[3]

It was, as always, an extravagantly festive event. On August 10, some 500 guests of H.J. Heinz Chairman and Chief Executive Anthony J.F. O'Reilly gathered under chandeliers in a mammoth white pavilion set up at the swanky Leopardstown horse-racing track outside Dublin. More than half were flown in from around the world, put up at Ireland's finest hotels, and feted at a lavish three-day bash. Guests included H.J. Heinz Co. executives and directors, Wall Street analysts, and assorted politicians, tycoons, and friends. In recent years, Paul Newman, William Kennedy Smith, and the CEOs of PepsiCo, Sara Lee, and Clorox have joined in the fun.

From a gala ball at O'Reilly's own Georgian mansion to the main event, the Heinz 57 Phoenix Stakes, no expense was spared. And with Heinz picking up the tab, O'Reilly was clearly the star of the show. Arriving last to the pre-race luncheon, he and his wife, Chryss, stepped gingerly from a blue Bentley. As they made their entrance, O'Reilly began working the room, offering handshakes, jokes, and whispered asides with a politician's natural ease.

"When he walks into the marquee, the whole place comes alive," recalls a recent guest. "Short of a United States President's arrival, I've never seen anything like it."

Wherever he goes, whatever he does, 61-year-old Tony O'Reilly projects a commanding presence. A world-class salesman, bon vivant, and raconteur, O'Reilly has reigned as king of the US$9.4 billion food powerhouse for the past 18 years. And perhaps nowhere is that truer than in the corporate boardroom at Heinz's Pittsburgh headquarters, where O'Reilly is first among equals on a board that includes many insiders, business associates, and even personal friends of the charismatic CEO. "Tony is larger than life, and he knows it,"

---

[3] This case was prepared for teaching purposes and does not purport to illustrate the effective or ineffective resolution of specific managerial situations.

says Heinz director Donald R. Keough, 71, a former Coca-Cola Co. president and longtime friend.

In part, that is because he has performed: Through much of his tenure, shareholders have had little to complain about. He revived the company in the 1980s, becoming a Wall Street star. Even though growth is no longer red-hot, Heinz still does about as well as its average food-industry peer.

So why has Tony O'Reilly become the next target of activist investors leading the corporate governance movement?

The answer has as much to do with the evolution of corporate governance as it does with O'Reilly or Heinz. For despite O'Reilly's performance, unhappy shareholders such as Teachers Insurance & Annuity Assn.-College Retirement Equities Fund (TIAA-CREF) and California Public Employees' Retirement System (CalPERS) believe it is a textbook example of what a board should not be: a cozy club of loyalists headed by a powerful and charismatic chieftain. Now that view is being put to the test. Since late last year, TIAA-CREF — the US$101 billion pension fund, which owns 2.7 million Heinz shares worth US$113 million — has been waging a behind-the-scenes battle with O'Reilly over governance. Early next year, CalPERS is expected to push for board changes at Heinz. "The board is way too large, way too dominated by very old men, and it has not had enough turnover," says Kayla J. Gillan, CalPERS' general counsel.

O'Reilly bristles at the notion that his board fails to measure up. "This is not a cronies' board," he insists. The current setup is simply "the best for Heinz Co." And in O'Reilly, shareholder activists face a formidable and powerful opponent. Heinz may no longer be a high-flier, but activists cannot point to the mediocre performance that allowed them to force change at companies such as American Express Co. and Eastman Kodak Co. Unlike other embattled CEOs, O'Reilly is waging a strong philosophical fight against the board reforms they demand.

For O'Reilly and the company he leads, the stakes are huge. Critics believe a stronger board would likely rein in his free-spending ways. O'Reilly's lavish bash was the 15th in a row, for example, even though Heinz is in the midst of laying off 2,500 employees. Heinz says the event, which also includes meetings with analysts and big customers, is an effective corporate marketing tool that is no more expensive than sponsoring a golf tournament.

A tougher board might also trim the generous options that have made O'Reilly one of America's highest-paid CEOs — even as his company's performance has slipped. And pressure on O'Reilly to pass the baton to his hard-charging No. 2, William R. Johnson, a move many on Wall Street would like, could grow. "I think Johnson is the right man for the times at Heinz," says Arthur B. Cecil, an analyst at T. Rowe Price Associates Inc., another big shareholder.

But the stakes go well beyond Heinz. The issues involved — what makes for an effective board or a good director — are at the core of a much broader debate about boardroom practices that is raging throughout Corporate America. After spending much of the past decade going after lackluster management, activist investors are turning a sterner eye on the job done by boards and directors, regardless of how a company or its stock are doing. If investors succeed in forcing tougher boardroom practices at Heinz, many other lackluster boards are likely to face similar pressure to shape up.

Such moves have gained momentum since November, when a National Association of Corporate Directors panel headed by governance guru Ira Millstein issued a sweeping set of guidelines that outlined "best practices" for boards. Early this year, TIAA-CREF began screening its corporate investments on 25 governance issues, from the ages of directors to their potential conflicts of interest with management. Where boards don't measure up, TIAA-CREF is prodding even well-run companies to strengthen the quality of their directors. CalPERS joined the fray in June by proposing its own strict board guidelines. Within months it, too, plans to target those that fail to make the grade. Even the Business Roundtable is getting into the act, in part to head off tougher measures by activists. It plans to publish its own set of principles on September 10.

The list of best practices favored by the activists today is extensive. Since the aim is to ensure that directors ally themselves with shareholders, not management, the guiding principle is director independence. Governance experts believe boards should have no more than two or three inside directors, and key audit, nominating, and compensation committees should be composed entirely of outsiders. All director retainers should be paid in stock. Extras, such as pensions, which activists fear compromise independence, should be eliminated. No director should earn consulting, legal, or other fees from the company. Moreover, interlocking directorships — execs who serve on each others' boards — should be banned. Activists believe they encourage members to look out for each other.

Still, the new board standards have come in for some vociferous criticism. Many executives — and, indeed, many investors — remain skeptical. Although hundreds of companies are considering them, so far only a few — Ashland Inc. is one — have adopted them in any significant way. Citing such top companies as Walt Disney Co., which has also been criticized for weak boardroom practices, many directors dismiss the guidelines as rigid and academic. More to the point, they say, they bear no correlation to performance. "I'm not for blanket rules," says John C. Bogle, chairman of mutual-fund giant Vanguard Group and a director of Mead Corp. "When you get into valuations of a stock, it is hard to know where one would put governance with fundamentals like dividend and earnings growth and financial strength."

To many observers, Heinz could well be a poster child for poor corporate governance. For its size and prominence, the company stands nearly alone in its failure to meet many of the new guidelines. Heinz's board immediately popped up on TIAA-CREF's radar last year because it failed to meet the fund's basic standards. And in BUSINESS WEEK's first ranking of corporate boards, published last November, Heinz' was the third worst in the United States, behind only Archer Daniels Midland Co. and Champion International Corp. But far from backing down, O'Reilly and his associates firmly dismiss such guidelines as procedural frippery. "These are philosophical differences that will be debated for years," says Benjamin E. Thomas Jr., Heinz's corporate secretary. "I don't think there is empirical evidence out there to show this stuff matters."

If shareholders are doing well, O'Reilly and other skeptics ask, does the makeup of the board — or the rules under which it operates — really make a difference? In the past, the answers might well have been no. But governance experts now recognize it took years of decline and board inaction at such companies as American Express, GM, and Westinghouse Electric before a looming crisis forced reforms. So activists are focusing on avoiding a meltdown in the first place. "The key to good governance is to keep a well-performing corporation from becoming a poor-performing one," says B. Kenneth West, the ex-chairman of Harris Trust & Savings Bank who is a senior consultant for governance at TIAA-CREF.

That is what makes Heinz a near-perfect candidate for this fight. It is not like General Motors Corp. in 1992. In fact, Heinz isn't doing badly. Excluding a US$420.9 million restructuring charge, the global food giant posted a 9.6% rise in net income, to US$722.8 million, in fiscal 1997, ended on April 30. Moreover, O'Reilly has made several moves long demanded by Wall Street during the past year. In mid-1996, he finally anointed William Johnson his heir apparent by naming him president and chief operating officer. In March, O'Reilly unveiled with much fanfare Project Millennia, a reorganization plan under which at least 25 plants will be closed or sold.

That is still far from O'Reilly's glory days. After taking the helm in 1979, he wowed investors by slashing expenses, stealing market share, and expanding globally. Profits and sales took off, as did Heinz' stock. Total shareholder returns averaged 31% a year in the 1980s, nearly double the Standard & Poor's 500-stock index's 16.8%.

But Heinz has offered up far more modest performance of late. Since the start of the decade, operating earnings have grown 43%; by contrast, rival Campbell Soup Co. has increased its income by 140%, to a projected US$1.5 billion for fiscal 1997. And over the past five years, Heinz' annual shareholder returns of 13.9% have consistently underperformed the S&P, as well as the S&P food index. Only a runup since Johnson's appointment as president — the stock has gained 35% — has allowed Heinz to catch up with its food-industry rivals.

Nevertheless, the Heinz board continues to pay O'Reilly like a superstar. His total compensation of US$182.9 million in the past six years ranks him among a handful of the best-paid CEOs. In five of those six years, he has won the dubious distinction of being among the five CEOs cited by BUSINESS WEEK as giving shareholders the least for their money. While much of that stems from gains on options granted early in his tenure, the hefty awards have continued even as performance has slipped. Indeed, the board has been so generous with O'Reilly's options that he is now Heinz' largest individual shareholder, with 1.6% of the stock.

A comparison with Campbell Soup Co. is telling. Last year alone, O'Reilly got a new options grant on 750,000 shares. That is more than the 646,800 shares Campbell Chairman David W. Johnson got in the past seven years combined. Still, O'Reilly defends his hefty options packet. "There could be no more honorable or fairer way [to be paid] in American capitalism," he insists.

That's not the only contrast between Heinz and Campbell that rankles shareholder activists. Once under duress itself from investors for being a lackluster, family-dominated sleeper, Campbell ousted the CEO in 1990 and hired outsider Johnson from Gerber Products Co. Since then, the company has become a pioneer in corporate governance: In 1992, Campbell became the first major company to publish board guidelines (see table below).

The shift appears to be paying off. Since 1992, Campbell's annual shareholder returns of 20.9% have far outdistanced those of Heinz. "You have to wonder how Campbell, with a model board, is outperforming Heinz," says Charles M. Elson, a law professor at Stetson University College of Law and a governance expert. "This is a captured and incestuous board. That may explain the difference."

Of course, there are other differences. Share repurchases, acquisitions, and a steady stream of new products have helped. Campbell also has had greater pricing flexibility, thanks to its dominance of the United States soup market. But Johnson views an active, independent board as a source of competitive advantage, and he credits the directors with helping engineer the turnaround. In approving a new strategy last year, for example, the board retained its own investment banker and legal counsel. "The directors helped me by asking the right questions," says Johnson.

By contrast, the Heinz board is very much an O'Reilly creation, and its lackluster reviews have much to do with the sheer force of his personality. The Irish-born O'Reilly is no ordinary CEO. A former rugby star in Ireland, O'Reilly was 33 when he was hired as managing director of Heinz' subsidiary in Britain in 1969. Four years later, he was tapped as president of the company, and in 1979 as CEO. He is one of the world's most charismatic businessmen. "He has a million stories and tells all of them well," says Heinz director Richard M. Cyert. "When you sit down to lunch with him, it is like going to a movie theater for entertainment."

But that charisma may have a downside. Critics believe it has led to a board that's far more deferential to O'Reilly than it ought to be. "Most of the directors are more mesmerized by Tony than critical in any way," says an outside consultant who worked with the board for years. "Whatever Tony wanted, Tony got." O'Reilly, Johnson, and seven of Heinz' nine outside directors disagree; two others did not return phone calls. Maintains director Cyert: "He frequently goes around the room to see how people feel about an issue. They shall argue back and forth. It is not necessarily tough on Tony, but it shows the independence of the board."

Does it? The independence of the Heinz board is at the core of the dispute between O'Reilly and the governance crowd. For starters, Heinz' board remains loaded with insiders. Ten of the 19 board members are current or former Heinz employees. Governance experts believe that having so many insiders lends too much support for O'Reilly. "Why would an insider challenge the boss?" asks Elson. "That is a nice way to lose your job very quickly."

As if that were not enough, Heinz' board is overloaded with aging directors. The average age of Heinz' board is more than 66; only one of the nine outside members is below the age of 65. And rarely do directors leave: 85-year-old Joseph J. Bogdanovich, for example, joined in 1963. That flies in the face of the most controversial aspects of the new guidelines: that boards ought to have mandatory retirement ages — and even term limits. CalPERS has argued that board members who stay for a decade or more should no longer be considered independent.

O'Reilly not only dismisses his critics, he argues vehemently that companies are better off with many inside directors. "If you have only one insider," he says, "the only person who talks to that board is the

CEO, and every view is filtered through one mind to the board." Heinz President Johnson, a four-year board member who spoke on behalf of the inside directors, insists that they say what they think. "I am sure there were times when Tony or a couple of other senior guys were rolling their eyes when someone said something he wished he hadn't heard," says Johnson.

O'Reilly and his directors also insist that age and length of service are irrelevant. "Most of us are rather aged, but we are quite viable," declares 77-year-old Eleanor B. Sheldon, a Heinz director of 18 years. Although forced to retire because of age from the boards of Citibank, Equitable, and Mobil, she remains at Heinz.

Just as jarring is the fact that most of the outside directors who gather around the sierra chica granite table in Heinz' windowless boardroom are longtime colleagues or friends of O'Reilly, and not one outsider is a sitting CEO. Indeed, how the powerful executive maneuvered over the past 18 years is nothing less than a study in how to craft a board of directors.

As was common when O'Reilly became CEO in 1979, many board members had crossed paths elsewhere: Three outsiders also were directors of Mobil Corp., where O'Reilly had become a board member. Within a year, O'Reilly joined the Heinz board's nominating committee. By 1984, he took over as committee chairman and began to dominate the selection process.

To governance experts, that is a huge no-no. To foster independence, they believe board selection should remain in the hands of outside directors. They also frown on cross-directorships, since that can lead to a "you scratch my back, I'll scratch yours" mentality among directors who sit on boards together. But at nearly every turn, O'Reilly hand-picked his new directors — almost always from boards he already sat on or from organizations affiliated with Heinz.

His very first recruit, in 1983, was William W. Scranton, a fellow director at Mobil. A year later, he tapped Cyert, then president of Carnegie Mellon University, a beneficiary of Heinz Foundation grants and a fellow director with O'Reilly at Allegheny International, a company that eventually declared bankruptcy amidst a financial scandal. In 1987, O'Reilly recruited his third outsider, Nicholas F. Brady, then chairman of Dillon, Read & Co., an investment bank Heinz had been doing business with for 4 years. Brady had also served on the NL Industries board with two other Heinz directors. A year later, a fourth Mobil director, Samuel C. Johnson, joined the Heinz board.

As O'Reilly continued to find familiar candidates, Heinz' nominating committee didn't even bother to meet. O'Reilly's next recruit was Coca-Cola's Keough, with whom he served as a director at Washington Post Co. as well as on the board of trustees at Notre Dame University. He joined the board in 1990, the second year in a row that Heinz' nominating committee failed to convene even once. And even in recent years, as the governance movement has led many companies to begin looking further afield for their directors, O'Reilly's M. O. has not changed. On director Brady's recommendation, O'Reilly brought aboard in 1994 Washington attorney Edith E. Holiday, a longtime Brady aide. The newest outsider on the board is former United States House Speaker Thomas S. Foley, whom O'Reilly describes as a friend for more than 15 years. When Foley retired as Speaker of the House of Representatives in 1996, O'Reilly organized an extravagant tribute to him in the Capital Hilton ballroom.

O'Reilly insists the shared experiences allow him to better evaluate potential directors. He defends his role as nominating committee chairman, claiming it allows him to get better talent. Adversaries counter that his role simply ensures he has virtually free rein to hand-pick his own directors. Complains Robert A.G. Monks, a principal in Lens Inc., an activist investment fund: "Everybody knows it is a matter of personal loyalty to the guy who put him or her there."

He and other experts also point to another troubling issue: O'Reilly has treated his board as generously as it has treated him. In three of his first four years as CEO, O'Reilly and directors hiked the pay of all outsiders and added lifelong director pensions. Later, O'Reilly added other raises and perks, including a US$1 million donation to charity after a director's death. Along with annual retainers of US$30,000 and yearly grants of 300 shares of stock, directors receive US$1,500 for each meeting they attend. In all, it's pretty generous — about 20% above average for the nation's 100 largest companies, according to consultants SpencerStuart.

Slow Mover

No less problematic is the fact that the board's executive committee, which has the authority to act when the board is not in session, is composed entirely of insiders. Chaired by O'Reilly, the committee regularly meets the day before the full board. Most companies restrict their purpose to emergency business. Not Heinz. In six of the past seven years, its executive committee has met more often than the board. By comparison, Campbell Soup's five-member executive committee has only one insider and has met once in three years. "O'Reilly has created two classes of directors: those that make the decisions and those that bless them," charges John M. Nash, president of the National Association of Corporate Directors. O'Reilly makes no apologies, arguing that the executive panel is more of a "reporting committee" that helps prepare for the full board.

The question, of course, is whether any of this matters. Would a different board — younger, less familiar with each other, or with O'Reilly — have overseen Heinz any differently? O'Reilly and his directors say no — and they deny that oversight has been weak. "This isn't a show-and-tell board," says Keough.

Even O'Reilly's harshest critics concede that the charge is impossible to prove, since only O'Reilly and his directors see what goes on in the boardroom. But they believe plenty of signs show that O'Reilly and his managers are not being held to very tough standards. Heinz was the slowest of the major food companies to restructure, and many on Wall Street believe it did not go far enough. Analysts have also complained that Heinz has inflated its earnings through aggressive accounting. Heinz denies that allegation.

Moreover, though O'Reilly has also been frequently criticized for devoting extensive time to his outside interests to the detriment of Heinz, the board has made no move to challenge him. Among other things, O'Reilly is nonexecutive chairman and director of three companies he owns — Independent Newspapers, Fitzwilton, and Waterford Wedgewood. He's also chairman of a Dublin law firm that does work with Heinz. All told, O'Reilly travels some 300,000 miles a year on the company's Gulfstream. "There is no doubt that he is often out of the country, and not only on Heinz business," says one analyst. "I think that's hurt the company." Retorts director Brady: "Three-quarters of O'Reilly is better than 100% of most people. He is that talented."

He's also tenacious — and those who want Heinz to reform its board are in for a long fight. In the past, outside efforts to get Heinz to improve its governance practices have failed. While TIAA-CREF and CalPERS are stronger adversaries than Heinz has faced before, O'Reilly clearly has plenty of board support.

So far, that has added up to a stalemate. After a series of letters from TIAA-CREF and a meeting with West, asking O'Reilly to trim the insiders, he still refuses to budge — the only one of seven companies targeted by TIAA-CREF to do so. In fact, in June, O'Reilly added one more inside director — giving current and former executives a board majority. Meanwhile, activists want most of the old-timers to go, and some have asked that directors' pensions be eliminated and a larger share of directors' compensation be paid in stock.

Although O'Reilly says he might concede on the last two issues — if the board wants it — he insists he won't significantly reduce the number of insiders. "Outsiders are outsiders. They simply are not committed to the board in the same way as people who have their careers at stake here. Boards that listen to one man will be the prisoners of that man."

Perhaps. But many who have looked at the rarefied and privileged realm of Heinz' board, believe the company's inside and outside directors alike already are prisoners to one man: O'Reilly. If there are no board changes soon, the lobbying behind the scenes by TIAA-CREF could erupt into a public boardroom brawl. If it does, investors may finally get a chance to weigh in on whether they think boardroom practices really do matter.

Does good governance pay?

Rival Campbell Soup is a leader in adopting innovative board practices. Its shares have outperformed Heinz, a governance laggard, as well as the market. Here's how they compare:

Best practices	Campbell	Heinz
Majority of outside directors	Only one insider among 15 directors	Ten of 19 members are insiders
Bans insiders on nominating committee	Yes	No: CEO is chairman of panel
Bans former execs from board	Yes	No: Three directors are ex-Heinz execs
Mandatory retirement age	70, with none over 64	72, but six directors are grandfathered
Outside directors meet without CEO	Annually	Never
Appointment of 'lead director'	Yes	No
Governance committee	Yes	No
Self-evaluation of board's effectiveness	Every two years	None
Director pensions	None	Yes
Share-ownership requirement	3,000 shares	None required

Data: 2000 Proxy statements, *Business Week*, 2000.

Independent directors or O'Reilly's cronies?

Some shareholders and corporate governance activists charge that Heinz' board is overloaded with loyalists and friends of O'Reilly. Here is the list of outside directors:

SAMUEL C. JOHNSON: (69) Former chairman of S. C. Johnson & Son; served with O'Reilly on Mobil board.

EDITH E. HOLIDAY: (45) Attorney who worked with Nick Brady when he was Treasury Secretary under Bush; joined board in 1994.

WILLIAM P. SNYDER III: (79) Longest-serving director. Former president of Shenango Furnace Co.; on board since 1961.

HERMAN J. SCHMIDT: (80) Former vice-chairman of Mobil Corp.; on board since 1977; fellow Mobil director with O'Reilly.

NICHOLAS F. BRADY: (67) Joined in 1987 when he was chairman of Dillon Read & Co., investment banker to Heinz. Now, Heinz is putting US$5 million in his investment fund.

DONALD R. KEOUGH: (71) Former Coca-Cola Co. president; served with O'Reilly on the Washington Post Co. board for many years.

ELEANOR B. SHELDON: (77) Described as a "social scientist." Board member since 1979; served with O'Reilly on Mobil board.

RICHARD M. CYERT: (76) President of Carnegie Mellon University, a beneficiary of Heinz Foundation grants.

THOMAS S. FOLEY: (68) O'Reilly friend for over 15 years. Former United States House Speaker joined board in 1995.

Data: 2000 Proxy statements, *Business Week*, 2000.

A man of many interests

Besides H. J. Heinz, Tony O'Reilly is also involved in a panoply of businesses around the world. Among his major investments:

Business	Details	O'Reilly's Stake (millions)
Independent Newspapers of Dublin	Ireland's largest newspaper chain	$332.9
H. J. Heinz	Largest individual shareholder	254.0
Fitzwilton	Includes china maker Waterford Wedgwood	71.4
Arcon	Irish oil-exploration company	71.4
Australian Provincal Newspapers	Chain of small newspapers in Australia	41.3
Dromoland and Ashford	Irish castles converted into hotels	19.5

Data: *Business Week*, 2000.

Putting More Stock in Good Governance

How much is good governance worth? These days, corporate chieftains, shareholder activists, and academics are hotly debating that question. Even as funds such as TIAA-CREF and the California Public Employees' Retirement System (CalPERS) seek to impose boardroom guidelines on companies such as H. J. Heinz Co., critics of the somewhat rigid rules say they are trying to do the impossible. Investors simply can't tally the benefits of a strong board of directors, in part because what goes on inside the boardroom is invisible to outsiders.

But as the battle over boardroom standards heats up, institutional shareholders and governance gurus are gathering evidence to prod often reluctant chieftains and their directors into reform. A number of recent studies show that well-governed companies not only make more money than the poorly governed, but investors are likely to give them a higher stock market value.

In one yet-unpublished study, Yale University economist Paul W. MacAvoy looked at the performance of 275 companies ranked on governance by CalPERS in 1994. Those that CalPERS considered well-governed boasted an extra 1.5–2% on average in annual returns to shareholders. "Over a decade, we're talking about returns of 15–20% more to shareholders," says MacAvoy. Another study of 205 corporations in 14 industries by professors at the University of Pennsylvania's Wharton School found that companies with "ineffective governance structures" often rewarded their CEOs excessive pay in relation to performance.

But perhaps the most compelling evidence that good governance pays off comes from a McKinsey & Co. study. Investors were asked how much they would be willing to pay for shares in two well-performing companies. The difference between the two theoretical companies: Only one of the boards followed good governance practices, such as having a majority of outside directors.

The investors surveyed — 50 institutional money managers who together oversee assets worth US$840 million — told McKinsey they would fork over an average premium of 11% for the stock of the company with good governance practices. Perhaps more telling, chief executives and directors were willing to pay an even higher premium. Directors said they would pay about 14–15% more, while CEOs said they would ante up an extra 16%. "This is the first time anyone has demonstrated that investors place a high value on good governance," says Ira M. Millstein, the governance guru. "We'll be able to use this study to convince boards to become more pro-active."

Applying the study's numbers to Heinz would suggest that the company's market value would grow US$1.6 billion if investors thought it was well-governed. That's hardly chump change. McKinsey estimates that Heinz would have to increase its pretax profits by more than US$140 million annually to gain 11% in stock price.

Hypothetical

Why the big jump? Some investors surveyed said they believed that good governance would help boost performance over time, bringing a higher stock price. Others felt good governance decreases the risk of bad news — and when trouble occurs, they rebound faster.

Of course, McKinsey's numbers are based on a hypothetical; there is no telling whether investors would make the same decisions if they had money on the line. And in real life, so many disparate factors go into assessing a stock's value that it's impossible to put a price tag on a well-run board. Even staunch supporters such as Millstein caution that guidelines and policies offer no guarantees. He concedes that the best standards in the world will not do much good if directors do not take their responsibilities seriously. Nevertheless, without the ability to peek inside the boardroom, investors will have to settle for the next best thing: measuring a company's commitment to governance via the independence, quality, and accountability of its board.

Higher premiums for well-run boards

McKinsey & Co. asked institutional investors, chief executives, and directors to compare two well-performing companies and state whether they would pay a premium for the one with better governance. The results:

Group	Premium (%)
Institutional Investrs	11
Directors	14
Chief Executive	16

Data: McKinsey & Co.

Thinking Points

1. Assess the chairmanship of O'Reilly against the principles set forth in the chapter. Do you think he passes?
2. Compare Campbell's and Heinz. Do you think their corporate governance practices are responsible for their performance differences?
3. If you were on the board of Heinz, what would you do to address your critics? Could you make the changes you think is important?

I'd Like the World to Buy a Coke[4]

In 1954, Roberto C. Goizueta answered a help-wanted advertisement for a chemical engineer in a Havana newspaper and went to work for The Coca-Cola Co. Twenty-six years later, the Cuban-born executive triumphed in a bruising battle for Coke's top job. Named president in May of 1980 and elected chairman and chief executive 10 weeks later, Goizueta had overcome long odds and bested worthy rivals to command one of the world's great enterprises.

But Goizueta could hardly afford to rest on his laurels. The company he headed was mired in a hodgepodge of unrelated ventures, from shrimp farming to winemaking. Its crucial bottler system was badly decayed, with important markets left in the hands of weak operators. There was no strategic vision, and creativity was stifled by a blind adherence to tradition and a refusal to take risks. Worst of all, Coke's stock had fallen by half, and the company was barely turning a profit.

Over the next 12 months, in a period of astonishing activity, Goizueta set in motion a series of initiatives that would set the course for Coca-Cola for the next 17 years. From the time he became chief executive until his death in 1997, Coke's sales more than quadrupled, from US$4–US$18 billion, while its market capitalization ballooned from US$4.3–US$180 billion, a staggering 3,500% increase. The blueprint for that record — one of corporate America's best — was largely drawn up during Goizueta's first months in office.

In June of 1980, Coca-Cola Co.'s new president, Roberto C. Goizueta, was eager to get started — to put his mark on the company and pull it into the modern era. Goizueta set out first to cure the soda company's most glaring problem, its troubled bottling system. Next, he would call his managers to Atlanta and purposefully shake them to their roots, questioning every assumption that they held about the

---

[4] This case was prepared for teaching purposes and does not purport to illustrate the effective or ineffective resolution of specific managerial situations.

business. Only then would Coca-Cola be ready to receive Roberto Goizueta's vision for the future — a vision that respected tradition but held nothing sacred except progress.

Within six weeks of becoming president, Goizueta had a dramatic plan for revamping Coke's network of bottlers. The franchise system of independent bottlers created at the turn of the century had served Coke well, allowing it to expand nationwide with a minimum of capital. But now those operations were in the hands of third-generation owners, many of whom had grown complacent and lacked the capital to keep pace with technology and with changes in their markets.

Goizueta presented his plan to 15 of Coke's top domestic bottlers at an all-day meeting in Atlanta. The approach, he explained, would be one of shared responsibility and shared opportunity. Both sides would have to work hard to improve their relationship — and their businesses. He promised a more aggressive, focused, and responsive approach from Atlanta but also demanded that the bottlers get tougher, leaner, and more competitive. "If your sales decline for a single week, we want to know why," he said.

Then, Goizueta unloaded his most dramatic and far-reaching news. It was time to "refranchise" the Coca-Cola bottling system, he said. The company intended to weed out weak operators. Coke's recent purchase of its Atlanta bottler and an investment in its New York bottler were just the start of a broader program of investment. Coke bottlers looking for an exit strategy would find a ready buyer in Corporate Coke, which planned to refurbish weak franchises and put them back out for sale to stronger members of Coca-Cola's system.

Dramatic Shift

A stronger bottler system would mean better distribution for Coke as it battled Pepsi in store aisles and soda fountains across the country and would make the bottler's businesses more valuable. It was a dramatic cultural shift for Coke and a signal to the bottlers that Goizueta, whom many had lobbied against in his struggle for the top job, was willing to enter into a new partnership. Ultimately, Goizueta's plan would lead Coke to invest billions as it built the best beverage distribution system in the world.

Bringing new discipline to the bottling system, though vital to Coke's future, was relatively simple compared with the vast cultural changes Goizueta would soon wreak throughout the worldwide organization. But first, he needed to wrest the last remaining power from his mentor, Robert W. Woodruff, the revered former chairman known simply as "the boss," who had saved the company from bankruptcy during the Great Depression and was now its biggest shareholder. Even at age 90, Woodruff was able to use allies on the board and his position as head of the powerful finance committee to retain ultimate control at Coke. Before the Goizueta era could begin, Coke's new leader knew, the Woodruff era had to end.

Goizueta wasted no time. At his first board meeting as chairman-elect in early September, 1980, he made a series of moves that brought the Coke board closer to modern notions of corporate governance and at the same time expanded his authority. First, he imposed three-year terms for board members, eliminating open-ended service. Then, he pushed through a by-law prohibiting renomination of board members after their 71st birthday, an edict designed to flush out Woodruff and his cronies.

But Goizueta's most important move was to seize control of the purse strings from the finance committee, the vehicle Woodruff had used to exert control over the previous CEO, Paul Austin. To shore up Coke's faltering operations, Goizueta needed capital, particularly borrowed capital. He could not abide the committee's persistent vetoing of pleas to issue debt. And he did not want it to block a plan he was developing to reduce Coke's imprudently high dividend payments.

Goizueta made his move at the September board meeting. Without warning Woodruff in advance, Goizueta proposed adding to the finance committee the company's two top executive officers — himself and, very soon, Coke President Donald R. Keough, Goizueta's most trusted associate. Woodruff missed the September board meeting, and he howled when he heard 10 days later that Goizueta had outflanked him. "Not until today did Mr. Woodruff learn about the action taken," Woodruff's assistant, Joseph W. Jones, wrote to Garth Hamby, corporate secretary. "This is contrary to his concept of the function of the finance committee." But the rules were changed for good and by the spring of 1981, Woodruff would drop off the committee altogether.

The flurry of activity with bottler buyouts and boardroom maneuvering did not mean Goizueta was ignoring the nuts and bolts of the company. During the summer and early fall of 1980, he roamed Coke's headquarters tower, peppering executives with questions in what amounted to a detailed study of every aspect of Coke's business. Goizueta placed special emphasis on Coke's financial intricacies, grilling his subordinates on everything from market size to complex rates of return. Given his lack of sophistication with corporate finance, he was blessed that his predecessors had left him an uncomplicated balance sheet, with only US$31 million in long-term debt at the end of 1979. Goizueta knew enough, though, to recognize that he could unlock the power of Coke's assets by leveraging the balance sheet.

"The Spanish Inquisition"

The Spanish Inquisition started innocently enough. Coke executives from around the world were accustomed to flying into Atlanta each fall for a two-week business review. There they discussed their five-year plans and were handed a list of objectives that corporate managers had drawn up as their next year's budget. The budget meetings were full of cheerleading, wish lists, and hopeful promises, but there was little hard-nosed planning and almost no accountability.

Goizueta would have none of it. Five-year plans, he felt, were a waste of time. No one could predict with any accuracy what the world would look like in five years. He wanted three-year plans, and he told the executives that he would hold them accountable for meeting their three-year targets. He demanded that managers file their plans early so that he could dissect them. And instead of waiting passively for headquarters to dictate the year's goals, each division chief now had to present his own brief and be ready to defend it. "I want you to tell me what you need to do to expand your business, what kind of capital you need to do it, and what kind of net return you're going to get," Goizueta demanded of Coke's 17 division heads. Most were sent back to the drawing board to revise their plans.

As Goizueta immersed himself in Coke's budgets, he found that the company's finances were even weaker than he had feared. For years, no one had focused on the cost of capital or the economic return on investments. Handcuffed by Woodruff from borrowing money, Austin had used Coca-Cola stock to fuel an acquisition binge. But due largely to a generous dividend, the company's cost of capital was running about 16% per year, more than short-term bank borrowings would have cost in late 1980. Meanwhile, except for soft drinks, none of Coke's businesses — including wineries, water purification, plastics, and foods — were generating more than 10%. "We're liquidating our business, borrowing money at 16 [percent] and investing it at 8 [percent]. You cannot do that forever," Goizueta exclaimed.

The horrors Goizueta discovered during the Spanish Inquisition were not limited to Coke's financial mismanagement. Strategically, the company was adrift as well. As he broke down Coke's business into its widespread component parts, Goizueta found there was no coordination, no central planning, no strategic thinking. In Europe alone, Coke was pursuing three totally separate strategies in different countries, pushing packaging innovations in Belgium, line extensions of Sprite and Fanta in Germany, and bottling investment in Spain. "This company has no sense of direction whatsoever," Goizueta declared at one point. "None."

Logical and methodical as ever, Goizueta created a model by which he and his managers could assess Coke's businesses. Across the top of a sheet of paper, he named the company's operations. On the vertical axis, he listed what he considered the vital financial characteristics of any business: margins, rate of return, cash-flow reliability, and capital requirements. On that basis, Coke's concentrate business — the one on which Woodruff had built the company — proved a winner. Bottling was a little less stellar, but still a solid enterprise. Coke's foods business was further down the line because it ate up huge chunks of capital and was less predictable. Wine, water, and plastics were long shots at best.

At the start of the Spanish Inquisition, Goizueta was shocked to learn how little Coke's managers knew about the financial end of the business — ironically, a criticism that could have been leveled against him just a few months earlier. "None of our operating executives can read a balance sheet," he grumbled. By the time it was finished, he had taken them to school and issued one of the most far-reaching imperatives of his tenure. From that point on, Goizueta warned at one of the closing budget sessions, the corporation would charge its operating units a set percentage for the capital they used. Performance, he declared, would be judged on "economic profit," the unit's operating profit after a deduction for the cost of capital. Strategic planning would be taken seriously, Goizueta said, and objectives would be met. "Don't even come to us with a project that doesn't yield more money than the cost of money," he warned.

Future Shock

When the executives limped away from the Spanish Inquisition and returned to their posts around the world, the effect was both immediate and long-term. From Los Angeles to Kuala Lumpur, Coke managers reorganized the way they ran their businesses. They stopped keeping excess inventory of syrup on hand, just in case of an emergency. They quickly switched from stainless steel syrup containers to plastic and cardboard, saving Coke a great deal of money in one blow. They drew up detailed economic models before launching plans for plant expansions or other major investments. "When you start charging people for their cost of capital, all sorts of things happen," said a satisfied Goizueta.

The change of approach was desperately needed. Profits, which had grown 13% a year in the late 1970s, had stopped short, and forecasts showed they would be flat — zero gain — for all of 1980. The stock market certainly was aware of the troubles. Coke's shares had fallen 50% since their high of US$150 in 1973. Performance in the consumer marketplace was not much better.

To have a lasting impact on the numbers and on Coke's corporate culture, Goizueta realized, he needed to overhaul the way Coca-Cola did business, from the top down. It would be a long and difficult battle to mold Coke into a world-class company at every level. But his job, as he saw it, was to jolt Coke into the future — to shake up the managers and make them understand. The Spanish Inquisition had set the right tone, creating a healthy understanding of the need for change. But without an overarching vision, the revamping would not mean anything. The next step was to establish the guiding principles that would carry Coca-Cola through the 1980s, and a blueprint for how to implement those principles.

Two measures would set the process in place. First, Goizueta would create a mission statement for the company. Then, he would gather his top management from around the world and make them sign on, face to face, to his program. Booklets of platitudes had a habit of finding their way to bookshelves in managers' offices and staying there, ignored and useless. The follow-up conference would stop that from happening. It would give Goizueta a chance personally to lay down his vision and the law.

Goizueta wanted the mission statement to combine a broad vision of Coca-Cola Co. for the next decade with a set of specific strategic steps. He spent weeks bouncing ideas off board members, executives, and consultants — to the point that Keough and others scratched their heads at Goizueta's obsession with such a seemingly pie-in-the-sky project. With great fanfare, he unveiled the result at a board meeting on March 4, 1981. Printed on brown heavyweight paper, it was titled, simply, "Strategy for the 1980s. The Coca-Cola Company." Those who took it lightly, did so at their peril. For Coke's new chief, a statement of principles and objectives was a serious undertaking, a compact with the future that he intended to keep.

"Our Challenge," the statement opened, will be to enhance and protect the Coca-Cola trademark, giving shareholders an above-average return and entering new businesses only if they can perform at a rate substantially above inflation. "Our Business," Goizueta wrote, will continue to concentrate in soft drinks, emphasize leadership in other segments, and most likely expand into "industries in which we are not today." Only market segments with inherent real growth would be attractive. "Increasing annual earnings per share and effecting increased return on equity are still the name of the game," Goizueta wrote.

The statement concluded with a broad-based section about "Our Wisdom," a set of guiding principles that Goizueta believed would make Coke a leading company as it entered the final decade of the

20th century. As they worked their way into the 1990s, Goizueta wrote, Coke's employees must consider "the long-term consequences of current actions," sacrifice short-term gains when necessary, adapt to changes in consumer tastes and needs, and become a welcome part of every country in which Coke does business. Finally, every Coke employee must exhibit "the capacity to control what is controllable and the wisdom not to bother [with] what is not."

The Spanish Inquisition had proved Goizueta was prepared to launch the kind of guerrilla warfare needed to take Pepsi by the throat, regain leadership in all segments, and squeeze the potential out of the farthest reaches of Coke's vast system. The mission statement showed that Goizueta was also a high-minded corporate philosopher.

Coca-Cola's top managers got their introduction to the mission statement — and to an unambiguous agenda for the Goizueta years — at a conference in Palm Springs, Calif., in April of 1981. It is customary at big companies for new executive teams to invite their elite managers for a retreat, as a way to kick off the new regime. It is not, however, typical to open the session with a harsh kick in the pants, strong enough to shake up even the old-timers waiting to collect their gold watches. But after the Spanish Inquisition, Coke's management corps knew not to expect the predictable from Goizueta. Even so, no one could have anticipated the fusillade that awaited them in Palm Springs.

"No Sacred Cows"

The new chairman made it clear that nothing at Coke was so sacred it could not be sacrificed for the greater good of the company, and he laid waste to some of Coke's most cherished myths. If Coke's executives wanted to see world-class marketing, he said, they should look at Procter & Gamble Co., not Coca-Cola. The distribution system needed a face-lift. People needed to take bold risks to survive. Concocting soda-pop formulas and processing orange juice did not amount to world-class technical strength. And the culture of complacency must change. "The only company that continues to enjoy success is the company that keeps struggling to achieve it," Goizueta said.

Goizueta's concluding passage was filled with portent. "Just to give you an example that there are no sacred cows," he began, "let me assure you that such things as the reformulation of any or all of our products will not stand in the way" of seizing a real or perceived market advantage from a competitor. "The days are gone in which an inflexible adherence to a sacred cow will ever give renewed impetus [to] or breathe life into a competitor," Goizueta swore. In other words, the day of New Coke was not far away.

As he finished, the chief executive turned to a colleague. "Well," Goizueta said, "we're off to a start."

In fact, the conference in Palm Springs marked a clean break with Coca-Cola's past. But the wrenching changes that Roberto Goizueta imposed in his first year as head of the nation's biggest soft-drink company were just the beginning. Mistakes, such as the purchase of a Hollywood studio and the introduction of New Coke, still were ahead of him, but so were triumphs, such as Coke's invasion of Eastern Europe and the reinvention of Coke's marketing strategies. The basic principles that Goizueta outlined in those early days prepared Coke to rack up one of the most impressive records of shareholder returns in United States corporate history, and enabled him to transform Coca-Cola from a sleepy Southern soda maker into a global marketing powerhouse.

Excerpted from *I'd Like the World to Buy a Coke: The Life and Leadership of Roberto Goizueta* by David Greising, BUSINESS WEEK's Atlanta bureau chief. Copyright 1998 by David Greising. Reprinted by permission of the publisher John Wiley & Sons, Inc.

Thinking Points

1. What were the challenges facing Goizueta when he assumed the position of Chairman at Coca-Cola?
2. What were the key elements to Coke's turnaround and how much of that do you think was due to Goizueta's leadership?
3. In the light of Goizueta's leadership, how would you have seen your role and responsibilities if you were on the board of Coke?
4. Chairman Goizueta saw succession as a natural outcome of good corporate governance. Comment on this statement and think about how you would apply this principle to the board you are currently sitting on.

In Conclusion

Around the world is a call for the separation of the positions of Chair and Chief Executive. It is a fact that more than 70% of the Fortune 500 firms combine the positions of Chairperson and Chief Executive in one person. Known as duality, this board anomaly has been the source of controversy among corporate governance experts. Logically, the Chairperson is responsible to the shareholders for the monitoring of the top management and therefore cannot also be the Chief Executive. Recognizing this contradiction, Scandinavian firms as a group have chosen not to practice CEO duality. In Britain, listed firms are prohibited from practicing duality. However, due to tradition and the de facto power of top management, many boardrooms in the U.S. have evolved to combine the two roles. In response, the Sarbanes-Oxley Act of 2002, Section 4, has raised this as an issue for further study and potential regulation by the market regulators of listed firm.

Regardless of where an individual holds one or both leadership roles, it must still be recognized that *chairmanship* is a highly subjective activity. The effectiveness of a Chairperson is as much dependent on his personality and ability to command respect as it is on the process and mechanics of managing good meetings. By definition, every successful chairperson is a leader and therefore to be successful, he must understand the qualities of good leaders and seek to emulate them.

The role of the Chair is increasingly intellectually demanding. The complexities of global business require chairpersons to continually reinvent themselves and renew their understanding of the competitive and organizational environments that surround them. Therefore, effective chairpersons are those who are in touch with their world and who continually make inquiries into this world.

At the same time, because every individual, no matter how talented, has a limited capacity to process information, a successful chairperson is one who realizes he depends on this board to get the job done. Therefore he understands his limitations and is willing to empower his directors to realize their full potentials and to support the maturing and development of the directors in his charge — not competing with them but challenging them to give their best.

Chapter 3

Taking Back the Boardroom:
Ethics and Social Responsibility

Social Responsibility

... to leave the world a bit better, whether by a healthy child, a garden patch or a redeemed social condition; to know even one life has breathed easier because you have lived. This is to have succeeded.

Ralph Waldo Emerson

In the same way, that global trade is homogenizing the way business is conducted around the world, the globalization of information, spread of democracy, and softening of national boundaries is forcing business leaders to think beyond the dictates of short-term economics. This chapter focuses on the role that ethics plays in the boardroom and highlights the importance of thinking ethically in an era of broadcast television, investigative reporting, and the Internet. It addresses the connections between personal integrity and corporate ethics and presents an argument for the ethical nature of directors' duties. Finally, we end by discussing a framework for considering ethical issues and how to go about conducting an ethical audit.

There are three premises to this chapter. Firstly, the discharge of a director's duties is fundamentally an ethical exercise. The fiduciary relationship between a director and the corporation is based on trust. Practically, for all the reasons previously discussed, the corporation has no recourse when a director fails to exercise his faculties or his integrity to the maximum. Secondly, the law is incapable of contemplating every contingency so that the company depends on the director to exercise discretion when making business decisions. Finally, the law recognizes the primary responsibility of the director for ethical violations by the corporation. As the directing mind of the corporation, a director's fiduciary responsibility puts him squarely on the firing line for questions on ethical conduct. Many communities have extended a director's responsibilities to include social responsibility issues (e.g., the closing down a plant that results in the layoff of hundreds of workers). Therefore, to protect himself from charges of breach of duties, a director has to make decisions in a *transparent* manner and has to be *accountable* for his actions.

Transparency in corporate governance is defined as a state of affairs in which the decision-making *processes* in the boardroom are open for review. Transparency also implies that the standards and enterprise goals of the organization are apparent to those people with a material interest in the company. These standards determine the manner in which decisions are taken and define the domain beyond which certain decisions are simply not contemplated. Transparency is critical to the ethics of the corporation, how it discharges its social responsibility, and the legitimacy it commands from its public and private stakeholders.

Transparency is also critical to the efficient functioning of the capital market system on which the corporation depends for funds and other resources. Without transparency, the costs of contracting are increased as parties are forced to deal with the corporation at arms length and with costly safeguards built in. Transparency in corporate governance does not imply strategic transparency. Thus, the substance of corporate level decisions (for example, decisions related to R&D investment, strategy implementation, etc.) do not have to be transparent but the *logic*, some of which may be *ex post*, of the decisions have to be justifiable on the basis of the corporation's economic goals and objectives.

Accountability is simply accepting responsibility for the decisions. To do so, a board has to be structured such that executive offices have direct responsibility over various aspects of the corporation. While board decisions are taken as a whole, it is the responsibility of such persons to know the issues in depth, report to the board and make recommendations. In addition, the board must be self-monitoring, which implies that those responsible for recommending a course of action should not be the ones responsible for evaluating and ratifying them.

Part of how accountability is exercised in the boardroom is at the annual general shareholders' meeting where the owners of the corporation are given a chance to question the board on its handling of the affairs in the company. In fact, a mini-industry has developed over this process, in which representatives of the institutional investors use this occasion as a forum for preaching the values of shareholder sovereignty. In fact, it was at a 2001 annual meeting that a group of shareholders, questioning the cash management practices of Hollinger International and its Chairman, Conrad Black that triggered the events leadings to the collapse of Hollinger and the indictment of Black on criminal charges. The annual elections process, in which board members are re-appointed according to how they have served the shareholders' interests, can enhance accountability if it is conducted conscientiously with a view to protecting the interests of the firm.

An important consequence of the principle of accountability is illustrated in the corporate structure of a publicly listed company. The board sits at the apex of this structure from which all decision-making responsibility flows to the bottom and accountability flows to the top. The US has taken this principle to its logical conclusion by enacting laws that hold directors personally accountable for decisions that impact broad segments of society. For example, in the US, boards are personally liable *with no due diligence defense* for employee wages and benefits, taxes, and environmental violations. In addition, directors and officers' (D&O) insurance cannot be used to cover such violations. Thus, the law has both compensatory and punitive elements in order to solidify the principle of the board as the *directing mind* of the corporation and its full accountability for the actions taken.

Why is it Important to Talk About Ethics?

The law has imbued the corporation with personhood, meaning that it can enter into binding contracts, has legal obligations, can bring suit, and be sued. What the corporation does not have is a conscience. For this, the corporation has to rely on the board. Since the days of the first corporation, society has recognized that this social creation will have a significant and immediate impact on the affairs of humankind. It can bring benefits as well as destruction to social order, and the environment. Through deliberate short-term profit seeking or callous negligence, the corporation has been credited with numerous environmental and social disasters, such as chemical spills, oil spills, bacterial poison outbreaks, massive deforestation, nuclear contamination, pesticide contamination, gender discrimination, child labor practices; the list goes on. As the directing mind of the corporation, directors are increasingly held responsible for the societal impact of their companies.

July 1, 1997 is the date that the Asian Crisis is believed to have begun. What started as a devaluation of the Thai Baht, to correct problems with Thailand's real estate bubble, quickly escalated into a general collapse of the region. The "miracle economies" of Southeast Asia experienced their most severe economic crisis of the Post-War period. The causes of this crisis are many but there is an emerging consensus that poor managerial ethics and practices were major contributing factors to the chain of events that led to the collapse. Common among these practices are the use of related-party transactions, opaque strategic asset allocation decisions, and relationship-based managerial appointments. Anecdotal evidence suggests that 25 years of growth may have led to feelings of invulnerability in the boardroom, leading to poor vigilance and the lack of accountability.

Following this Crisis, corporations have become increasingly sensitive to their social responsibilities and are taking steps to improve their records in this area. Research has shown that corporations with strong ethical centers generally do better in times of crises. Agency theory clearly states that contracts are more stable and are less costly to write and enforce in an environment of trust, which requires transparency and a willingness to be accountable for mistakes. In poor economic conditions, trust becomes the most important factor that determines the stability of ongoing contractual relationships. Trust is developed over time when corporations demonstrate that they are reliable and trustworthy. It is also easier to build trust in a growth environment than it is to do so in a shrinking one because the cost of mistakes is easier to bear.

The ethical issues facing individual directors are many. From the more obvious legal violations to the gray areas of social responsibility,[5] directors are increasingly ask to take responsibility for issues outside of their functional expertise. In such situations, directors are asked to think, not as functional experts, but as members of the community in which their companies do business. In a global environment, this is even more difficult because a director has to understand the social and political issues of far-flung host country domains; Shell Petroleum in Nigeria, British Petroleum in Vietnam, Union Carbide in India, and Nike in Indonesia are such examples. Many directors are not prepared to deal in specifics with these issues. Yet, they are required to make decisions and take a stand. Unless a director is certain of his ethical stance on the broad issue, it will be easy for him to ignore his social obligation and make ill-informed and potentially disastrous decisions on specific ones.

Why Don't We all Simply Behave, as We Would Like Others to Behave?

The conflict between personal and corporate ethics is one area in which directors probably face the greatest challenges. On the one hand, it may not be possible or even desirable to impose one's personal ethical standards in the boardroom. On the other hand, it will be dangerous for a board of directors to allow its ethical standards to default to the lowest common denominator. Each director has to take a personal stand on the issues, and still come to a consensus because the directors are jointly and individually liable for all decisions taken by the board as whole. Thus, the board, through the leadership of the Chairperson, has to actively develop an ethical climate that sets the minimum ethical standards for the individual manager.

Directors face a great deal of peer pressure in the boardroom. Because the boardroom represents the inner sanctum of power, it has offered entry only to a select few. The process is usually informal and

[5] For example, should corporations engage in non-economic activities such as community activism and political action?

relies as much on word of mouth as on personal relationships. The Chairperson of the corporation typically handles the appointment process and personally invites members to join. In the US, more than 90% of the directors in Fortune 500 companies are male, Anglo-Saxon, and are successful managers of other large corporations. They are part of a tight social network; many have attended the same schools, and belong to the same social clubs. This combination of the informal appointment process, and tight social networks often creates a sense of obligation toward those who appoint the directors. Where the Chair is also the CEO, the typical appointment process immediately creates a conflict of interest for the director.

Traditionally, board meetings are genteel affairs pervaded by a 'don't-rock-the-boat' ethic. Unless the corporation is facing a crisis, a director seldom has occasion to raise uncomfortable questions about managerial practices in the 'gray' area and therefore may be hesitant when called upon to do so. Corporations with very long histories and strong cultures are often the ones with the greatest likelihood of passive boards. Directors in these corporations tend to have long tenures and therefore settle into a comfortable routine that defines their relationship with management (see for example, the case study on the board of Heinz in the previous chapter). However, in the 21st century, a broad swath of institutional shareholders including formerly passive mutual funds have become activist and more willing to engage in proxy battles to discipline boards that they perceive as not serving the corporation's interests. Corporate raiders like Kirk Kerkorian are sitting on increasingly large war chests with which they use to buy up the stock of companies such as General Motors to lend weight to their voices and force changes in the boardroom. Hence, boards who want to be seen as discharging their duties have to ensure that their actions are transparent and accountable.

Corporations often have inappropriate systems of evaluation and reward. Research has shown that CEO compensation is pegged closely to firm size. But the collapse of the *chaebols* (family based conglomerates) in Korea during the Asian Crisis and the continuing financial struggle of Airbus, General Motors, United Airlines, and other corporate behemoths demonstrate that firm size is not a guarantee of economic performance. Indeed there appears to be negative relationship when the firm grows beyond an optimal point because very large corporations can become bureaucratic, which restricts the flow of information and hence effective decision making at the top. Finally, in corporations that already face crises, the pressures to produce results can lead to short cuts, many of which involved the compromise of ethical standards. For example, the 1970s Lockheed bribery scandal that brought down a Japanese government is largely due to the desperation for business caused by cutbacks in United States defense spending.

The Connection Between Personal and Corporate Ethics

Ethics has been defined as the combination of virtue, character, and practical wisdom. There is no question that one cannot talk about corporate ethics without first discussing personal ethics. At the very least, we must acknowledge the role of personal ethics in defining corporate ethics. Firms are created and run by people. All companies begin life in the minds of individuals. These individuals imbue the prototypical firm with a sense of mission, purpose and view of the world. Whether it is Bill Gates and the well-known Microsoft paranoia, Sam Walton and the family values of Walmart, or Henry Ford and 'excellence is job 1' at Ford Motor, the founder is responsible for setting the ethical tone of the corporation.

While it is not the intent of this chapter to expound on the philosophical precepts of ethics, careful observation has shown that human beings are remarkably capable of self-deception. Bandwagon effects, stock market bubbles, and economic contagion are manifestations of the underlying phenomenon of self-deception. In an individual, self-deception can often lead to a slow erosion of personal integrity. In the corporation, the continual compromise of personal ethics leads to a rationalization of unethical conduct at the organizational level.

The longer a director has had to make hard decisions, the more prepared he is to make the next ethically challenging one. However, experience is no guarantee of success. Very few directors start the day by deciding that they will be unethical and yet such decisions continue to be made with alarming regularity. Instead of relying solely on experience, a director must continually clarify his own values through conscious reflection, and systematic ethical inquiry. Thus, when faced with making an unpopular decision, the director must examine himself for self-deception. Conscious and collected self-examination is the first line of defense against the erosion of personal integrity when faced with the pressure to conform to a lower ethical standard. A director must also be prepared to trust his instincts on the issue. These instincts, the result of family values, experience, and personal beliefs, can often tell us when something 'feels' wrong. Instead of suppressing these instincts by using common rationalizations (e.g., "it's industry practice", or "if we don't, our competitors will") we need to acknowledge them and consciously deal with them. A director ignores his conscience to his peril.

Ethical tests for the director

There are a number of test questions a director can ask to guide his conduct when he faces a thorny ethical question in the boardroom. The publicity test asks the question, "How would I feel if the newspapers found out and published it on the front page?" This test is often telling because many things that we would condone in private, we would not contemplate in public. The trusted friend test asks the question, "Would a respected and trusted friend or relative do this?" While we are often willing to compromise our personal standards, we often do not attribute such compromise to a role model we esteem. The reciprocity test is also known as the 'Golden Rule' test. It asks the question, "Would I like to be treated in the same manner that I am proposing to treat the other party?" The universality test is more philosophical and requires deeper thought as it asks the question, "What would the world be like if everyone behaved in the same manner that I did?" We often are willing to subject ourselves to a lower standard of behavior than we hold others accountable for. The truth is that if everyone behaved in the way he or she felt like, the world would be a chaotic and undesirable place to live in. Finally, the obituary test asks the question, "How would I like to be remembered 15 years from now?" The last test is the most difficult because in making decisions, directors often have to trade off the interests of stakeholders and while not all decisions are zero sum games, neither are all decisions positive sum games. In short, there will be winners and losers, and the losers will not remember the directors too fondly. What the last statement forces a director to consider is the possibility that a director's problem may not be to prevent hurt but lessen pain. This requires a great deal of compassion and creativity and while directors are not called to a higher standard of conduct than ordinary human beings, it is inexcusable that they allow callous negligence into the decision-making process.

Creating an Ethical Organization

There are four elements to a company's ethical climate and they all have to be in place before the right climate can be created. Some boards are aware of three but often miss the forth. For example, a company may have the right policies and procedures in place to ensure ethical behaviors but the exigencies of running a business may cause the management to compromise their standards, which may reduce the credibility of the company's stated goals and shared values. Through these elements, the ethical climate is continually being examined for internal consistency with its strategic goals and objectives, and shaped for alignment when these goals and objectives shift.

The first element is the company's shared values. Everyone seems to understanding the importance of compelling shared values. They pull an organization together and provide stability in a constantly shifting competitive environment. Shared values are not present in most organizations. However, there is strong evidence that superior companies have shared values.

The sum total of individual directors' values formed the shared values in the boardroom. Shared values are the often unwritten guiding concepts, or set of values and aspirations, which go beyond the formal statement of corporate objectives. Shared values are the fundamental ideas around which a business is built. They form the broad architecture for the future direction that the board of directors wants to infuse throughout the organization. Shared values are the way in which the board expresses to the firm's stakeholders. To be readily communicated, shared values need to be succinct.

In a sense, shared values are like the basic postulates in a mathematical system. They are the starting points on which the system is built, but are not themselves logically derived. Therefore, they are typically expressed at high levels of abstraction and may mean very little to outsiders who do not know the organization well. But for those inside they are rich with significance. However, the ultimate test of this value is not its logic but the usefulness of the system for ethical decision making that it creates.

The second element of an ethical climate is managerial example. This refers to the actual behaviors-in-use exhibited by management in the day-to-day life of the corporation. It has been said that we communicate our intentions by the way we behave. In the same way, we communicate our values or the lack of values by what we do. The most important behavior that managers have to watch for is the way they arrive at decisions. Known as 'procedural justice', this is particularly important for decisions on promotions and rewards as they have to be perceived as impartial and transparent. If employees are unclear on the way such decisions are made, convincing them to accept higher ethical values espoused by the corporation will be very difficult.

Thirdly, the board can shape an organization's ethical climate using appropriate performance measures and rewards. Research in equity theory and compensation systems informs us that people tend to behave as they are rewarded. Incentive systems should be designed to reward appropriate ethical behaviors and punish inappropriate ones. Such incentives should be integrated into the regular employee performance evaluation systems. For example, if a salesperson is evaluated and rewarded for selling more, thought has to be given to *how* units are sold, not just the number sold, so that there is an explicit consideration of ethical sales practices. Clearly, reward systems are not enough if employees are not trained to behave ethically and therefore, it is also important to back up the performance measurement and reward systems with ethics sensitivity training programs.

The final element and the most easily implemented is the system of recruitment and advancement used to staff the organization. It is critical that the management explicitly includes assessments of personal ethics in their recruitment practices. It is often expedient to recruit a 'star' performer from another organization while ignoring the methods such an individual used to get ahead. While boards are ultimately responsible to shareholders for the bottom line, it is disastrous for them to ignore ethical standards in the pursuit of profit. Therefore, ethical value systems have to be championed in the hiring and the promotion processes. I am not suggesting that we promote only the 'nice' guys. We need to promote the best performers but also those top performers who practice high ethical behaviors in getting to the top. This is not as impractical as it sounds because a board can instill the right values from the top and because these values are persistent, they will eventually shape the behaviors in the management team.

Finally, in order to put these four elements into practice, boards have to conduct regular ethical audits of themselves and their practices. Whenever a board encounters a business decision that has ethical or social responsibility implications, it should examine the social impact of such a decision concurrently with its examination of the decision's economic implications. The way to do this is through a formal ethical inquiry.

How to Avoid Common
Pitfalls in 'Gray-Area' Decisions

There are four steps to a successful ethical inquiry. The comprehensive ethical inquiry of a business decision rests on a simple principle, which is popularly known as the 'Golden Rule'. However, to apply the Golden Rule in a business decision is not always easy nor are the results always obvious. It is a given fact that business decisions often involve tradeoffs between parties with conflicting interests. Therefore, it is not always possible to satisfy the interests of all stakeholders. Sometimes, these interests have to be prioritized, which means that some interests will invariably have to be subordinated. However, recognizing that some interests have to be subordinated does not imply that we can safely ignore them or the impact of our decisions on those parties. The ideal outcome of a successful ethical inquiry demands that all stakeholder interests are explicitly considered and adverse impacts minimized to the extent possible, under a shareholder value maximizing constraint.

The first step to an ethical inquiry is to define the problem accurately. This is not as simple as it sounds because we tend to define problems in ways that are familiar to us. Thus, an economist will define a problem as one of efficiency, while a sociologist may define the same problem as one of organization. For example, a factory closing decision is often cast as a purely economic one. However, it may indicate a more fundamental problem of poor capacity management, which means that unless the firm first deals with the lack of proper planning processes, a factory closing will not solve the problem in the long run. Defining a problem accurately requires the board to use a variety of viewpoints, usually those of affected stakeholders. The board has to understand the genesis of the problem, and the human interests involved at the time the problem happened. Therefore, by defining the problem accurately, the board can detect and attack the root causes of the problem, rather than simply treat the symptoms. To do this requires accurate information, cooperative management, and intensive reflection by board members. Therefore, the first step to a successful ethical inquiry must begin with a managerial brief, followed by a retreat for the directors to consider the issues independent of managerial influence.

The next step is to define the affected parties and their interests. Those making the decision have to ask themselves if there is a conflict between their personal interests and the interests of the corporation, which is its long-term survival. If there is a natural conflict, then those making the decision should recuse themselves and designate a non-interested party to handle the process. For example, the executive directors will naturally be in a position of conflict when faced with a takeover offer. Thus, the final disposition of a takeover offer should rest with the non-executive directors, and while the executive directors may be heard on the issue, the board's charter should be written to ensure that they cannot influence the outcome. By identifying the stakeholders in a decision, the board is able to get clarity on the reasons for the stakeholders' positions. Using the same example, different stakeholders may view the board's disposition of the tender offer as maximizing shareholder value, assuring the job security of employees, realizing a strategic advantage in the marketplace or protecting the independence of company management. Identifying these reasons will surface the interests being served by the decision and, therefore, allow board members to assess the strength of the stakeholders' claims.

The third step of the ethical inquiry is to understand the impact of the decision on stakeholders with material interests in the outcome. First of all, board members have to place themselves in the shoes of the affected parties, and try to understand how the decision may cause injury. Sometimes, it makes sense to bring these affected parties into the discussions and to invite input. But the board must do this without creating implied promises of relief. In Germany, the doctrine of co-determination has ensured that the interests of employees are always considered whenever a board makes a strategic decision impacting the welfare of its employees. While it is not always desirable or even necessary to have labor representation on a board, labor representatives can be included in the deliberations when it is appropriate because this will help the board assess any long-term impact. For example, a takeover offer is often accompanied by a plan for factory closings or employee layoffs. The impact of such layoffs on morale and productive capacity should be assessed with the help of human resources executives and labor representatives and if they find that the benefits are temporary, alternative arrangements may be considered. Thus, even though the board is not responsible for implementation, they must be sensitive to the concerns of the employees, as employee support for a merger will lead to a greater probability of success.

The final and most important step of a successful ethical inquiry is for the board to understand the impact of the decision on the company. Here, the test of public disclosure can be applied. If the public found out about this decision, would be company be seen in a poor or good light? Would there be public embarrassment or acclaim? While a board must never be held hostage by the possibility of bad public reaction to its decision,[6] it has to realize that a negative reaction can signal a problem with their decision outcome. Together with

---

[6] For example, rather than bow to public pressure, Bata International chose to keep its factories open in apartheid-era South Africa because the board felt that it was doing more good in creating jobs for the Black African population.

understanding public reaction, the board has to prepare for the possibility that their decisions may be misunderstood and take proactive steps to prevent the misunderstanding from happening.[7] At the same time, the board will have to decide how much negative impact it is willing to accept for its decision as this will clarify the extent to which the board is willing to make tradeoffs.

...And in the Final Analysis

Board members have to realize that even though they represent the corporation as a body, they are individually responsible for the decisions that are taken. Therefore it is critical that individual directors first clarify their own values. Then they have to realize that the corporation's values are only as strong as the weakest individual values. Thus, the task of the board is to ensure that it creates the highest ethical values in the corporation and to hold all its members to that standard. To do so, the board can employ the lens and levers for creating an ethical climate and reinforce this through the individual examples set by its members.

The continuing globalization of markets is increasing the pressure for corporations to adopt standards of performance acceptable to foreign shareholders. The dispersion of ownership continues to increase for many European and Asian firms as they list in non-domestic, usually American, stock exchanges. Because foreign shareholders do not share the same national and cultural concerns as domestic shareholders, their demands are purely for maximum shareholder returns and they will be intolerant of any deviation from this standard of performance. In this environment, boards are called upon to make more trade-offs between

---

[7] For example, special interest groups and the popular media excoriated Burroughs-Welcome PLC for the initial pricing of its drug, AZT. However, what they did not know was that the company had a long history of investing in the research for cures of rare diseases with very small market demand. The company had spent more than US$100 million, and did not know if they could ever recover the costs because the demand for AZT was unknown at the time. Few companies were willing to spend that kind of money at that level of risk. Burroughs-Welcome did so because of its strong sense of social responsibility but because it did not effectively communicate its intentions to the public, it was punished.

shareholders and stakeholders. As the firm increases its exposure to foreign capital markets, domestic stakeholders will lose out. In Asia, the need for foreign capital is acute with the result that foreign share-holders now have more say in how the corporation should deploy its resources. This will bring boards into direct conflict with the firm's stakeholder groups (such as employees, government, and suppliers) whose claims they may have previously considered less paramount.

It has become increasingly critical for boards to be proactive in their public relations efforts. It is no longer possible for this function to be seen as part of marketing and relegated to the lower levels of the organization. Managing stakeholder expectations has become as important as managing the firm itself. In the following case example, an anatomy of an ethical crisis is presented. Consider how the crisis started and whether at any stage along the development of the crisis an independent and alert board could have done something about it. Consider also if there ever was a time during the history of this crisis that the board reached a point of no return beyond which it would never be able to do anything. When was this point reached and could this point have been anticipated? Do you think something like this could happen to your company? How do you know?

A Corporate Kleptocracy: The Saga of Conrad Black and Hollinger International[8,9]

A typical Chicago juror 'does not reside in more than one residence, employs servants or a chauffeur, enjoy lavish furniture, or host expensive parties'.

Conrad Black in 2007 on why he won't get a fair trial

THE city of Chicago has played host to the trials of some notorious crooks. Al Capone met his fate here, as did his fellow mobster Frank "The Enforcer" Nitti. The next high profile case involving Conrad Black, the founder of Hollinger International and a Canadian-born tycoon who became a British peer could rival anything from that gangster era. He faces charges of racketeering and criminal fraud that could put him behind bars for a lifetime. Black, who once boasted, "Some people are offended by extreme opulence but I find it sort of entertaining," regarded private jets, Rolls Royces and luxury homes in London, New York, Toronto and Palm Beach, Florida as a God-given right.

The child of a wealthy Canadian businessman, Black grew up with an ingrained belief that he was above the rules that everybody else abided by. When he was 14 he stole copies of exam answers and then sold them to other students. Instead of feeling remorse when

---

[8] This case was prepared for teaching purposes and does not purport to illustrate the effective or ineffective resolution of specific managerial situations.
[9] Sources: *Edmonton Journal*, Final Edition, March 11, 2007, p. A4; *The Express*, 1st Edition, March 10, 2007, p. 32; *The Toronto Sun*, Final Edition, March 11, 2007, p. 10; *National Post*, Final Edition, March 3, 2007, p. 1; *Financial Post*, Final Edition, March 6, 2007, p. 1; *Financial Post*, Final Edition, March 3, 2007, p. 1; *The Evening Standard*, March 13, 2007, p. 18.

caught, he felt both proud of his crime and victimized. According to prosecutors, the depth of looting, by some estimates up to 95% of Hollinger's profits, is surpassed only in audacity and size by Enron a half decade earlier.

It all started in October 2001 Tweedy Browne, a little-known New York investment firm, wrote a letter of complaint to the independent directors of newspaper publisher Hollinger International Inc., alleging abusive management fees of up to US$40million were being paid out by the company to Black.

"Black's companies, it seemed, were not doing that well," says journalist Jeff Randall, "but Conrad and Barbara were flourishing. Their lifestyle was fabulous and they were spending fortunes. Shareholders in New York began to wonder how he was footing all those personal bills. "The answer rapidly became clear. Hollinger [the company that Black was CEO of] was making money," says Randall, "but much of it, 95%, appeared to be going to Black and a small group of senior managers, leaving little for other shareholders.

Black was acting as if he owned the company." "Conrad treated it as a private company," said BBC broadcaster Andrew Neil, "Public ownership was just something that got in the way. Shareholders were people to come up with the money but, once they handed over the money, it was his money." He ignored the complaints from shareholders, whom he viewed with utter disdain and bullied senior executives into sanctioning allegedly illegal transfers of money — tens of millions of pounds in a single afternoon — that would satisfy his greed. "The board Black selected functioned more like a social club or public policy association than the board of a major corporation, enjoying short meetings followed by a good lunch and discussion of world affairs." When one director questioned him about what he felt was the misuse of funds, Black hissed: "This is my company." says Tom Bower, author of *Black and Amiel, Dancing on the Edge.*

In November 2003, Richard C. Breeden, the former chairman of the powerful U.S. Securities and Exchange Commission, chairing a special committee of the board filed a wide ranging internal investigation report (see the Appendix for an abstract of the report) charging Lord Black and his executives with a breach of fiduciary, and creating and nurturing a culture of 'corporate kleptocracy' within Hollinger. This report would later become the bulwark of the Federal government's lawsuit against Black. The crux of the report centered on "non-compete" payments.

When a business is sold, the vendors frequently promise not to start again; after all, they may retain considerable knowledge and expertise which they could use against the new owner. If the vendor is a company, the non-compete payments are generally made to it, as the owner of the asset being sold. In 1998, after 12 years of trying, with his empire up to the gunwales in debt, Black abandoned his ambition to compete with Rupert Murdoch across the world and decided to break up Hollinger International. Over the following three years, six sales of US newspaper groups realized more than US$800 million. Each sale contained non-compete clauses, but instead of paying the money to Hollinger International, Black arranged for money to be paid up the chain of companies he controlled, but did not fully own.

A pre-trial memorandum from Amy J. St. Eve, the U.S. District Court Judge, explained the mechanism: "[The buyer] was no worse off the non-competition payment... The end result, however, yielded a significant personal gain to Defendant Black. By virtue of his owner-ship interests in Hollinger International, Hollinger Inc., and Ravelston, Black could gain an increased share of earnings merely by transferring money between companies. "For example, if US$100 was transferred from International to Inc., Black would net US$36 because Black owns 15% of International and 51% of Inc. For every US$100 trans-ferred from International to Ravelston Black loses US$15 but gains US$65, for a personal net gain of US$50."

The non-compete fee in Hollinger International's sale of Community Newspaper Holdings in late 1998 was set at US$50 million, of which US$12 million was paid up to Hollinger Inc., giv-ing Black a US$6.3 million gain. Since Hollinger Inc. was a skeleton company whose only significant asset was its holding in Hollinger International, the idea of it being able to compete with the purchaser of the newspaper assets was preposterous. There is another bonus in the scheme: under a quirk of Canadian law, non-compete payments escape income tax.

By November 2005, in a new conference in Chicago by Patrick Fitzgerald, a top prosecutor in the United States Attorney General's Office read a criminal complaint against Black, along with four of his lieutenants, indicting them with 17 counts of fraud, money laundering, obstruction of justice, racketeering and tax evasion.

Between the mailing of the letter and the 2005 indictment, Black would lose his homes in London and New York, his prized Daily Telegraph and Sunday Telegraph newspapers, a seat on the board of the Canadian Imperial Bank of Commerce, and a friendship and business partnership of more than 35 years.

The following is a timeline of the career and fortunes of Conrad Black and Hollinger International, the newspaper company that he founded with David Radler.

Pre-Crisis Period

August 25, 1944: Conrad Moffat Black is born in Montreal to wealthy brewery executive George Black and wife Betty.

1971: Black co-founds Sterling Newspapers Ltd. with friends David Radler and Peter G. White after buying a number of small papers in his 20s.

1978: Upon the death of mentor Bud McDougald, Black becomes chairman of Argus Corp., a platform from which he creates the Hollinger group.

1978: Marries Shirley Hishon, with whom he has two sons and a daughter. (Shirley changes her name to Joanna at Black's behest in 1990 and the marriage ends in 1992.)

1985: Hollinger buys the Daily Telegraph in the UK, which propels him into a world where he cavorts with the super-rich and powerful. Making acquaintances with Margaret Thatcher, then Britain's Prime Minister, he begins a long campaign to acquire a peerage and a seat in the House of Lords.

1992: Marries Barbara Amiel, former Toronto Sun editor and a well-known columnist living in London. They become a celebrity couple and are on many top-level guest lists in Britain. By this time, Hollinger controls 60% of Canada's newspapers, as well as hundreds of dailies in the US, UK, Australia and Israel. The Chicago Sun Times and Jerusalem Post are among Black's holdings.

1993: Black publishes his autobiography, *Conrad Black: A Life in Progress.*

October 1998: After buying the Financial Post from his partners, including Sun Publishing, Black launches the National Post to combat what he sees as an "over-liberalizing" of editorial policy in Canadian newspapers.

1999: Hollinger is the third largest publisher in the world with revenues of more than US$2 billion. The British government moves to make him Lord Black of Crossharbour, but Canadian Prime Minister Jean Chretien, a frequent target of Black's newspapers, refuses to approve the move. Black is unsuccessful in a court challenge to the Chretien ruling.

2000: Hollinger sells most of its Canadian media holdings, including 50% of the National Post, to the Asper family's CanWest Global media empire.

Crisis Period

2001

October 2001: Determined to get his British title despite Chretien's opposition, Black renounces his Canadian citizenship and becomes Lord Black of Crossharbour (the name of the area where Black's Daily Telegraph is located in London).

Two weeks before Conrad Black takes his place in Britain's House of Lords as, Tweedy Browne & Co., a New York based major shareholder of Hollinger's non-voting stock, sends a letter to the blue-chip directors, among them former U.S. Secretary of State Henry Kissinger and Marie-Josee Kravis, the wife of multimillionaire leveraged buyout specialist Henry Kravis, of Hollinger International, complaining about about Hollinger's "management fees," which had climbed to as high as US$40 million from US$8.5 million in 1996.

The letter, also sent to Black, is ignored.

2002

May 23, 2002: At Hollinger's annual meeting in New York, Lord Black grilled by Laura Jereski of Tweedy Browne who had worked at the Wall Street Journal as a financial reporter about US$74-million in "non-compete agreements" linked to a series of newspaper sales paid to Hollinger executives, including Black and David Radler. She argues that the money should have gone to Hollinger International.

2003

March 2003: Hollinger International posts a loss of US$239 million for 2002. The financial statements say the company continued to pay management fees to Black's Canadian companies totalling US$28 million. Another major shareholder, investment manager Cardinal Capital Management of Greenwich, Conn., demands answers about excessive executive compensation and agreements with Black's Canadian companies, Ravelston Corp. and Hollinger Inc. that seem to disadvantage Hollinger International.

June 17, 2003: Black agrees to an internal investigation by a special committee of the board of directors, made up of three directors with no ties to the chairman and CEO, into the non-compete fees paid to Lord Black, other Hollinger executives and Ravelston Corp. The committee, chaired by prominent investment banker Gordon Paris, brings in as its adviser Richard Breeden, former Chairman of the United States Securities and Exchange Commission.

November, 2003: The Ontario Securities Commission and the United States Securities and Exchange Commission announce investigations.

November 19, 2003: The special committee reports it has uncovered US$32.2 million in previously undisclosed payments to Black, three other Hollinger International executives, and Hollinger Inc., their Toronto-based holding company, that allegedly have not been authorized by the board of directors.

Black steps down as CEO of Hollinger International, but retains the title of Chairman, describing his departure as a "retirement." His chief operating officer, David Radler, is also forced out, along with lawyers Peter Atkinson and Mark Kipnis. Jack Boultbee, a senior vice-president and accountant at Hollinger, refuses to deal with the special committee and is fired. He sues for wrongful dismissal.

November 21, 2003: Hollinger's audit committee quit after the full board rejects their proposed changes. Hollinger International announces past earnings were overstated by US$17 million because of unauthorized non-compete payments made to Lord Black and others.

December 22, 2003: Black refuses to answer questions before the United States Securities and Exchange Commission, citing his Fifth Amendment right against self-incrimination.

2004

January 17, 2004: Hollinger International removes Black as chairman, but he remains as director, and announces a US$200 million US lawsuit against him and David Radler. Black reneges on his pledge to pay back US$24 million, his and Hollinger Inc.'s portion of the US$32.2 million payments uncovered by the special committee, claiming he has been duped into agreeing to do so.

January 18, 2004: Black says he will sell his controlling stake in Hollinger Inc. for US$423 million to Britain's billionaire Barclay brothers. But United States Securities and Exchange Commission object to the sale and take the matter — and Black's refusal to repay US$24 million as agreed — to court in Wilmington, Delaware, where Hollinger is incorporated.

The trial pits Black on the stand against Breeden. Breeden testifies Black has tried to bully the special committee members, threatening to sue them and take away their houses if they continued to pursue him.

February 13, 2004: Black files US$850 million lawsuit in Toronto for defamation against members of the special committee and Breeden.

February 26, 2004: Delaware Chancery Court Judge Leo Stine blocks the sale of Hollinger Inc. to Barclay Brothers. The Court finds

Lord Black "breached his fiduciary and contractual duties persistently and seriously."

March 8, 2004: Black is removed as chairman of the London-based Telegraph Group by its directors.

April 30, 2004: Hollinger International amends its US$200 million lawsuit to claim US$1.25 billion in damages from Lord Black and adds his wife, Barbara Amiel-Black, as a defendant.

June 22, 2004: Hollinger International sells the Telegraph Group to the Barclay Brothers for US$1.65 billion.

June 24, 2004: Hollinger International sells the former HQ of the Chicago Sun Times newspaper to Donald Trump.

August 31, 2004: The United States Securities and Exchange Commission makes public a report by the special board committee of Hollinger International that alleges "racketeering" and "corporate kleptocracy." (see Appendix for an abstract of the key findings). Black's holding company, Ravelston Corp., dismisses the report, saying there were "factual and tainting misrepresentations and inaccuracies."

September 2004: A group of Canadian investors launches a class-action lawsuit against Black and his associates, seeking at least US$4 billion in damages.

October 1, 2004: Black sues the Hollinger International special committee for US$1.1 billion, claiming it defamed him.

October 4, 2004: Black wins a partial victory when the special committee is told by a Chicago judge it had not proved racketeering in its civil lawsuit.

October 29, 2004: Hollinger International refiles the lawsuit against Black and the other former executives, dropping the claim to US$542 million from US$1.2 billion damage.

November 2004: Catalyst, a shareholder in Hollinger Inc., files a complaint about self-dealing by Black and his associates. An Ontario court judge orders an investigation into past transactions at Hollinger Inc. and longtime Black allies, including Amiel-Black, are fired from the board.

November 2, 2004: Black steps down from the board of Hollinger Inc. and announces a plan to privatize the company.

November 15, 2004: United States Securities and Exchange Commission files civil fraud charges against Black and Radler.

2005

March 18, 2005: The Ontario Securities Commission files notice that it intends to charge Lord Black, Hollinger Inc., and three former associates with violating Ontario securities laws.

March 23, 2005: United States Attorney General's Office open a criminal investigation into Black and Radler's activities.

March 28, 2005: The Ontario Securities Commission blocks Mr. Black's attempt to take Hollinger Inc. private.

April 20, 2005: Ravelston Corp., the company at the top of Black's media empire, is put into Chapter 11 bankruptcy proceedings. Along with Mr. Radler, Black resigns as officer and director of Ravelston Corp.

April 20, 2005: Ravelston applies for bankruptcy protection.

May 20, 2005: Black, his chauffeur and an aide are videotaped by a security camera taking boxes of files from Hollinger Inc.'s 10 Toronto Street headquarters, despite a court order barring Black from removing documents.

August 18, 2005: Radler, former Hollinger lawyer Mark Kipnis and Ravelston Corp. are indicted on fraud charges that carry maximum jail sentences of 35 years.

September 20, 2005: Radler, Black's friend and trusted partner for more than 35 years, reveals he has secretly negotiated a plea deal in Chicago that allows him to acknowledge his guilt on a single count of fraud in exchange for his co-operation in the pursuit of Black and his other former associates. Under terms of the deal, Radler will serve 29 months in jail, possibly in Canada, and pay a fine of US$250,000. Mark Kipnis, the former Hollinger lawyer, is also charged with criminal fraud, as is Black's private holding company, Ravelston.

October 7, 2005: US government seizes US$9 million from sale of Black's New York apartment.

November 3, 2005: Black sues the US government, claiming it didn't have right to seize the US$9 million.

November 17, 2005: The U.S. attorney's office in Chicago charges Black and two other executives associated with Hollinger International, Peter Atkinson, who a friend says "co-operated" with the special committee investigating Hollinger until "he realized he was being used", and John Boultbee, CFO of Hollinger International, with eight counts of criminal fraud in an alleged scheme (bonuses disguised as non-compete payments linked to newspaper sales) to divert more than US$80 million from the company. More charges are laid against Kipnis.

November 29, 2005: Mr. Kipnis pleads not guilty to the new fraud charges.

December 1, 2005: Black is photographed and fingerprinted by the FBI, then appears in a Chicago courtroom to plead not guilty to eight counts of fraud. Mr. Atkinson, former executive vice-president, pleads not guilty to six counts of fraud and is released on US$1.5 million bond.

December 7, 2005: Jack Boultbee, pleads not guilty to eight counts of mail and wire fraud. He is freed after posting bail of US$1.5 million.

December 15, 2005: Black is further charged with obstruction of justice, tax evasion, money laundering, and racketeering. The first charge relates to the removal of boxes of documents from Hollinger's Toronto offices.

He is also accused of abusing corporate perks, specifically that he used corporate money to help pay for the lion's share of his wife's US$60,000 birthday party, and flew her on Hollinger's jet to the French Polynesian island of Bora Bora for a vacation.

2006

June 26, 2006: Bail is increased by US$1 million after prosecutors accuse Black of lying about the value of his personal assets.

September 8, 2006: Black is arraigned in Chicago on fresh criminal charges for tax evasion.

September 15, 2006: Black confirms he has begun the process of regaining his Canadian citizenship.

December 8, 2006: Hollinger Inc. sells 10 Toronto Street headquarters.

2007

January 31, 2007: Arguing that he will not get a fair trial because a typical Chicago juror 'does not reside in more than one residence, employs servants or a chauffeur, enjoy lavish furniture, or host expensive parties', Black asks US federal judge Amy St. Eve to keep facts about his wife, Barbara Amiel, and his spending habits out of the trial. Judge refuses the request.

March, 2007: Ravelston, the holding company formerly controlled by Black, pleads guilty in Chicago to one count of fraud.

March 14, 2007: Jury selection begins in the United States District Court, Northern District of Illinois, Eastern Division. US federal judge Amy St. Eve gives prosecutors approval to put "co-conspirators" on the witness stand to testify against Black although no one in the case is charged with conspiracy.

Report of Investigation by the Special Committee of the Board of Directors of Hollinger International Inc.

**Gordon A. Paris, Chairman Graham
W. Savage Raymond G.H. Seitz**

**Counsel and Advisors Richard C.
Breeden & Co. The Law Offices
of Richard C. Breeden
Counsel O'Melveny & Myers LLP**

August 30, 2004

Full report can be found at: http://www.sec.gov/Archives/edgar/data/868512/
000095012304010413/y01437exv99w2.htm

Introduction and Executive Summary

The Hollinger Chronicles

The Special Committee of the Board of Directors of Hollinger International Inc. submits this Report to the U.S. Securities and Exchange Commission and the Honorable Blanche M. Manning of the United States District Court for the Northern District of Illinois pursuant to Section III.4 of the Order of Permanent Injunction dated January 16, 2004 in the matter of United States Securities and Exchange Commission vs. Hollinger International Inc. The Report covers the results of the Special Committee's investigation, since it was formed in June 2003 in response to allegations of fiduciary duty violations and other misconduct at Hollinger.

The Report chronicles events at Hollinger over the decade since it first became a U.S. public company in 1994. Hollinger is a publishing company, but the story of the last decade at Hollinger, which is the subject of this Report, is not about Hollinger's valuable publishing assets or the quality of the staff at its many publications. Rather, this story is about how Hollinger was systematically manipulated and used by its controlling shareholders for their sole benefit, and in a manner that violated every concept of fiduciary duty. Not once or twice, but on dozens of occasions Hollinger was victimized by its controlling shareholders as they transferred to themselves and their affiliates more than US$400 million in the last 7 years.[10] The aggregate cash taken by Hollinger's former CEO Conrad M. Black and its former COO F. David Radler and their associates

---

[10] For ease of reference, this Report presents all monetary amounts in U.S. dollars. To the extent that a conversion from a foreign currency was required and amounts related to a specific transaction, the amounts were converted to U.S. dollars at the closing exchange rate on the date preceding the transaction. For all other conversions, an average annual exchange rate was applied.

represented 95.2% of Hollinger's entire adjusted net income during 1997–2003.

At the outset, the energies of many people went into building Hollinger into a major publishing enterprise. Over time, however, Hollinger went from being an expanding business to becoming a company whose sole pre-occupation was generating current cash for the controlling shareholders, with no concern for building future enterprise value or wealth for all shareholders. Behind a constant stream of bombast regarding their accomplishments as self-described "proprietors," Black and Radler made it their business to line their pockets at the expense of Hollinger almost every day, in almost every way they could devise. The Special Committee knows of few parallels to Black and Radler's brand of self-righteous, and aggressive looting of Hollinger to the exclusion of all other concerns or interests, and irrespective of whether their actions were remotely fair to shareholders.

The Special Committee believes that the events at Hollinger were driven in large part by insatiable pressure from Black for fee income from Hollinger to prop up the highly levered corporate structure of Ravelston and HLG, and to satisfy the liquidity needs he had arising from the personal lifestyle Black and his wife had chosen to lead. The intensity of the pressure for tens of millions in cash payments to Black, irrespective of corporate performance or the fairness of transactions to shareholders, led to a series of abusive transactions in which Hollinger was a victim of Black and Radler's ravenous appetite for cash.

The cash that the insiders pursued so ravenously did not come from taking an aggressive share of the growth of an expanding firm, or from gains generated through the value of outsized equity grants. The bulk of what Black and Radler were taking from Hollinger was cash, and that cash did not come from earnings or the creation of value for all shareholders. Rather, one scheme after another was devised to siphon away Hollinger's opportunities, its cash flow and a share of its balance sheet. For years Black and Radler found excuses for transferring existing cash or assets to themselves, even if it required dismantling Hollinger for their own benefit.

Black and Radler (together with Ravelston and HLG, the corporate vehicles that they controlled and utilized in their improper acts) were the principal actors with the greatest responsibility for conceiving and directing most of the events described in this Report. Others facilitated or assisted efforts to skim cash from Hollinger improperly, or failed to detect and prevent the looting of the Company. The Report describes the actions of those individuals as well.

The Committee has already commenced the Illinois Action against Black, Radler, Amiel-Black (Mrs. Black), Colson and Boultbee as individuals, and against Ravelston and HLG as corporate vehicles, seeking US$1.25 billion in damages suffered by Hollinger from the individual acts and events described in the Report, and from a long course of fraudulent activities in violation of federal racketeering statutes. As part of the relief sought in the Illinois Action, the Committee's complaint seeks an order permanently barring Black, Radler, Boultbee, Ravelston, and HLG from "conducting or participating in the conduct of the affairs of [Hollinger]" pursuant to 18 U.S.C. §1964 (a) to avoid what would otherwise be a certain resumption of the repeated illegal acts that are chronicled in the Report. Related issues have also been litigated in the Delaware Court of Chancery before Vice Chancellor Leo E. Strine, Jr.[11] Earlier this year Vice Chancellor Strine found, among other things, that Black had "persistently and seriously" violated his fiduciary duties to Hollinger, as well as the Restructuring Agreement he entered into with Hollinger in November 2003 as a result of the Special Committee's work.

The Committee's investigation has been completely independent, and as thorough as possible. We have sought to evaluate fully and fairly the conduct of numerous people in a large number of transactions and to identify appropriate remedial actions on behalf of the Company and its shareholders. Our Report includes a detailed review of dozens of individual payments and transactions during the period 1997–2003. We interviewed more than 60 witnesses in depth, and reviewed nearly 750,000 pages of documents as background for our analysis. The Committee has met on more than 40 occasions, together with our

---

[11] *Hollinger Int'l, Inc. v. Black*, 844 A.2d 1022 (Del. Ch. 2004). *Hollinger Inc. v. Hollinger Int'l, Inc.*, 2004 WL 1728003 (Del. Ch. July 29, 2004).

advisors, and more than half of these meetings have been in person and involved extended discussion of our investigative findings.

A Corporate Kleptocracy

The problems traced in this Report are not new.[12] Indeed, Hollinger does not appear ever to have been run in accordance with accepted governance principles in the world of public corporations. While individual issues and transactions can and will be the subject of dispute and interpretation, the evidence reviewed by the Committee establishes an overwhelming record of abuse, over-reaching, and violations of fiduciary duties by Black and Radler, the two controlling shareholders. To fully gauge the level of Black and Radler's disregard for shareholder interests, one must step back from individual transactions and note the myriad of schemes, fiduciary abuses and fraudulent acts that were used to transfer essentially the entire earnings output of Hollinger over a seven-year period to the controlling shareholders. In this case more than most, one must not overlook the forest for the trees.

Hollinger was not a company where isolated improper and abusive acts took place. Rather, Hollinger was a company where abusive practices were inextricably linked to every major development or action. For most companies, operating in compliance with law and following ethical practices are key objectives, and specific concerns of the CEO. At Hollinger, Black as both CEO and controlling

---

[12] In 1982, the SEC sued Black and Norcen Energy Resources, Limited (an indirect subsidiary of Ravelston of which Black was Chairman) for fraud in connection with transactions relating to the stock of The Hanna Mining Company. The SEC's suit charged that among other things, Black and Norcen had "made untrue statements of material facts, omitted to state material facts necessary to make the statements made not misleading, and engaged in fraudulent, deceptive and manipulative acts and practices" relating to purchases by Norcen of stock in Hanna, and a subsequent tender offer for Hanna's shares. Both Black and Norcen were found to have made false and misleading statements to Hanna, as well as in SEC disclosure documents, as part of an effort to gain control of Hanna. Black was permanently enjoined from future violations of antifraud requirements of U.S. securities laws. See Securities and Exchange Commission Litigation Release No. 9719, 1982 SEC Lexis 1253, July 20, 1982.

shareholder, together with his associates, created an entity in which ethical corruption was a defining characteristic of the leadership team. Indeed, at Hollinger during the years covered by this Report transactions or strategies were particularly attractive if they offered opportunities for extraordinary payments to the control group. For example, while delevering the Company had real advantages, the US and Canadian community newspapers sold off by Black and Radler had the highest returns of any Hollinger business. However, their sale offered opportunities to Black and his Ravelston associates to divert tens of millions in sales proceeds to themselves, and then to use that cash in part to buy many of the publications at reduced prices or for nothing at all. No matter its effect on Hollinger, that was a winning strategy for Black and Radler.

Over the years success or failure at Hollinger came to be measured largely by how much cash — and even chunks of the Company — could be transferred from Hollinger to Black, Radler, Ravelston or their affiliates and not by earnings per share, share price, market share, return on equity or any other measures of how the Company was actually performing. Indeed, Hollinger's equity market capitalization stagnated for years as the insiders turned more and more to transferring cash that could have been earnings at Hollinger into fees for Black and Radler. From March 31, 1995 through March 31, 2003 (shortly before the Special Committee was formed), Hollinger's stock price rose 15.1%, from US$6.74 to US$7.76 per share.[13] During the same period the S&P 500 rose 69.4% and the Dow Jones rose 92.2%.[14] Someone who invested US$1,000 in Hollinger on March 31, 1995 would have had US$1,151 on March 31, 2003, compared with US$1,694 for someone who invested in the S&P 500 and US$1,922 for an investor in the Dow Jones average at the same dates. An investor in Hollinger therefore ended up with US$771 less at the end of these years compared with someone who had invested an equal

---

[13] Hollinger's historical stock prices have been adjusted for stock splits and dividends. Source: Commodity Systems, Inc.

[14] Many people believed that Hollinger's stock traded at a discount to market valuations due to what Burt called the "Conrad Black discount."

amount in a basket of the Dow stocks. This was truly awful performance for the stock.

Delaware law establishes a standard of "entire fairness" for judging transactions between controlling shareholders and the controlled company. To protect the non-controlling shareholders (here, the majority) from the acts of controlling shareholders,[15] any transactions between a controlling shareholder and the controlled company must result from a process used to negotiate terms that is "entirely fair," and the substantive economic terms themselves must also be "entirely fair." As controlling shareholders, Black and Radler, as well as Ravelston and HLG, were bound by the limits of the entire fairness doctrine in all their dealings with Hollinger. Nonetheless, the Report documents dozens of transactions in which the Committee believes Black and Radler (as well as Ravelston and HLG) violated their fiduciary duties by engaging in transactions that were not fair — economically or procedurally — to Hollinger and its non-controlling majority shareholders.

A fundamental element in many of these transactions was Hollinger's basic control and ownership structure, which involved a layered control pyramid as shown in the diagram below. At the top of the control pyramid, Black and Radler exercised ultimate control over Hollinger (at all times covered by this Report) through their collective 80% control of Ravelston. Ravelston is a closely held Canadian company that represented the second layer in Hollinger's control pyramid, immediately below Black and Radler.

---

[15] The entire fairness doctrine would typically apply to majority shareholders, who have their own natural economic reasons not to see damage to the company that would reduce the share price. Because of the dual voting structure at Hollinger, the controlling shareholders did not own a majority or anything close to that of total equity. In this structure the entire fairness doctrine is even more important, to prevent exactly the type of transactions that were Black's specialty. Absent this fiduciary duty, or a functioning sense of ethics, a controlling minority shareholder could with impunity take actions that would damage the public company but transfer an even greater economic advantage to the controlling shareholder. At Hollinger this exact situation took place regularly, with unfair fees to Ravelston weakening Hollinger but making Black and Radler rich.

Black and Radler's Effective Economic Ownership in Hollinger
As of December 31, 2002

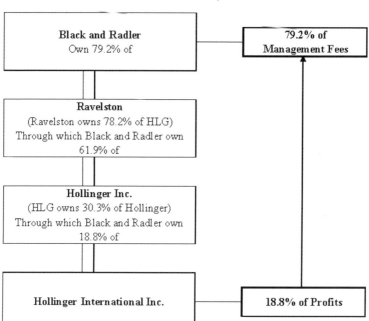

As shown in the Report, Ravelston has exercised outright voting control of HLG, the third layer in the control structure, since 1997. However, even in 1995 and 1996 Ravelston exercised control as a practical matter even though its voting percentage was under 50%, while the remaining interests were dispersed.

HLG (and therefore Black indirectly) has held absolute voting control of Hollinger since Hollinger's IPO in 1994. That control is maintained through a dual tier voting stock structure under which "Class B" voting shares of Hollinger, held solely by HLG, have ten times the voting power of "Class A" common shares owned by the public. Under this structure, HLG's share of Hollinger's total equity has fallen from approximately 65% after its IPO to less than 19% today, without HLG or Black losing absolute voting control of Hollinger.

Repeated abusive practices

Our Report describes at length many individual instances of what the Special Committee concluded were deliberate acts designed to take cash or assets out of Hollinger and to transfer them on unfair terms to Black and Radler and their associates directly, or indirectly through HLG or Ravelston, as well as other abusive or illegal acts or practices.

Only a small sample of these events includes:

- Taking US$9.5 million of corporate cash in late 2000 without notice to Hollinger's Board, which was accomplished with falsified closing documents used to provide a pre-text for the transfer. Kipnis, the internal lawyer, facilitated the unauthorized transfer of cash with falsified documents and was paid a US$100,000 special bonus at Radler's direction.
- Taking US$5.5 million of corporate cash in early 2001 without notice to Hollinger's Board, which was accomplished by creating fictitious agreements not to compete with one of Hollinger's wholly owned subsidiaries. The phony payments were then back-dated to the prior year which enabled them to be hidden through accounting offsets.
- Diverting to Black and Radler through Ravelston nearly US$200 million in excessive and unjustifiable management fees. The requests for such fees were accompanied by misrepresentations and failures to make full disclosure of relevant information to the Audit Committee, grossly inflated charges for personnel costs, and in effect billing the Company for debt service and other costs unrelated to services provided to Hollinger.
- Causing Hollinger to pay more than US$90 million in supposed consideration for the execution of non-competition agreements by Black, Radler, Boultbee, Atkinson, Ravelston, and HLG in connection with sales of publications belonging to Hollinger. More than US$47 million of this amount went directly to Hollinger officers who should not have required any individual compensation to adhere to agreements to which Hollinger was a party, while approximately US$26 million went to Ravelston in a duplication

Table 3.1.   Hollinger International

	2003 (%)	2002 (%)	2001 (%)	2000 (%)	1999 (%)	1998 (%)	1997 (%)	1996 (%)	1995 (%)	1994 (%)
							Ravelston and HLG Ownership Percentages			
Ravelston Equity Interest in HLG	78.2	**78.2	77.8	68.6	67.1	59.8	62.6	49.3	49.5	49.2
HLG Ownership Interest in Hollinger										
Voting power	65.0	*72.6	71.8	73.3	75.2	73.9	84.3	77.8	88.2	94.7***
Equity Interest	18.2	*30.3	32.1	37.0	41.1	41.3	59.9	51.2	66.5	64.2***

*As of August 2004.
**As of April 2004.
***As of Hollinger IPO.

of payments that had already been made to Ravelston's principals individually. All of these payments were made on terms that were unfair to Hollinger and represented unjustifiable waste of assets that rightfully belonged to all Hollinger shareholders.

- Filing proxy statements and other disclosure documents with the SEC that contained false statements, or omitted to include material information regarding fees and other forms of compensation or related party transactions that sometimes involved transfer of tens of millions of dollars out of Hollinger. For example, the compensation table in Hollinger's proxy statements does not show Black and Radler as receiving *any* compensation from Hollinger as their share of US$226 million in management fees from 1996 to 2003.[16] In an average year, Hollinger failed to disclose in its proxy statement as much as 96% of the compensation the Committee believes was received by its top five officers.

- Transferring income-generating Hollinger assets to entities secretly controlled by Black and Radler for free, or at prices known to be below market value. This was accomplished by concealing key facts from, or making misrepresentations to, Hollinger's Audit Committee and Board.

- Taking approximately US$80 million in Hollinger cash as "loans" to HLG, without paying market levels of interest, using Hollinger's own cash to repay debt that HLG owed to Hollinger, or simply not repaying HLG debt to Hollinger at all. Black and Radler freely used Hollinger's cash and credit to benefit HLG without adequately compensating Hollinger, in part to maintain HLG's stranglehold control of Hollinger.

- Allowing sales proceeds to Hollinger to be reduced by US$39 million in order to offset a side deal negotiated by Black in which CanWest agreed to pay Black and Radler US$3.9 million in perpetuity through Ravelston. This was accomplished by misrepresentations to

---

[16] The proxy statements do state that Black and Radler, among others, are affiliates of Ravelston and that Ravelston (and Moffat Management and Black-Amiel Management) received the management fees although they do not disclose how much compensation.

the Audit Committee and the Board, and was not properly disclosed in SEC filings.

• Causing Hollinger to spend US$9 million over a five year period to purchase papers and memorabilia of former US President Franklin D. Roosevelt without authorization, in furtherance of Black's personal interests, and using the materials to decorate his personal residences in Palm Beach, New York and other locations.[17]

• Paying Black and his senior associates US$5.3 million in "incentive compensation" on Hollinger Digital transactions by disregarding US$67.8 million in investment losses. Black and others misrepresented to the Board the characteristics of an incentive plan that was unusual and off market. Black and others wired Digital "incentive payments" to what appears to have been a shell Caribbean entity variously referred to as "Argent News" or "Argent Barbados."[18]

• Cutting the interest rate on a US$36.8 million loan Hollinger had made to HLG from 13% to 4.9% without authorization, or any compensation to Hollinger. Black and Radler directed this action to benefit themselves, HLG and Ravelston even though it cost Hollinger more than US$3.9 million per year in reduced interest payments.

In these and many similar transactions, insiders benefited financially from Hollinger on unfair terms. The Special Committee found endemic failures to disclose material facts to the Board, as well as repeated failures to seek proper authorization for related-party transactions that transferred Hollinger's assets to HLG, Ravelston, Horizon or to Black and Radler directly. In many cases the participants in these transactions claimed that they could not remember critical facts or important details of transactions. The Special Committee found numerous examples where recipients of Hollinger's cash appear to have tried to disguise the true nature of related-party transactions,

---

[17] Hollinger recently accepted an offer through Christie's to sell the largest group of FDR papers for US$2.4 million, compared to a purchase price in 2001 for the same materials of US$8 million.

[18] "L'argent" is French for "money."

or to hide them completely from the Board. These duplicitous actions make it difficult to ascribe the wrongful actions we document in the Report to anything other than deliberate intent.

Management fees

From 1997 to 2003, Black and Radler received "management fees" of US$218.4 million through HLG and Ravelston. For many years, this system of management fees paid to Ravelston was a simple but effective device for camouflaging just who was providing exactly what services for what price. That camouflage was important because the Special Committee does not believe Hollinger's compensation practices could ever have withstood the light of day. Indeed, the Special Committee found that a principal purpose for bundling compensation through Ravelston was to prevent others from realizing just how much Black and Radler were really taking out of Hollinger.

After careful analysis the Committee's compensation experts concluded that US$196.9 million of the aggregate US$218.4 million in management fees represented compensation to the five senior officers, and they noted that they had never seen non-compete payments used to compensate individual corporate officers as was done on a massive scale at Hollinger. In the Committee's view, the maximum upper limit for a Ravelston management fee to have been fair and reasonable to Hollinger would have been the amount that Hollinger would have paid to retain its own management directly on a full time basis.[19] In practice, Ravelston changed a fee that was tens of millions higher than this every year. Consequently the Special Committee believes that the

---

[19] If Black had recovered his actual costs and charged Hollinger the same or less than it would otherwise have to pay on the open market, the system could have operated in a manner that was fair and reasonable to Hollinger shareholders. In actual practice Black and Radler hired clerical and financial staff to service Hollinger (and to assist with other personal business interests in which Hollinger did not have an interest), and then bundled the direct and indirect costs of that clerical and financial staff together with (i) the compensation and profits Black and Radler wished to receive and (ii) whatever other costs of Ravelston Black and his associates needed to cover, including debt service obligations to HLG.

entire US$218.4 million in management fees did not satisfy the entire fairness standard, and that the so-called "Ravelston structure" did not benefit Hollinger in any way. Indeed, Hollinger could have retained the top five officers of several publishing companies that were both larger and more successful than Hollinger for what it paid in management fees to Ravelston and still had millions left over.

The Committee found that in setting the management fee that Ravelston proposed to charge each year, Black and Radler decided what they wanted or needed to charge, not what was fair and reasonable to Hollinger in light of the services actually provided. The only real reason for the Ravelston structure was to shift cash to Black and Radler in amounts far greater than any direct compensation package could ever do, and to avoid even a discussion with the Board of how much compensation Black and Radler should receive. This cash could then be used in part to maintain and increase their investment holdings in HLG, to buy up Hollinger's assets through Horizon, or for other purposes beneficial to them.

The Hollinger Board did not decide what Black and his associates should each receive in salary, bonus, and equity incentives as is required by Hollinger's Compensation Committee charter, and as is the nearly universal practice of established public companies. Instead, Black decided who got what, and he simply built that amount and whatever else he wished into the management fee. The Board acquiesced to Black and Radler's decisions and never even purported to set a target level of compensation it considered reasonable.

Shareholders could not learn what compensation Black and his Ravelston associates were receiving by reading Hollinger's proxy statement, as most of the compensation Black, Radler, and the others at Ravelston received just was not there.[20] For example, the Special Committee determined that Hollinger's five most highly compensated officers (all Ravelston shareholders) received US$57.2, 116.8 and 60 million, respectively, in compensation in 1999, 2000, and 2001 (including non-competition payments, but excluding stock

---

[20] The aggregate management fees were disclosed although investors had no way of knowing that the vast bulk of this represented compensation to the individuals.

option grants). However, Hollinger's proxy compensation table for those same years only disclosed US$1.2, 5.4 and 2.8 million (excluding stock option grants, though non-competition agreements were not disclosed). Out of total compensation of US$234 million for the five individuals in 1999–2001, only US$9.4 million or 4.0% was disclosed in the Hollinger proxy, while approximately 96% went undisclosed, as was generally the case every year.

Black's public defense of the Ravelston management fee system has been that the amount of the management fee each year was approved by the Audit Committee. Yet the Hollinger Board was never given truthful and accurate information that would let it understand how much Black or Radler made directly and indirectly in annual compensation from Hollinger. When the Audit Committee approved the Ravelston management fees, it did so without knowing the level of compensation this was generating for Black and Radler, and therefore they could not compare this with compensation for the CEO and COO at other publishing companies. The Audit Committee also did not know — or even have a rough estimate of — how much more the Ravelston fee cost Hollinger compared with what it would have cost Hollinger to follow normal compensation and hiring practices for senior executives. The Special Committee believes the Audit Committee needed to know these and other material facts (and Black had a duty to tell them) before it could form a reasonable business judgment concerning the size of the management fee that would be fair and reasonable to Hollinger. The Special Committee also believes that instead of its inert behavior, the Audit Committee should have required Black and Radler to disclose the necessary information to it so it could perform an independent analysis. At the same time, the Special Committee does not believe this lessens Black's and his colleagues' violations of their fiduciary duty of loyalty, or justifies the legitimacy of a system that was used to plunder Hollinger on a vast scale.

Non-compete payments

While the grossly excessive management fee was the single largest source of the cash Black, Radler and their associates improperly took out of Hollinger, the device of the "non-compete" payment was probably the most unusual and offensive practice of the Ravelston crew. In a series of transactions from 1999 to 2001, Black and his associates (including both HLG and Ravelston) collected a bonanza of more than US$90 million purportedly as compensation for executing non-competition agreements with buyers of publications Hollinger was selling. The amount of these payments was unilaterally determined by Black and Radler, who in doing so were negotiating simultaneously for themselves and for Hollinger. Evidently sitting on both sides of the table made reaching an agreement on non-compete fees easier.

These payments became a potent device for skimming a small percentage of Hollinger's cash into the hands of individual officers of Hollinger every time publications were sold. The entire rationale offered as an excuse to justify these unprecedented payments was contrived by Black and his Ravelston colleagues.[21] Buyers of publications from Hollinger generally did not ask anyone other than Hollinger to provide non-compete agreements at all, and they never asked for HLG, Ravelston, Black, Radler, Boultbee, or Atkinson to be paid for any such agreements. Instead, Black or Radler, sometimes through Kipnis, told buyers that they wanted HLG, Ravelston or the individuals to provide these agreements in addition to what the buyers wanted, which was a non-compete covenant from Hollinger as seller. It was presented as something extra for the buyer, on top of an agreement with Hollinger, whether or not the buyer saw any value in receiving these extra agreements.

Officers of several buyers from Hollinger during the period told the Special Committee that they had not even heard of some of the corporate entities offered up to provide non-compete agreements, and that their concerns were with Hollinger rather than any other

---

[21] The device of allocating a portion of the sales price for a community newspaper to a non-compete agreement is not unprecedented, particularly in the case of founder-sellers. This can also be a de facto source of seller financing if the non-compete component is taken over time. Neither the Special Committee nor its compensation consultants could find examples of transactions in which large public companies paid non-competition payments to their own officers while still employed in connection with contracts signed by their own company as seller.

entities. Even in CanWest, where the buyer did want a non-compete from Black and Radler as well as Hollinger, CanWest did not specify that any payments be made to Ravelston, or to Black, Radler and the other individuals. Where buyers demurred on the offer of getting a non-compete from HLG (as in CNHI I) or from others, Black and Radler would insist. Once a non-compete was referenced in an agreement with a buyer, even though they themselves usually suggested it, Black and Radler then had a pretext for telling the Board that they had done something onerous and deserving of a special payment. The non-compete payments were in effect a device for allowing Black and Radler to take a cut of the sales proceeds from every Hollinger deal. In other transactions Black and Radler and their associates paid themselves ostensible non-compete fees even when there was no third-party transaction, or when the agreement with the buyers was silent on the matter.

The Special Committee believes that it is utterly nonsensical to claim that senior corporate officers such as Black, the CEO, and Radler, the COO, should be paid anything personally simply to go along with agreements that Hollinger had signed (let alone payments of tens of millions of dollars). They had fiduciary duties to Hollinger, and once Hollinger signed a non-compete agreement with a buyer of assets that commitment should have bound Black and Radler for as long as they served as officers of Hollinger. Since Black and Radler were bound not to violate Hollinger's agreements as long as they were officers, that meant that neither HLG (which did not have any other employees) nor Ravelston could compete with someone else even if they wanted to do so. Therefore, there was no logical or rational justification for why buyers from Hollinger would need an agreement from those entities either. The entire concept of these payments was simply bizarre.

As long as Black and Radler remained officers of Hollinger, they could not compete with CanWest, CNHI or anyone else in the newspaper business with whom Hollinger already had a non-compete, and the Hollinger Board could also simply have refused to allow them to have *any* other business activities as a condition of their positions and fees. They could also have been given protection against the possibility they might leave Hollinger or be terminated through employment contracts, severance agreements or post-employment consulting agreements that would not have cost Hollinger anything if they continued serving as officers. A buyer could also have been offered indemnification against any of the individuals leaving Hollinger and causing competitive damage to the buyer as an alternative to a "non-compete" agreement from anyone other than Hollinger. Thus there were several less costly alternatives available to Hollinger to avoid the types of payments that were made. Since Black and Radler decided they should award themselves these payments, these other alternatives were never pursued.

The Special Committee concluded that while serving as officers of the Company, none of the Ravelston personnel should have been entitled to collect a toll on Hollinger's ability to sell assets or to skim off the sales proceeds in any amount. For them to do so was a fundamental breach of their fiduciary duties. These payments were so far off normal practice that it is no wonder Black described them in a letter to Radler as "the splendid conveyance of the non-competition agreements from which you and I profited so well ..."

The Hollinger Board was not even told about approximately US$38 million of these non-compete payments when they were made. The Board did not have any opportunity to question in advance whether those fees were necessary and in Hollinger's interest. In transactions they were told about, the Board was not fully and accurately informed of a range of facts.

In the biggest of the transactions, the US$2.1 billion sale of Canadian publications to CanWest, Hollinger directors were given false and misleading information to help win Board approval of nearly US$52 million in fees directly and indirectly to Black and his associates. As part of the CanWest transaction, Black negotiated a side deal (in addition to direct payment of the US$52 million) under which CanWest would pay Black and Radler (through Ravelston) US$3.9 million in "management fees" each year. Black then agreed that CanWest could *reduce* the price it was paying to Hollinger by US$39 million to offset the fees CanWest had agreed to pay Black and Radler. Black personally negotiated the annual US$3.9 million payment even though he knew that the deal involved a loss of US$10 in sales proceeds to Hollinger for every US$1 in annual fees he and Radler received, a massive conflict of interest.

Shareholders were told in a Form 8-K filed with the SEC in December 2000, that the sales prices in the CanWest deal were set using "arm's length negotiations." However, when Black cut his deal for tens of millions in non-compete and management fees at Hollinger's expense, nobody was negotiating on behalf of Hollinger's shareholders. When the Board reviewed the US$52 million in direct payments to Black and the other recipients, Black never revealed that he had initially sought a US$12.3 million annual payment from CanWest, which would have reduced the sales price paid to Hollinger by US$123 million instead of the eventual US$39 million. Black and Radler later asked for US$20 million (but at closing they actually received US$26 million) in payments from Hollinger to Ravelston to compensate them based on their claim that Ravelston voluntarily lowered the fee it sought from CanWest, and that Hollinger received a higher sales price as a result. Of course, Hollinger did receive more than it would have gotten if Black had his way, though Hollinger received US$39 million less than it would have gotten if Black had not taken any personal side deal from CanWest. This argument is similar to a bank robber asking a bank to pay him a reward because he stole only a portion of what he might have taken.

The performance of the Audit Committee and the Board in reviewing the non-compete payments was unacceptable. While it was bombarded with misinformation, the Audit Committee nonetheless allowed Black and Radler as interested parties unfettered rein to direct the amounts and the allocation of non-compete payments to themselves. There never was any economic justification for repeated non-compete awards to Black and his associates, and these payments of tens of millions of dollars amounted to a gift of a percentage of Hollinger's balance sheet. Any such proposal from Black, if not rejected out of hand, should have received heightened and intense scrutiny from the Audit Committee, but that never happened. Indeed, after tens of millions in non-compete fees and sharp reductions in the size of Hollinger's business, the Board never seems to have asked why the Company needed to continue to pay tens of millions in annual management fees to Ravelston.

As with the abuses in connection with management fees, however, the Special Committee does not believe the failure of the Audit Committee to perform a reasonable analysis of these implausible fees justifies or excuses the taking of these fees in the first place. Black and Radler's fiduciary duties required them to refrain from arranging these transactions that were patently inequitable to Hollinger (which never received any portion of the fees in CanWest).

Unauthorized Transfers of Hollinger Cash

In the fall of 2003, the Committee discovered that more than US$32 million in cash had been transferred from Hollinger to Black, Radler, Atkinson, Boultbee, and HLG without any notice to the Audit Committee or the Board, or any approval of the transactions. In one case Radler simply ordered Hollinger employees to pay himself, Black and two others US$9.5 million in cash at the closing of a transaction, even though the related agreement did not provide for any such payment. He then authorized the employee who helped implement the cash transfer to pay himself a US$100,000 special bonus. As set forth in more detail in the Report, the Committee believes that this US$9.5 million, and millions more like it in other situations, was intentionally transferred without any intent of disclosing it to the Board.

This US$9.5 million cash diversion took place at the time of the CNHI II closing in November 2000, less than two months after Black and Radler obtained Board approval for the US$52 million in non-compete payments from the CanWest proceeds. The Committee does not know why this US$9.5 million transfer was not submitted to the Audit Committee and the Board as happened in CanWest. However, we believe that individuals may have feared that disclosing US$9.5 million in new payments in the same month in which the US$52 million was to be paid to the same people might have provoked even the compliant Hollinger Board to refuse to go along. Had the Audit Committee been provoked to retain counsel of its own or to make any independent inquiries, it might have discovered that there was not any provision for the US$9.5 million in payments in the deal with CNHI, and that might have led to discovery that the US$52 million had not been requested by CanWest, either.

Only three months later, in February 2001, Black, Radler, Boultbee, and Atkinson, the same individuals who received the payments in CanWest and who secretly took the extra US$9.5 million, signed back-dated, spurious agreements not to compete with a wholly owned subsidiary of Hollinger. In the February 2001 action, the individuals paid themselves US$5.5 million for signing up to an agreement that did not mean anything. The Board was never told that these officers helped themselves to this US$5.5 million, or that they had done so based on backdated sham agreements that were simply a fraud on Hollinger.

Deceitful practices become the norm

As noted, in the early years of Hollinger's existence Black and Radler proved effective at increasing Hollinger's business, principally through acquisitions. Radler was widely regarded as accomplished in cutting expenses and improving earnings at the community newspapers. Black and Radler had built the Hollinger entities over a sustained period, and most members of the Board believed they were accomplished managers.

Unfortunately, the early relationship with Hollinger turned parasitic over time. After applying the percentage ownership interests up the control layers in Hollinger's ownership structure, Black and Radler had roughly a 19% beneficial interest in Hollinger's profits. However, they enjoyed nearly 80% of Ravelston's profits. That was the simple math that appears to have prompted many of Black and Radler's actions. When Hollinger's stock price multiples did not prove attractive (a reflection of poor performance, high leverage and related-party issues), the Company was increasingly run to produce extraordinary payments to the controlling Hollinger shareholders, rather than to increase value for all shareholders. Over and over again in the course of our work, we have sought to unravel complex situations only to discover a common denominator: the transfer of money and assets out of Hollinger and into the hands, directly or indirectly, of Black and Radler on terms that would never have been acceptable in an arm's length transaction with an unaffiliated party.

In some situations, insiders knew that they were taking Hollinger's cash or property without authority, or on terms rigged to their advantage. Insiders often knew they were not giving the full picture to the Board, and at times they had to know they were giving the Board information or rationalizations that just were not true. Self dealing, misrepresentation and other abusive and unethical practices had become so deeply ingrained in the corporate culture that they became commonplace, and perhaps indistinguishable from normal everyday practice for some of the key actors. The endless quest for huge cash payments to Black and Radler displaced ethics, fiduciary duties or any other considerations.

Examples of misleading conduct abound. Black and Radler limited their direct ownership in Horizon, their side newspaper business, to 49%, while Radler secretly hid an additional 24% ownership stake with a nominee, and gave false court testimony under oath that the nominee was independent. By limiting their direct ownership interest to 49% and hiding the remaining indirect 24% interest, Black and Radler were able to tell the Board when it reviewed transactions they recommended with Horizon that it was an enterprise in which they would "assist the financing and take equity positions." Had it been disclosed that this was an entity 73% owned by Black and Radler, the transactions would most likely have been more carefully analyzed.

In another case, Black and Radler caused Hollinger to disclose in a Form 10-K a year later than required that money taken without authorization and solely on their own initiative was supposedly paid "to satisfy a closing condition." The participants knew this was untrue, and that the disclosure omitted more than half the money taken and changed the dates when the money was paid.[22]

---

[22] This misleading disclosure filed almost a year and a half after the events may have been intended to create a defense against any later charge that the participants had taken the money with criminal or fraudulent intent, while minimizing the chances the Board would ask questions regarding the unauthorized payments.

Hollinger under Black and Radler lost any sense of corporate purpose, competitive drive or internal ethical concerns. The internal focus became exclusively how to generate opportunities to suck cash out of Hollinger and into Ravelston, if not into the hands of Black and Radler directly. The pace and scale of the effort to siphon away Hollinger's cash is noticeable in the minutes of the Audit Committee's meeting of February 22, 2000. In a meeting lasting 65 minutes, Black and Radler won approval for (i) US$38 million in management fees to themselves through Ravelston, (ii) the Hollinger Digital incentive plan (through which the "senior executive group" received US$5.3 million) and (iii) the sale for US$1.00 of Hollinger's *Skagit Valley Argus* and the *Journal of the San Juan Islands* to Horizon (then secretly 73% owned by Black and Radler) with a "working capital adjustment" that turned into a US$162,000 payment from Hollinger to Horizon to take its properties. In roughly one hour, Hollinger's Audit Committee considered more related-party payments than many companies consider in their entire existence.

Personal expenses

Another form of "compensation" at Hollinger was the payment of personal expenses of Black and his wife, and of Radler and his family, by Hollinger. Hollinger was used as a piggy bank for the Blacks, with shareholders paying for large and small expenses that would not typically be considered eligible for corporate reimbursement. As described in the Report, Hollinger bought a Challenger aircraft (US$11.6 million) for Radler, and leased a Gulfstream IV (at a cost of US$3–$4 million per year) for the Blacks. Operating both of these aircraft cost the Company over US$23 million from 2000–2003, an expensive fleet for a Company as small and poorly performing as Hollinger in those years. The jets were used for some business activities, but they were also used indiscriminately to fly the pair to and from their collections of homes without any plausible business connection. Initially the jets were paid for by Ravelston, which for US$40 million in fees each year could afford to get Black and Radler to work. In 2000, a time when the Company was completing the disposition of many of its far flung newspaper assets, this expense was shifted onto Hollinger without any commensurate reduction in Ravelston's management fee.

A much more unusual corporate "expense" occurred in 2000, when Black and his wife "swapped" Park Avenue apartments with Hollinger. The apartment owned by the Blacks (which they had purchased for US$499,000 two years earlier) was "priced" in the swap by crediting it with 70% appreciation from its acquisition cost. The apartment owned by Hollinger (which it had purchased for US$3 million six years earlier) that the Blacks were acquiring was "priced" in the swap by crediting it with zero appreciation. Both apartments were in the same building, though the apartment owned by Hollinger was greatly superior due to its size and location on a higher floor. Based on New York City Finance Department data for actual appreciation on Upper East Side properties for the dates in question, the Blacks obtained Hollinger's apartment for US$2.5 million below its value due to the rigged appreciation assumed in the deal. The apartment Hollinger took back in the rigged swap was then used to house personal domestic staff for the Blacks, personal friends visiting New York and on occasion visiting executives for corporate purposes.

Hollinger's proxy statement for 2000 falsely stated that Black had exercised an option to purchase the apartment at "then fair market values." In reality, Black acquired the Hollinger apartment in 2000 at what its market value had been in 1994 when Hollinger bought it. The deal was a real estate time machine for Black.

Apartments were not the only deal the Blacks cut for themselves in living expenses. Food, cell phones, perfume, and other routine living expenses, including tips by Mrs. Black while on shopping trips, were expensed to Hollinger. Black's corporate expense reports charge the company for items such as "handbags for Mrs. BB" (US$2,463), "jogging attire for Mrs. BB" (US$140), exercise equipment (US$2,083), "T. Anthony Ltd. Leather Briefcase" (US$2,057), opera tickets for "C&BB" (US$2,785), stereo equipment for the New York apartment (US$828), "silverware for Blacks' corporate jet" (US$3,530)

"Summer Drinks" (US$24,950), a "Happy Birthday, Barbara" dinner party[23] at New York's La Grenouille Restaurant (US$42,870),[24] and US$90,000 to refurbish a Rolls Royce owned by Ravelston for Black's personal transportation.

These expense amounts pale in comparison to Hollinger's cost in other deals Black engineered for himself or his wife. As described in the Report and in the Illinois Action, Black gave his wife a "no show" corporate post that paid her over US$1.1 million but did not require her to do anything. Amiel-Black was separately compensated for her services as a writer, though Hollinger paid for her pens, pencils, modems, computers and other office equipment as well as the operating cost of a private telecommunications network (something not given to other columnists) to connect her from multiple locations. Black's expense practices evidence his attitude that there was no need to distinguish between what belonged to the Company and what belonged to the Blacks. In Hollinger's world, everything belonged to the Blacks.

The efforts to avoid taxation

Another finding of this Report is that Black and his Ravelston associates, particularly Boultbee, frequently coupled their maneuvering to avoid accountability with aggressive schemes to avoid personal taxation. Not satisfied with receiving US$20–$40 million a year in excessive

---

[23] Eighty guests including Oscar de la Renta, Peter Jennings, Charlie Rose, Barbara Walters and Ron Perelman enjoyed dinner at US$212 a plate, including Beluga caviar, lobster ceviche, and 69 bottles of fine wine. Black paid an additional US$20,000 toward the cost of the evening. At least Black's choice of venue for his wife's birthday was less expensive than Dennis Kozlowski's party for his wife on Sardinia that was charged in part to Tyco.

[24] The majority of these items were charged to Hollinger corporate credit cards and paid in full by Hollinger. The Special Committee has found no evidence that these items were reimbursed to Hollinger on behalf of Black and Amiel-Black, though the Company's internal controls and recordkeeping practices concerning payables at the time were not comprehensive.

management fees, Black and the Ravelston insiders then directed significant portions of those fees to Moffat Management and Black-Amiel Management, which were empty shell companies registered in Barbados. Even though these entities did nothing to earn fees, and did not have either employees or real operations, paying management fees to them on the pretense that they performed services allowed the recipients the prospect of transforming a portion of the enormous management fees that would otherwise most likely have been taxable in Canada (where the payments were received), or possibly the U.S. (where services were largely performed), into dividends received in Barbados (where nothing occurred).[25] Similarly, not content with receiving more than US$5 million in "incentive" payments for losing US$68 million on Hollinger Digital investments, Black and other recipients members of the "Senior Executive Group" (but not Perle) had most of their Hollinger Digital payments wired to a different shell entity in Barbados.

The opportunity to turn compensation for personal services (though in part unauthorized and obtained with misleading information) into tax-free income in Canada was a factor in taking the US$53 million[26] in non-compete payments in CanWest, and probably also in the decision to return for another US$9.5 million in Hollinger cash that could be made to look like non-compete payments at the time of CNHI II in November 2000. The backdating of the sham agreements with APC in February 2001 may also have been done in part to claim tax-free treatment in 2000, although the backdating also allowed the US$5.5 million payments to be netted out, and effectively hidden, on Hollinger's books in 2000.

---

[25] Boultbee told the Committee that the reason for this structure was that income at these entities would only be subject to income tax at a rate of 2.5%.

[26] While the Board approved non-compete payments of US$51.8 million in connection with the CanWest transaction, Black and Radler decided to pay themselves and their fellow recipients US$1.1 million in "interest" on the payments due to them, even though their noncompete agreements had only been in force for one day. This represented an interest rate of more than 775% per year.

Private company behavior in a public company

Hollinger was a public company, with all the fiduciary duties and disclosure obligations that entails. However, though the form of a public company existed, the substance did not. Black and Radler created a governance structure at the formation of the Company that gave them voting control irrespective of their level of equity ownership. In the short run that structure left them free to violate ethical norms or fiduciary duty standards without serious risk of challenge. Black named every member of the Board, and the Board's membership was largely composed of individuals with whom Black had longstanding social, business or political ties. The Board Black selected functioned more like a social club or public policy association than as the board of a major corporation, enjoying extremely short meetings followed by a good lunch and discussion of world affairs. Though pleasant and not unrelated to Hollinger's editorial positions, this level of Board involvement was not what the business of Hollinger and its web of conflict situations required from its Board. Actual operating results or corporate performance were rarely discussed. Burt recalls Black changing the subject when he tried to ask questions about the financial performance of *The Telegraph*, for example. Elemental disclosure requirements and fiduciary standards were routinely violated, and Black generally did what he pleased.

Black unquestionably saw Hollinger as "his" company. Healy told the Special Committee of an unpleasant telephone exchange with Black following the 2002 annual meeting when Healy suggested informing Thompson of certain information. According to Healy, Black hissed at him: "This is my Company, I am the controlling shareholder and I'll decide what the Governor needs to know and when … ." KPMG's Pat Ryan recalled a similar Black tirade in 2002, after Ryan raised questions with the Audit Committee about the CanWest non-compete payments.

In Black's own words, the public company structure was useful because it allowed the "relatively cheap use of other people's capital." Black saw the system he had created as one endless opportunity to confer rewards on himself and his colleagues. He did not appear to acknowledge that fiduciary standards for public companies created meaningful limits on his dealings with Hollinger.

While the Special Committee does not believe that most of the fraudulent and abusive practices described in the Report would be tolerated in a private company any more than in a public company, a private company would not present the same type of fiduciary issues that inevitably were raised in a public company where Black and Radler could decide for themselves how they wished to use the capital of disenfranchised public investors. In a typical private equity setting, Black and Radler would have had to deal with empowered and active equity investors who would take the time to oversee internal practices and cash flow, as well as with knowledgeable debt creditors. The public company format left Black and Radler free to prey on relatively uninformed and completely powerless equity investors to the extent Black's hand-picked Board would allow.

The Report describes an exchange in early 2000 between Black and Asper, the late CEO of CanWest, that contrasts different approaches to fiduciary standards. When Black asked Asper to give him a post-transaction management fee of US$12.3 million per year in return for a reduction of US$123 million in sales proceeds to Hollinger, Asper told Black to "give us an accounting of what services the [US$12.3] million covers and what and who is provided at what cost."[27] In a handwritten note to Black, Asper noted that CanWest's management costs ran about US$2 million each year to Hollinger's US$38 million. Asper pointed out to Black that at CanWest the management fees were to cover salaries "actually paid to members of the Asper family, at modest market rates, with no overhead, or profit."

Asper's suggestion to Black that "market rates, with no overhead, or profit" was the right standard for fees charged by a controlling shareholder to a public company fell on deaf ears. In 2000, Ravelston's management fee to Hollinger as a percentage of total revenues was approximately 10 *times* greater than similar costs at CanWest. In that

---

[27] This was a simple question the Hollinger Audit Committee should long since have asked Black. Rather than even trying to answer Asper, Black immediately cut the fee he asked for by approximately 68%.

same year, the top five officers of Hollinger had total compensation the Committee estimates at US$122 million, including nearly US$53 million in non-competition and interest payments received from the proceeds of the CanWest transaction. This represented a nearly unbelievable 30.2% of Hollinger's 2000 adjusted EBITDA, and 61.6% of Hollinger's adjusted net income. For an encore, Black and his four senior officers received total compensation in 2001 that the Committee estimates was more than US$69 million, representing 73.4% of Hollinger's adjusted EBITDA in a year Hollinger reported a net loss of over US$337 million. Cash compensation to management at such levels (whether paid directly or indirectly), and in such a proportion of corporate cash flow, is stunning in its audacity and its utter disregard for either market practices or the legal standards of fiduciary behavior.

Repeated disclosure issues

The record of Hollinger's disclosures under Black and Radler's leadership shows repeated instances of incomplete, inaccurate or nonexistent disclosures, as well as Black's own refusal to testify before the SEC after asserting the Fifth Amendment privilege against self-incrimination in response to questions involving his leadership of Hollinger.[28] For example, until 2003 Hollinger's proxy statement compensation tables did not include disclosure of even US$1 in compensation to Black, Radler and the other Ravelston executives resulting from more than US$226 million in management fees Hollinger paid to Ravelston since 1996.

In 2003, there was finally belated footnote disclosure in the proxy statement that, referring to compensation in 2001, listed US$13.2 million for the five senior officers as "an allocation of the economic interest in the management fee." However, Ravelston charged Hollinger US$30.7 million in management fees in 2001, not US$13 million.

---

[28] Black argued that he should retain his privileges as Chairman of the Board at Hollinger notwithstanding his assertion of the Fifth Amendment protections. Most public companies automatically terminate employees or officers who refuse to answer questions under oath before the SEC.

This curious disclosure does not say what compensation was actually received by whom, and it also only accounts for 43% of the fee actually paid to Ravelston that year, even though the five senior executives hold an 84.2% interest in Ravelston. Approximately US$15 million of Hollinger management fees evidently just disappeared.[29]

Evaluating the Board's Conduct

The Committee believes that Black and Radler were by far the most culpable people in causing damage to Hollinger by taking more than US$400 million and operating parts of the Company for their own benefit, and consistently violating their fiduciary duties as they pushed through one unfair transaction after another. These were the truly "bad actors" involved in the *Hollinger Chronicles*. The Committee focused its most intense efforts in the early stages of the process on determining the scope of wrongdoing by those who took the money. The Committee's suit on behalf of the Company in the Illinois Action seeks to make Hollinger's shareholders whole by recovering at least US$1.25 billion in damages stemming from the actions of these individuals and the corporate vehicles that they utilized to carry out their schemes.

Though the persons who took funds or assets from Hollinger improperly are the primary offenders, the consistent inaction of the Hollinger Board also resulted in squandering opportunities for stopping abusive acts before the damage was too great. The simple fact that the members of the Audit Committee did not learn what was going on in the related-party transactions and did not stop the looting of the Company by its controlling shareholders of necessity raises the question of "where was the Audit Committee?" There is not a good answer to that question.

---

[29] Investors can only speculate where this US$15 million went, though the Special Committee believes that it is approximately equal to the amount Ravelston would have needed to pay HLG to meet its liquidity needs. Hollinger money used to pay Ravelston's debts should almost certainly be deemed to be disclosable indirect compensation to each of the Ravelston shareholders.

The Audit Committee and the Board were given false information (and were not told other material facts) about the non-compete payments and management fees. However, it is also true that they did not do much if anything on their own about either the non-compete payments or the excessive management fees. The Audit Committee could have hired its own compensation consultants and its own counsel without any affiliations to Black given the perpetual nature of conflict situations built into Hollinger's structure. Instead it only hired independent counsel or advisors in rare circumstances. The Audit Committee relied for most advice on Black, Radler or other Ravelston personnel who had a direct conflict of interest. KPMG and Torys represented HLG and Ravelston as well as Hollinger, so the Audit Committee also knew or should have known that their views could be tempered or compromised when it came to related-party payments among the various entities.

The Report notes that the Audit Committee does not appear to have asked for any information concerning the components of the management fee, such as the breakdown between compensation for the back office personnel and payments to the senior officers. The Audit Committee did not inquire as to what indirect costs of Ravelston were being charged back to Hollinger, and it did not do any work to determine whether any such "costs" were related in any way to services performed for Hollinger. The Audit Committee did not seek backup documentation regarding any aspects of the proposed management fee each year.

The Report concludes that the Audit Committee's "review" of the annual management fee did not pass a threshold level sufficient to characterize what it did as a "review" (let alone a "negotiation"), and that any "approval" given was not based on any serious analysis. Indeed, in many cases approvals were not based on any analysis at all. The Audit Committee failed to take any of the steps, or to ask any of the questions, that might have made their review of both management fees and non-compete fees meaningful. They were inattentive, and they failed to be alert to the possibility that Black and Radler might be proposing vastly inflated or wholly inappropriate fees that were fundamentally unfair to Hollinger shareholders.

In performing our work, the Special Committee discovered a pattern of misleading statements to the Board and the Audit Committee surrounding related-party transactions. In addition to making false statements, we also found many cases in which Black, Radler, Kipnis or others failed to tell the Board or the Audit Committee key facts necessary to fully understand transactions or payments as to which partial information was given. "Lying by omission" can be just as misleading as making a false statement, and unfortunately both occurred in connection with Hollinger's Board.

Perhaps the most dramatic of the affirmatively false statements occurred during the Board's review of the proposed CanWest non-compete payments. As described in the Report, Black, Radler, Boultbee, and Torys, the outside lawyers, all knew that CanWest's original drafts of the purchase agreement had not required (or provided for) any specific payments for the non-compete agreements that it expected to receive at closing. Nonetheless, Radler told the Audit Committee that CanWest had insisted on the specific amounts of non-compete payments, which was simply untrue. Black later told shareholders at the annual meeting that it had been the independent directors that had negotiated the amount of the payments, which also was not true.

The Audit Committee was also misled by Kipnis' memo prior to the meeting, and his and Radler's statements at the Audit Committee meeting on September 11, 2000, that Ravelston had generated increased sales proceeds for Hollinger by voluntarily modifying its contract rights. The Audit Committee's cursory review and discussion failed to recognize that this was nothing more than a fairy tale. Ravelston had not given up any rights, as its agreement with Hollinger continued in force unchanged.[30]

These and other misleading statements to the Board at the time of the CanWest deal had the effect of characterizing payments that were entirely discretionary as having been required by the buyer.

---

[30] As noted earlier, Black actually attempted to do the exact opposite of what was claimed, by seeking to reduce the price CanWest would pay to Hollinger by US$123 million in exchange for a side deal for US$12.3 million in annual management fees from CanWest.

The Audit Committee and the Board agreed to the payments, but they did so thinking that they did not have a choice if they wanted the CanWest transaction to be completed for the good of the Company. As outrageous as these misrepresentations to the Board were, they do not in our view relieve the Audit Committee from the responsibility of obtaining independent confirmations of the reasonableness and necessity of these payments.

Approximately six months after the original CanWest transaction closed, the Board received an extraordinary memo from Kipnis. It advised the Board that they had been misinformed as to information regarding the non-compete and break fee payments in late 2000. They were advised that this misinformation included the fact that CanWest had not actually specified the amount of the non-compete fees that would be paid. The misleading information given to the Board was described as "inadvertent." The Board was asked to ratify a modified variation of the original payments, with Ravelston now receiving a "non-compete" instead of a "break fee" payment. The Board approved the request with virtually no discussion, even though they had expressly been told that they had been given incorrect information at the time of the CanWest closing when they awarded US$52 million to management.

Under the proposal Kipnis conveyed, the "new" rationale for paying Ravelston the US$20 million, it had already received as a "break fee" became compensation for signing a non-competition agreement. Upon receipt of these "corrections," the Audit Committee evidently did not ask why Ravelston needed a non-compete fee on top of individual non-compete payments to Black, Radler, Atkinson, and Boultbee, leaving no one else at Ravelston who realistically could compete with CanWest. Once told that CanWest did not dictate who should receive the US$52 million, the Audit Committee should have re-examined the size and appropriateness of all of the payments, and it should have revisited the question of why Hollinger was paying any of the US$52 million to its officers (each of whom was already fully paid through Ravelston) rather than keeping this money for its shareholders.

Almost all of the payments relating to "non-compete" agreements involved false statements to the Board, failures to tell the Board the full story, or failures to tell the Board anything at all. For example, in the two Osprey transactions, Black and Radler simply took payments of more than US$5 million without telling the Board or the Audit Committee anything at all. Black and Radler subsequently advised the Board of the Osprey payments, and sought (and obtained) an express ratification based on a misleading portrayal of the events.

Throughout most of this time, the Board was hearing consistent stories from Black or Radler on the one hand, and Kipnis on the other. The Board did not have any reason to think Kipnis would knowingly give the Board false information, and his comments made statements by Black and Radler all the more credible. The Board did not know, however, that Kipnis had in effect cast his lot with Black and Radler who, among other things, controlled both his employment and his compensation.

The Audit Committee's failure to perform any independent analysis of the management fee and the non-compete requests was influenced by the trust they had in Black and Radler to be honest, and their belief that Black and Radler were capable executives. Thompson in particular would never claim to be a businessman, or an expert in financial analytics. However, he is a highly experienced lawyer, and he understands the fiduciary duties that Black and Radler had as controlling shareholders. Thompson knew that if Black and Radler charged Hollinger more than a fair and reasonable amount, they would be violating their duties under Delaware law. At that stage, Thompson probably could not believe Black and Radler would consciously disregard the fiduciary standards they knew governed their related-party transactions.

Unfortunately, Thompson seems to have trusted Black and Radler to honor their fiduciary duties when it turned out that he was dealing with individuals who had long since ceased to pay attention to those concerns. Thompson did not realize that Black and Radler might be regularly feeding inadequate or misleading information to the Audit Committee. Thompson largely accepted Radler's assertions that the management fee was as low as Black and Radler could make it, never believing that Radler would make that assurance to his face while proposing a fee each year that was tens of millions of dollars higher than it would have cost Hollinger to perform the services for itself (or than it was costing Ravelston). He failed to apply the critical part of former President Reagan's famous dictum to "Trust, but verify." Thompson, Burt, and Kravis similarly failed to respond critically to the repeated demands for non-compete payments even though they should all have know these payments were highly unusual from the numerous boards on which they had served.

Thompson knew that various other people were aware of the management fee levels and did not suggest serious problems. Neither KPMG nor Torys told the Audit Committee that there was an issue of whether the amount and nature of these fees might violate fiduciary standards, or that costs unrelated to Hollinger like Ravelston's support obligations to HLG might be getting dumped into the management fee. Similarly, neither KPMG nor Torys expressed any contemporaneous concern with the proposed non-compete agreements. Thompson was not alerted, either expressly or by informal warnings, to the need to be more vigilant by KPMG, Kipnis, or by anybody else.

The Special Committee believes that the misrepresentations and partial information given to the Audit Committee, coupled with the lack of warnings from any of Hollinger's outside advisors, was a significant part of the reason why the Audit Committee behaved with such lassitude in the face of the abusive transactions. These reasons do not seem enough, however, to justify the Audit Committee's passivity and its acquiescence to everything Black proposed.

The Special Committee believes that another very significant reason for the lack of vigor in the Audit Committee was the overall control structure of Hollinger, and the impact that had on the perceptions of all the Board members. As noted above, Black expressly characterized Hollinger as *his* company. In his view, he and Radler built Hollinger, they ran it as they saw fit, and it was their job to figure out its next steps. Black definitely saw it as within his prerogatives to decide how much he and others would receive from Hollinger, and every Board member at least implicitly understood that Black would remove anyone who offered serious resistance to his dictates. That just wasn't done in *his* company.

Unfortunately, most members of the Board also saw Hollinger as Black's company. They were not selected by institutional shareholders for board seats, they were selected by Black. Black was infinitely skilled in reinforcing the aura that he, not the Board, had ultimate responsibility for decisions at Hollinger. Board members knew that the dual tier voting system meant in practice that Black named every board member, and was free to replace anyone who disagreed with him. No shrinking violet, Black would not hesitate to push the Board wherever he wanted them to go.

The fact that Black and Radler had given themselves voting control of Hollinger irrespective of their actual equity stake should have put directors on a state of high alert against actions that were not in shareholders' overall economic interests. However, psychologically it may have reinforced the tendency among Board members to see the Company as one that Black was free to direct. Once established, the mindset that Hollinger was not like other companies due to the control rights held by Black undoubtedly affected attitudes, beliefs and levels of effort by the Board. Unfortunately, the inherently dangerous aspects of a dual voting structure, separating governance power from economic interest, make heightened sensitivity and scrutiny highly important to protect the interest of non-controlling shareholders. Hollinger did not get either sensitivity or scrutiny, and the shareholders paid the price.

The Report also reviews the conduct of the other independent members of the Board, Dr. Henry A. Kissinger and Mr. Shmuel Meitar.[31] The Report concludes that Kissinger and Meitar were acting reasonably in relying on the reports of the Audit Committee that it had reviewed the various related-party transactions and found them to be fair to Hollinger. Both Kissinger and Meitar have a statutory right under Delaware law to rely on corporate officers and on board committees, and while they certainly could have done more in reviewing the numerous transactions, their good faith reliance on the Audit

---

[31] Other former independent directors would be in a similar situation to Dr. Kissinger and Mr. Meitar. The Committee does not consider Richard Perle to have been independent, and discusses his role and culpability separately.

Committee and Thompson's reports to the Board were reasonable in our judgment.

As a group, the Hollinger Board (and particularly the Audit Committee) was not alert and did not notice when Black and Radler were driving their bloated fee requests past them. While they were fed distorted information by Black and Radler, they did little to seek independent advice of their own. Even without their own advisors, they should have been concerned that the total amounts paid to Black and Radler under one pretext or another represented essentially 100% of the Company's adjusted net income for 7 years. This financial fact raised the possibility that Black and Radler were violating their fiduciary duties on a massive scale.

Whatever their prior somnolence, since formation of the Special Committee in June of 2003, the independent members of the Board and the Audit Committee have contributed substantially to the Special Committee's efforts to protect shareholder interests in the face of Black's threats and litigation over the Restructuring Agreement, and his ability to dictate actions contrary to the interests of the majority, non-controlling shareholders. Burt advocated creation of a strong Special Committee shortly after major shareholders filed a Schedule 13D challenging a number of issues on fiduciary grounds. Thompson also supported forming a Special Committee with strong powers. Both Thompson and Burt, along with other independent directors, supported the cleanup of management the Special Committee proposed following its discovery of the unauthorized payments. At the time of the Restructuring Agreement in November 2003, the independent directors supported the Special Committee's conclusion that Black must step down from his executive positions, and they later supported his removal as Chairman when he refused to answer questions of the SEC under oath.

The independent directors also supported the strategic process as contemplated in the Restructuring Agreement. They met on many occasions to review alternatives available to protect shareholder interests, and they adopted a poison pill to protect the Company's ability to block indirect transfers of HLG stock that would frustrate the strategic process. The strategic process has thus far benefited all share-holders by obtaining an outstanding result in the US$1.3 billion sale of the Telegraph Group. While current performance does not elimi-nate the fact of Board lapses in the past, the Special Committee believes that in assessing the consequences that should flow from those lapses, the entire record of the Board, both before and after for-mation of the Special Committee, should be considered.

As a result of the Board's support of the Special Committee's rec-ommendations in November 2003, the looting of the Company through the Ravelston management fees has stopped, and earnings have increased commensurately. Fees to Ravelston of more than US$2 million *per month* have stopped, generating savings to date in 2004 of US$18 million for Hollinger. The Company has incurred new expenses to offset the Ravelston services that are less than US$4 million *annu-ally* including all senior executive compensation and the cost of incre-mental growth in the finance department.[32] The Special Committee has also recovered more than US$42 million to date from Black, Radler, Atkinson and HLG with the support of the Board, and the Special Committee is forcefully prosecuting its litigation to recover US$1.25 billion in damages in the Illinois Action.

The members of the Board at Hollinger currently play an impor-tant role in carrying forward other initiatives that are of substantial importance to Hollinger's shareholders. These include completing the auditing of Hollinger's financial statements and returning the Company to full compliance with its reporting obligations under the securities laws, completing the strategic process through, at a mini-mum, fair and equitable distribution (or other use) of the proceeds from the sale of the Telegraph Group, and putting in place new

---

[32] Despite Black's agreement in November 2003 that the Services Agreement would be terminated and that the management fee for the first half of 2004 would be sub-stantially reduced, Ravelston has continued to send invoices to Hollinger as if the 2003 management fee level had been approved for use in 2004 by the Audit Committee or anyone else at Hollinger. If Black were to regain power at Hollinger, no doubt it would be a high priority to resume the bulk transfers of Hollinger's shareholder equity to Ravelston, as well as distributing tens of millions to Ravelston retroactively.

internal controls to assure both the integrity of the Company's financial statements and compliance with all applicable laws. The Board has to consider recommendations flowing from this Report for certain changes in governance to prevent repetition of the systematic violations of fiduciary duties and federal disclosure obligations that have occurred in the past, as well as to ensure that the Company complies with its obligations under its Consent Decree with the SEC and other legal obligations.

Finally, the Board should play a very important role in the future in insuring that Hollinger is able to recover the funds wrongfully diverted from it. Having conducted a thorough and independent investigation to determine that the Company is entitled to recover more than a billion dollars in damages for violation of Delaware and federal law, action must be taken to guarantee that these claims can be pursued in the courts until they are adjudicated or otherwise resolved in the interests of Hollinger's majority, non-controlling shareholders. The obvious interest of those whom the Report concludes have taken hundreds of millions of dollars improperly and illegally will be to find a way to assert control over the Company to prevent it from litigating these claims to a successful conclusion, thereby potentially destroying this enormously material asset that belongs to the Company and its shareholders.

In the end, the Special Committee believes that there were several dominant factors in the events that took place at Hollinger. One was the insatiable demands for cash from Black, whether to prop up his empire or to fuel his political and social ambitions in multiple countries. Black kept coming back to the Hollinger well again and again. The intensity of the pressure for payments to Black irrespective of corporate performance or the fairness of transactions to shareholders led to most of the abuses documented in the Report.

A second factor was the inherently flawed governance structure at Hollinger dating to its IPO, and centered on the two-tier voting structure. The "two-tier" system, with one class of shares having ten times the votes as the other class, severed the link between equity ownership and participation in corporate control. The multivoting shares gave Black the power to control Hollinger absolutely, even though he owned only a relatively small and shrinking percentage of its equity, and hence less and less interest in its profitability. At the same time, he held undiminished power to dictate the Company's actions, and to pay massive fees to himself that steadily bled the Company's financial strength even as it was dismembered to raise cash. Black as a small equity holder had the power to force transfers of funds to an entity where he was a large equity holder, even if doing so was a violation of his fiduciary duties.

In this case, Black had hammerlock control over Hollinger irrespective of a relatively small layer of real equity interest. He used that control actively and aggressively to promote his interests, even when the results were directly contrary to the interests of Hollinger's majority shareholders and grossly unfair. His control rights insured that, come what may, and no matter what anyone else thought, Black could take what he wanted, and his appetite for cash was simply ravenous.[33]

Black's ultimate control could not eliminate the requirements of Delaware law that the business of a company be managed by a board of directors. However, Black had the votes to replace any member of the Board, and they all knew it. Black called the shots, and he wanted a Board filled with prominent people who would not make waves. Black got what he wanted, until he pushed so far beyond the limits of acceptable behavior that he triggered the formation of the Special Committee and its investigative process.

The Audit Committee (and the Board) had the responsibility of considering carefully the conflicts it was presented with, and for making a prudent business judgment in the interests of all shareholders. Instead of analysis and evaluation, they acquiesced to Black's demands. This was exactly the wrong approach. On Black's part, he did not seem to possess the wisdom or judgment to recognize when he was approaching or exceeding the limits of tolerable behavior as a fiduciary for Hollinger's shareholders, and the Board failed to force him to adhere to reasonable limits.

---

[33] While the Audit Committee could refuse to approve a related-party transaction, Black held the voting power ultimately to elect every member of the Board.

Filing of the Report with the SEC and the U.S. District Court satisfies an obligation of the Company under the SEC Consent Decree. It also marks the substantial completion of the first, investigative phase of the Special Committee's work. However, the completion of the Report by no means represents the conclusion of the Special Committee's work.

The purpose of conducting the investigations was to determine whether wrongdoing took place at Hollinger. We concluded that wrongdoing took place on a far more extensive scale, in both time and the amount of damages to the Company, than anyone had previously realized or suggested. In January 2004, the Special Committee on behalf of the Compansy brought the Illinois Action seeking actual damages of US$380.6 million, interest of US$103.9 million, for total actual damages of US$484.5 million plus further interest that may accrue.

Our work also made us realize that the Company had not been victimized by isolated wrongdoing, but by a persistent and repeated course of illegal conduct. While the provisions of the federal racketeering laws are not typically invoked in matters of internal corporate behavior, this is not a typical case. Indeed, the illegal actions committed by Black and Radler as officers of Hollinger, acting also on behalf of Ravelston and HLG, created exactly the type of situation that the federal RICO statute was intended to help control. RICO allows Hollinger to recover treble damages plus attorney's fees, and the Illinois Action therefore seeks recovery of total damages of US$1.25 billion from Black, Radler, Ravelston, HLG, and various of their associates. The Illinois Action also seeks an order from the District Court barring the defendants from "conducting or participating in the conduct of the affairs" of Hollinger to prevent any recurrence of these unlawful actions.

The Special Committee's investigation showed that Hollinger had been willfully and deliberately looted by its controlling shareholders. It is a strong word, but it is an appropriate word to describe what took place at Hollinger over the past decade. Having conducted a thorough investigation and assembled what we believe is an overwhelming body of evidence, it is imperative that the Company now be able to hold the responsible parties accountable for their actions, and to recover for shareholders the damages inflicted on the Company. The Special Committee believes that its work will not be completed until appropriate judicial relief is obtained on behalf of the shareholders whose money was taken through illicit and improper means.

Thinking Points

1. As a director of Hollinger, what would have been your duty on November 1, 2001 at the time of the first complaint by investment firm Tweedy Browne?

2. What would have been your liability exposure by the time the indictments on Conrad Blank were filed in November, 2005? What would have been your primary defense against these liabilities, if any?

3. How is it, that with a blue chip board, Hollinger shareholders can find themselves in this position? Is the law sufficient to prevent such abuses? What does it take?

Chapter 4
Taking Back the Boardroom: Organization and Process

Just How Much is Good Corporate Governance Worth?

We asked investors to compare two well-performing companies and state whether they would pay more for stock of one of these companies if it were well-governed. Two-thirds of the investors said they would. As one respondent put it: "Companies with good board governance practices have a shareholder-value focus."

Among those willing to pay more for good governance, the average premium specified was 16 percent. Based on the entire survey group, including those who said they would not pay more, the average premium was 11 percent.

There are three main reasons why investors will pay a premium for good governance. Some believe that a company with good governance will perform better over time, leading to a higher stock price.

Others see good governance as a means of reducing risk, as they believe it decreases the likelihood of bad things happening to a company.

Still others regard the recent increase in attention to governance as a fad. As this group sees it, the stock of a well-governed company may be worth more simply because governance is such a hot topic these days.

Robert F. Felton, Alec Hudnut, and
Jennifer van Heeckeren, 1996,
Putting a Value on Corporate Governance,
The McKinsey Quarterly, Number 4, Page 170

This chapter is designed to discuss organization in the boardroom. *Why* a board should be organized is one of the key lessons that effective directors have to understand. *How* a board should be organized should also be instinctive to good directors. This chapter discusses three principles that drive an effective board structure with special attention to committee and directors' roles in committees. I will also discuss key activities that each committee should be doing and the organizational processes that should support these activities. A well-structured board is one that is fully informed of the ongoing status of the firm's strategy. To be informed, the board has to be involved in the strategic planning process. I will discuss why directors' involvement may be advantageous and when it may pose problems. There are many levels at which the board can be involved and this chapter will present a framework to position a director's involvement so that it will add value to and not detract from the management's contribution.

Many countries have enacted codes of conduct for boards of directors. The Cadbury Code was the first formal codes of conduct. Later versions, the Greenbury Code and the Hampel Report, are now the standards by which the London Stock Exchange judges companies fit for public listing. While there has not been a standard code in the US, many similar codes have been spawned by such organizations as the National Association of Security Dealers (NASD), the National Association for Corporate Directors (NACD), and the California Public Employee Retirement System (CalPERS). The most sweeping revision to the 1934 Securities and Exchange Commission Act, known as the Sarbanes-Oxley Act of 2002, while not strictly speaking a code, lays the foundational principles on which revisions of the listing requirements and the codes they spawn are based. Around the world, such organizations as the Toronto Stock Exchange (Dey Report), the Shareholders Association of Japan, the Paris Stock Exchange (Vienot Report), and the Organization for Economic Cooperation and Development (OECD) have also chimed in with their own codes. They are based on the agency theory definition of the fiduciary relationship between directors and shareholders.

Central to the formulation of codes of conduct has been the concept of board accountability. Accountability means that directors understand and accept the consequences of their actions, taking steps to ensure that recourse is available for those parties affected by the decisions that the board makes. Accountability, corporate directors can easily find themselves in violation of a duty or statute without realizing it. The case examples at the end of the chapter illustrate guidelines or codes of conduct adopted by two corporations (Intel and GM) and a major institutional investor (CalPERS). Closer examination of these codes reveals that there are four ways to achieve accountability.

The first is through ownership. Ownership allows the law to enforce the fiduciary duties of directors on behalf of the owners or shareholders of the firm. The second way to achieve accountability is through the statutory regulatory environment. Directors are responsible for a host of regulations not covered by their fiduciary responsibilities but simply because their companies have significant social and economic impact on the communities in which they do business. The third way is through the actions of social and community pressure groups such as Transparency International, Greenpeace, UNESCO, and the World Bank. Progressive boards in such companies as Royal Dutch Shell, the Body Shop, and Motorola are adept at levering these social forces to align managerial behaviors. The last way in which corporations can be held accountable is through the judicious use of structure and processes in the boardroom.

The Paradoxes of Corporate Governance

The structure and processes of the boardroom have evolved to deal with three major paradoxes in the art of governance. Firstly, the board is the highest authority in the company and yet has to deal with the reality that the management controls the information required to exercise oversight. Secondly, board members are expected to provide critical judgment on the performance of the corporation, which requires directors to be personally close to management, and yet remain as objective observers of managerial behavior. Finally, while individual directors rely on each other to make good decisions, they have to be individually accountable for these decisions.

The implications of the paradoxes are that excellence in corporate governance requires the board of directors to finely balance these tensions. Second, effective boards should not seek to eliminate the paradox because they are inherent in the nature of governance but should instead use the paradoxes advantageously. The key to solving the paradoxes is to create a board structure that is independent of managerial influence, and yet responsive and sensitive to managerial concerns.

Understanding Power in the Boardroom

In order to understand how to create a board structure that is independent of managerial influence, and is responsive to managerial concerns, a director must understand the concept of power. The process of governance is about the exercise of power, which is exercised by virtue of the legal authority that boards have over the management, that management has over the employees, and that governments have over the corporation. Because the board sits at the apex of the managerial structure of the modern corporation, it has power *de jure*.

Power is also gained by having control over sources and channels of information, because information is a valuable commodity that drives the decisions boards make. As the management is in a better position to understand the day-to-day problems and opportunities facing the firm, and because they control the channels that convey this information to board members, they have power *de facto*.

Finally, power comes from having control over resources. Institutional shareholders can withhold such resources as legitimacy and capital by selling their shares, and thereby threaten the corporation with a takeover. Such power, wielded by the shareholders, reduces the discretion of the board to misallocate corporate assets. However, evidence strongly suggests that the management has most of the power and that the other sources of power do not work well to countervail that of the management's.

Boards do not have power *de facto* because they do not control all of the sources of power, i.e., information and resources. The practical matter is that boards will never have more information than the management and they will never be able to influence the market's view of the firm to a greater degree than the institutional shareholders. Therefore, to gain power *de facto*, directors must organize themselves in the boardroom.

Organizing to Solve the Paradoxes

"Organization" connotes a level of formality that many boards are not comfortable with because it suggests that the 'gentleman's agreement' and friendly handshake with management is *not* the right way to govern. Indeed, unless a board is organized, it cannot have joint accountability and joint responsibility. An organized board is better prepared to assign responsibilities in ways that allow individuals to contribute their expertise in order to be fully involved in decision-making. While the law courts do not usually place themselves in the shoes of directors to assess the viability of business decisions, they do frown on acts of negligence in decision-making. Organization leads to effective due diligence by forcing the board to acquire, analyze, and use information in systematic and productive ways. By doing so, the board is able to involve the efforts of all of its members and to extract the very best from each. In short, organization allows the board to perform its duties at arms length from the management, reducing the chance for it to be co-opted by management. An arms length relationship creates a slight tension in the boardroom to make it easier for members to question the management without feelings of reservation.

An effective board uses the committee structure to ensure that the information flowing from the firm is fully exploited at the top. In addition, such boards use the committee structure to share and devolve power to individual directors. The committee structure forces the decision process to be transparent by publicizing the contributions of individual members in the minutes. The committee structure ensures that all decisions truly reflect the thoughts and feelings of the entire board, rather than just the few directors who have been there longest or who are closest to the Chairperson.

Two things are accomplished by formally dividing the work of governing among several people. Firstly, as there can be an information overload before and during board meetings, important details are not missed when considering the issues. It is important for information to flow continually between management and the board, even though the entire board may only meet periodically. A committee structure allows individual directors to meet more often, deal with problems or opportunities as they arise, and manage the information overflow problem before the general meetings.

The Principles of Good Structure

Internal and external information that are strategically relevant, useful, and timely are needed to create the appropriate standards and to assess the performance for top management. Thus, to maximize shareholder wealth in the long-term, a board must have information processing capabilities with feedback mechanisms to measure the performance of the corporation. To achieve such a structure, the board has to have a balance of outside and inside directors where outside directors provide objective oversight while inside directors provide information and expert opinion.

Balance has a number of dimensions. The board has to be balanced in terms of the sets of skills and experience brought to the decision-making process. Experience can come from long tenure within the industry the firm competes, life experience in terms of gender, and social experience in terms of profession. Many boards, such as that of Johnson & Johnson, include stakeholders such as doctors who use their products.

In order for the board to fulfill its monitoring and information dissemination functions simultaneously, it must have executive and non-executive directors. Many corporate governance experts recommend that a preponderance of the membership should be non-executives, with key executives taking on an informational role. Leadership is critical for exploiting the synergies created by such a structure, which begins with defining clearly the roles of the chair and CEO. Thirdly, outside directors must be given the opportunity to interact with each other and have easy access to corporate information. For example, Intel and GM have formal meetings for outside directors in which the executives do not participate.

The Principles of Good Process

Creating a committee structure is not enough to guarantee good governance. It is also important to have the right processes in place to support that structure. Here, the board must adopt policies that will allow the creation of the appropriate processes. Appropriate process requires them to be formalized because this, together with the adoption of objective standards of performance, reduces discretion at the individual level. Given that strategic decisions have to be ratified by the entire board, the processes should be designed to minimize individual discretionary decision taking but not individual critical thinking.

Part of designing right processes is to ensure that the right people carry them out. Generally boards do not pay much attention to the problem of director identification and recruitment. Directors are often brought onto the board through an informal process of personal networking and word-of-mouth. This tends to limit the pool of talent from which companies can draw their board membership. It also contributes to the over-extension of an individual director's time resources, leading to a lack of attention to the business of the corporation during board meetings.

Today, many boards strictly define what they mean by non-executive directors (see for example, the guidelines for corporate governance at Intel and GM at the end of this chapter.) Savvy companies do not leave this up to the law, as it has not specifically addressed this question since it holds both executive and non-executive directors equally liable. However, for good corporate governance, a firm must encode these definitions in its charter because doing so will enhance the transparency of the director appointment process.

Today, more firms are formalizing the director recruitment process through the use of corporate governance committees. This committee may in turn bring in such executive recruiters as Heidrick & Struggles or Egon Zehnder who specialize in placing directors. Additionally, an effective board is one that is skilled in the use of incentives and compensation to evoke the right behaviors from the management and its own members. Such boards make use of formal performance evaluation processes tied to contingent compensation programs. Many boards engage compensation consultants to conduct best practices surveys, recommend the right mix of incentives and rewards, and to develop appropriate evaluation instruments for their boards and top management teams.

The next characteristic of a good process is that it must be a closed loop system. A closed loop system simply means that information, which is introduced and analyzed, must find its way back to the users. In addition, 'closed loop' also means that the system must be capable of self-assessment and self-correction. This calls for a feedback and correction mechanism, which consists of a periodic assessment of a director's performance, an annual assessment of the committee chairs by the Chairperson of the Board, a variance analysis between work plan and actual committee output, and an overall evaluation of the effectiveness of the committee's contribution to the whole board. In specific committees, such as the strategy committee, part of the evaluation can be tied to whether major competitive challenges were adequately anticipated and fully accounted for. Finally, because the board is required to perpetuate itself, it has to develop a way to formally review its own performance. This is critical because unless the board takes regular measurements of its progress and activities, it will not know the skill sets and aptitudes in future directors.

Effective boards are those that meet frequently. Although there is a constraint on how many times a board can meet, it is clear that the standard quarterly meeting is not enough even as the business of the corporation becomes more complicated. In a global corporation, such meetings may have to take place in foreign locations and as such may entail more time commitment from directors. Between regular meetings of the full board, committees should also schedule their own meetings. This will allow non-executive directors to discuss the issues without feeling constrained by the presence of management. Progressive boards build these meetings into the annual meeting calendar. In today's world, teleconferencing and email have made it easier for committees to convene meetings across long distances. The acceptance of faxed signatures by most courts has made it possible for resolutions to be passed even though members are not physically in the same location. The benefits are enormous as decisions can be made more quickly with fresher information and with less regard to time zones. While the dynamics of a the 'virtual meeting' have to be managed differently from a physical one, as board members become more Internet savvy the barriers to communicating in disembodied form will fall.

The Committee Structure

In this chapter, I review the functions of four committees. Boards are allowed to organize themselves in any way they see fit and the law does not dictate or prevent them from doing so. According to the principles I laid out, the board should organize in a way that allows it to effectively address the business of the corporation. Therefore, committees should be set up to deal with key strategic issues faced by the corporation on an ongoing basis. For example, if the corporation is involved in the mineral extraction business, the board should have an environmental compliance committee to ensure that the corporation is not only acting in accordance with the law but is also actively discovering ways to improve the environment through its activities. Although the law holds the entire board liable for all decisions that are taken, the real work of the board happens in its committees. The job of these committees is to gather, analyze, and draw implications from the data, often using expert consultants to help them, and to make recommendations to the whole board. Most large global corporations today have the following committees in common: the audit committee, a compensation committee, the governance or nominating committee, and a strategy committee.

The audit committee: Who watches the watchers?

As committees go, probably the most important is the audit committee. At the minimum, each board should have one. For listed companies, audit committees are statutory requirements in most countries. Among OECD countries, there is an additional requirement at audit committees be populated only with non-executive directors. The need for such a committee is obvious. The board is ultimately responsible for the information that is propagated and, therefore, has to assure for itself the integrity of this information. In addition, the board is also required by the law to appoint the external auditors and, therefore, has to first understand the needs and the financial accounting system of the corporation.

Generally, the audit committee should consist of a minimum of three members, including the Chair, all of whom should be independent non-executive directors. The 2002 Sarbanes-Oxley Act is particularly concerned with the operations of the audit committee of the board. This is due to the widely held belief that the collapse of Enron, Worldcom, Adelphia, Hollinger International, and other high profile cases were in great part due to the inaction, incompetence or inattention of the audit committees of the board, in conjunction with the lack of independence of the external auditors. In general, the Act calls for the SEC to establish mandatory listing standards with respect to audit committees in each of the following criteria. First, each member of the audit committee must be independent, which requires that a director not receive any compensation from the company other than as a director or committee member and not be affiliated with the company or any subsidiary. This legal definition precludes nominee directors of substantial shareholders from serving on the audit committee, which places a great deal of pressure on companies to recruit proactively. The law provides for a minimal definition and boards that are serious about the audit function often go further by imposing more stringent constraints (see for example, the case study at the end of this chapter).

The audit committee must be responsible for the appointment, compensation and oversight of the work of the independent auditor. Then, the committee must establish procedures for receiving confidential, anonymous submissions by employees regarding questionable accounting or auditing matters (i.e., formally establish whistleblower provisions in the company). The committee must have authority to engage independent advisers as necessary and be provided with adequate funding. The audit committee must pre-approve the rendering of non-audit services by the independent auditor. This approval can be given on a general basis as part of approval of the engagement. Independent auditors are to report to the audit committee on critical accounting policies and practices of the company, on alternative treatments within GAAP discussed with management and on written communications such as management letters and schedules of unexplained variances. Companies will be required to disclose whether at least one member of the audit committee is a financial expert and, if not, why.

The New York Stock Exchange goes further by proposing that the chairman of the audit committee have accounting or financial management experience.

The chief function of the audit committee is to act as the board's liaison with the chief financial officer to obtain periodic updates on the performance of the organization with respect to its strategic plan and its competitors. In addition, the committee is also responsible for overseeing the external audit. During the external audit, the committee's responsibility is to quiz the auditors regarding the condition of the firm's finances and its operating procedures. Although the committee does not ratify the audit results — the board does — it must be sufficiently well-versed in the operations of the corporation to quiz the external auditor on its findings and to independently verify the effectiveness of the auditors, the auditing process and the veracity of its results. The committee should recommend periodic changes of the audit company or the partner in charge of the corporation's accounts to ensure that the auditor does not become 'too cozy' with the management.

The audit committee interacts with the management to review the auditor's findings and to decide on the steps that the management must take to address the auditor's concerns. In addition, the committee must also review the involvement of management in the audit process, to ensure that they did not exert undue influence, and to define the role that management should play during the audit process.

Although the audit committee has seemingly critical duties, the law does not impose a higher standard of duty other than those duties already imposed on all directors. The role of the audit committee is to recommend to the board as a whole, and not to take independent decisions. Therefore, while the audit committee has an important task, it is the entire board that is held accountable for their work. Therefore, non-audit committee board members should not take a backseat in the decision-making, assuming that they are free from the responsibility of seriously examining the audit committee's recommendations.

The compensation committee: Paying for performance

While the boards of directors cannot and *should not* be involved in the day-to-day operations of the firm, they are still ultimately responsible for setting the strategic direction. By using a combination of policy, reward, and incentives, they are able to elicit the right strategic behaviors from management. Most boards have a compensation committee to do this.

The function of the compensation committee is to evaluate managerial performance, and set the appropriate reward and incentive structures. The activity of monitoring not only includes assessing the outcome of implemented decisions, but also overseeing the integrity of the assessment process. The work of this committee has become strategic because the right compensation structure ensures that the management is focused on the appropriate performance targets and therefore strongly influences the strategic plans they formulate for the firm. The best way to do so is to create incentives that align the interests of the Chief Executive Officer with those of the shareholders.

In addition, a well-structured compensation plan will also garner support from the firm's stakeholders. This is because CEO compensation continues to be a hot button issue among the unions, community activists, shareholder interests groups, and institutional shareholders; it represents a powerful signaling device. The structure of a compensation plan tells stakeholders what the board values. It also tells the stakeholders how serious the board is about governance. A well-governed top management team is not one that is necessarily poorly paid. Instead, a credible compensation package is one that is seen to reward the right behaviors, encourage the right attitudes and apply appropriate punishments for non-performance.

The compensation committee should be composed of non-executive directors. When executive directors sit on compensation committees they are placed in a great conflict of interest and may experience untoward pressure to view the CEO favorably, regardless of his actual performance. The Chair of the compensation committee is often the Chairperson of the board. However, where this Chairperson is also the CEO, the compensation committee chair should be the lead non-executive director.

The compensation committee usually deals with such expert consultants as Hay Management Consultants, in the setting of compensation, performance appraisal, and recruitment policies. However, while it has been common practice to abdicate responsibility for serious thinking about such issues to consultants, it is now becoming less possible for boards to do so. Consultants should be used with caution, as their primary objective is to secure the next contract. Their role is to provide information on industry practices and trends, and the analysis of facts but never to recommend direction. Instead, this last area falls within the preserve and responsibility of the compensation committee. Thus, it is preferable that the compensation committee works with a number of consultants.

The work of the compensation committee is broadening in scope. In some corporations such as Dayton Hudson, a major holding company of retail chains in the US, board members are also evaluated annually, which the compensation committee undertakes. Thus, directors who serve on compensation committees should be cognizant of the latest practices and laws in compensation and performance evaluation, which means that they should set aside time each year to be briefed by experts on the latest developments.

The nominating committee: Balancing the board

Many boards today, recognizing the increasing complexity of the governance function, have nominating or corporate governance committees. The job of the traditional nominating committee has broadened in scope, to the point that director nomination is only a part of what such a committee does. Because of this, the nomination committee has also been called the corporate governance committee in some companies. As corporations globalize their operations to tap worldwide markets, the need to respond proactively to the demands of host country legal and social institutions has increased. In many instances, because these responses are policy level decisions, they can only come from the board of directors. The need for a nominating committee is even more urgent in companies undergoing strategic change, because these changes can have important implications for the corporation's charter, its relationship with the shareholders, and therefore, the composition of the board.

The composition of the nominating committee should consist of both executive and non-executive directors. The executive directors provide knowledge of the impact of board policies on the operations of the firm, while the non-executive directors play a central role in crafting governance policies. Usually, the non-executive Chairman of the board is also the chair of the nominating committee. Where the roles of CEO and Chair are combined, a lead non-executive director is given the role.

When the work of nomination and governance are combined, the job of this expanded committee is to define the code of best practices for the board. Many companies have created governance guidelines that codify the structure and processes of the board. The committee also recommends the code of ethics that set the tone for managerial behaviors for the corporation. This committee is responsible for upholding and refining these guidelines to ensure a continual fit with the business of the corporation by regularly reviewing the meeting procedures and adjusting the timing of such governance-related activities as nomination to meet the company's needs. The committee works closely with the Chair and CEO to specify the competency requirements of the board and to identify potential candidates for nomination.

The governance committee is sometimes given the task of administering the shareholder relations function of the board. In this capacity, they work with the public relations function in the company to craft the public announcements related to governance issues. Additionally, they may oversee the social responsibility program or corporate giving programs that many large corporations now have. The board of a modern global corporation must lead the management and the key to achieving this is an adaptive system of governance actively managed by a nomination or governance committee.

The strategy committee: Leadership from the boardroom

Strategy committees are very common in the boards of large transnational corporations. The reason is that the business of a global corporation is very complex and understanding the nature of the corporation, particularly as it diversifies, requires the full attention of specialists on the board. The South Korean *chaebols* elegantly demonstrated that managers could easily lose sight of the mission of the firm when it diversifies without direction. The board, through its strategy committee, attempts to discipline the asset allocation process by reconciling these decisions with the strategic intent of the corporation. By involving directors in the process, management gets to benefit from an impartial external opinion of its strategic recommendations. Shareholders obtain an independent assessment of such decisions, and therefore, are assured of the best use of their money.

The strategy committee is composed of a mix of executive and non-executive directors. The executive directors are responsible for the informational link between the committee and the firm as they are in the best position to provide the relevant information in the most cost efficient way. The non-executive directors provide the independent view of the strategic recommendations and contribute their individual experiences to the management's thinking on the issues. In addition, the committee often relies on information provided by executives in the company, and therefore, may require a 'dotted' reporting relationship from the chief financial officer or the chief information officer. The strategy committee works closely with the audit committee during the annual reporting season and with the compensation committee at the beginning and end of the planning cycle. The chair of the strategy committee is usually a lead non-executive director to maintain the impartiality of the assessments the committee makes.

The strategy committee works with the management when the latter puts together the annual strategic plan. The operating maxim of the strategy committee is *'involved and not managing'*. The committee does not actually create the strategic plans nor do they manage the planning process. Instead, they serve as sounding boards for the management, ensure that the planning process is executed in accordance with the principles of transparency and accountability, that the appropriate standards for evaluating corporate performance are adopted, and make recommendations to the board during the annual strategic planning exercise. The maxim of *'involved and not managing'* is crucial for upholding the governance principle of separating monitoring and control. If the relationship between the board and management is contaminated by board interference, it would be impossible to keep the management accountable for its decisions.

As Figure 1 illustrates, at the board level, the strategy formulation process begins with defining and understanding the enterprise vision, which may be derived historically (for example, Bill Gates' 1982 vision of "a PC on every desktop in every home running Microsoft software" drove the strategic direction of the company for 20 years), as a matter of competitive exigency (Novell's "the network is the computer" comes from its need to find a unique competitive position in the PC operating systems market), or simply as a conscious creation of the board.

The board can ask itself a series of questions when attempting to articulate an enterprise vision. These questions are answered after a process of consensus building. The first question concerns the 'real' definition of the business and whether it continues to be appropriate. For example, Sony traditionally defined itself as being in the consumer electronics business, and therefore, devoted it resources into building

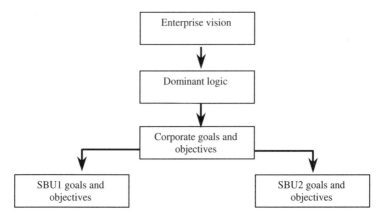

Figure 1.   The Board's view of the strategy process.

better and more innovative consumer electronic products. However, by the mid-1990s the board realized that the margins in this industry were shrinking. Chairman Akito Morita thus set out to redefine Sony from a product to an entertainment company by exploiting its core competencies in consumer electronics in a radically different way. This shifted the emphasis of Sony's asset allocation strategy, with the result that it is now a powerhouse in the entertainment business but with an edge over it competitors, because it controlled the technologies that drove the industry.

The strategy committee of the board thus translates the enterprise vision into the dominant logic of the corporation by trying to understand how its core competencies can be leveraged to achieve the enterprise vision. The dominant logic has seldom been articulated in a formal way but a board can deduce this by examining the way decisions have been made over time and identifying a pattern of behavior. For example, some corporations respond naturally to competition by avoiding price wars, while others may prefer to deter future entry by initiating heavy price discounting. Because the dominant logic is seldom articulated, a company that is unaware of its dominant logic may become trapped in a cycle of responding inappropriately to current competitive threats, because such responses may have worked in the past. The strategy committee can play a crucial role in strategic formulation by thinking actively about and surfacing the dominant logic of the firm. When articulated, the dominant logic can be a powerful force for self-awareness and strategic change. It provides an internally consistent way for corporate goals and objectives to be evaluated and harmonized.

Then the committee translates the dominant logic into a useful set of principles to guide strategy making. It does so by asking the question, "What are the firm's strategic objectives?" A re-evaluation of these objectives has to accompany the vision each time the latter changes. Although Sony moved from consumer electronics to entertainment, they continued to develop cutting edge consumer products such as the MiniDisc™ and the BluRay™ DVD standard. However, the company's strategic *objectives* shifted from simply selling more products to creating a total entertainment experience for its consumers. For Sony, consumer electronics became a gateway to influence the entertainment choices of its customers. To illustrate, Sony filled the Playstation™ game console with the latest graphical computing technologies but it did not make its profits from selling the consoles. The device was merely a gateway for the company to sell gaming software and other online entertainment where margins upwards of 90% could be achieved.

The primary activities of the strategy committee are to assess the strategic planning *process* and to recommend to the board the proposed strategic plan. To do so, the committee has to assess the logic of the strategic plan, the process by which the assumptions are derived, its financial implication, and long-term impact on the firm.

The strategy committee is responsible for evaluating the validity of the planning process and the quality of the recommendations. To evaluate the process, the committee has to determine the timeliness and completeness of the information used for planning. In addition, they have to understand the assumptions and evaluate whether they are reasonable. Often, the strategy committee may use facilitators to help them brainstorm in an off-site retreat. In their deliberations, the committee may also have some thoughts on the competency of the CEO since he leads the planning process. Here, the committee interacts with the compensation committee to assess the CEO's performance in this area.

To evaluate the quality of the recommendations, the committee members have to ask themselves two questions: The 'so what' questions, and the 'what if' questions. The 'so what' questions ask whether the strategic plan creates a sustainable competitive advantage. The firm achieves a sustainable competitive advantage by doing one or more of the following: reducing costs permanently, permanently increasing yields on expenses, improving quality to reduce customers' costs, and continually innovating ahead of its competitors. In order for intelligent 'so what' questions to be asked, the strategy committee has to understand the core competencies of the firm, which takes time, reflection and continual consultation with management. A well-crafted strategic plan, therefore, leverages the firm's core competencies at different stages of the value chain and in different markets with the result being a sustained contribution to positive cash flows and a maximization of shareholder value.

The 'what if' questions ask whether the strategic plan is robust. A management team that has spent time crafting the plan should put it to this test with the help of the board. The role of the strategy committee is to verify that this test has been applied by asking another series of questions. First, every plan has implicit assumptions about the industry growth rates, the rate of technological change, and the market power of incumbent competitors. These assumptions are not recognized in the financial models, and yet are routinely made to make modeling possible. For example, most plans do not build in the possibility of competitive retaliation or if they do may underestimate such actions. Second, because plans are made in the context of an industry, they often ignore the broader political-social context, which may indirectly affect market demand, preferences, and stockholder reactions. The committee must ask whether a failure in these assumptions might invalidate the plan's projections, and if management understands where the potential weaknesses of the plan are.

Specialty committees: When the board comes under fire

Depending on the business of the corporation, some companies have such specialty committees as environmental compliance, social responsibility, investor relations, special investigations, and community affairs. Many of these committees are composed of legal experts and community representatives or advocates, and they use consultants extensively for their work. The job of these committees is to provide an external link between the corporation and its stakeholders. Even in a strict regime of shareholder wealth maximization, it is the responsibility of a diligent board to understand the social, political, and legal forces in its competitive environment. Even if these forces are benign or friendly, they can change very quickly and an effective board is one that can anticipate and exploit these changes for the corporation.

In financial institutions, boards have risk assessment committees that are composed of experts versed in the latest financial instruments and markets and who understand the impact of these factors on the risk exposure of the corporation. These committees usually have executive directors as members with responsibilities in key areas of the institution that are exposed to risk. (For example, industrial and household credit, foreign exchange, derivative instruments, trade financing, and portfolio risk.)

Finally, all boards should be prepared to strike *ad hoc* committees whenever a situation requires it. Most importantly, they should have contingent recovery plans to deal with environmental disasters, natural disasters that hit corporate assets, man-made disasters, such as wars and technological failures, takeover attacks, adverse legal reversions, public relations scandals, and unanticipated executive turnover (i.e., deaths and resignations). While standing committees are unnecessary for such contingencies, one or more of these events will eventually strike the corporation in today's high velocity environments, and the board must be prepared. A well-structured board should be able to constitute an *ad hoc* committee with the right expertise and experience to deal with each of these events at a moment's notice. The difference between a successful resolution of a crisis and a slide into further disaster may well lie in the stakeholders' confidence in the management. For example, Johnson & Johnson's Tylenol™ poisoning scare was turned into a triumph for the company because the board acted quickly, decisively, and with great compassion. On the other hand, the Bhopal disaster continues to plague the image of Union Carbide today, more than 20 years after its occurrence, because the board did not respond appropriately by accepting responsibility and mobilizing corporate resources to deal with the situation.

Conclusion

At the heart of a well-structured board is the independent director. Independence has been the focus of much of the discussion around standards of practice and process in the guidelines put out by such organizations and companies as the National Association for Corporate Directors (NACD), OECD, New York Stock Exchange (NYSE), Toronto Stock Exchange (TSE), London Stock Exchange (LSE), Campbell Soup, and General Motors. Director independence or whether directors 'feel' right about a decision is based on the boardroom's culture and ethos, which is primarily driven by its structure and processes.

In the final analysis, a board discharges its duties to the corporation when it actively monitors and ratifies top management decisions, and is able to reliably perpetuate itself. It accomplishes these tasks by relying on the committee structure, which allows the board to acquire, analyze and act on information in the most efficient way possible. The committee structure defines the processes by which decisions are made and therefore ensures that the twin requirements of transparency and accountability for board effectiveness are met.

The end-of-chapter case example illustrates two sets of governance guidelines from well-known corporations (Intel and GM) who take their corporate governance responsibilities seriously. Compare and contrast the two guidelines. Notice that they are both remarkably similar even though the two companies compete in dissimilar industries utilizing different technologies. Notice also that these guidelines operationalize many of the California Public Employees Retirement System (CalPERS) principles and guidelines cited later.

After having studied these guidelines, do you think that there are objective standards of good corporate governance? Some commentators think not, referring to the differences in tradition, culture, and economic development among nations as factors that prevent a standard code from being adopted. Others such as Kayla Gillan of CalPERS and Robert Monks of LENS think that the principles for good corporate governance are universal. These people and their organizations are driving many of the efforts in crafting and pushing for the adoption of standard codes of best practices. They are taken seriously because their words are backed by billion-dollar investment funds. As illustrated by the Intel and GM examples, practices in today's boardrooms across the world are responding to their definitions of better corporate governance.

Corporate Governance Guidelines at Intel and General Motors[34]

Board Structure

	Intel[35]	General Motors[36]
Selection of Chair & CEO	• The Board should be free to make this choice any way that seems best for the Corporation at a given point in time. • The Board does not have a policy on whether or not the roles of CEO and Chairman should be separate and, if they are to be separate, whether the Chairman should be selected from the non-employee Directors or be an employee.	• The Board should be free to make this choice any way that seems best for the Company at a given point in time. • Therefore, the Board does not have a policy, one way or the other, on whether or not the role of the Chairman and Chief Executive should be separate and, if it is to be separate, whether the Chairman should be selected from the non-employee Directors or be an employee.
Size of the board	• The Board has 11 members in accordance with the Corporation's By-laws, and periodically reviews the appropriate size of the Board. The Board also has three Emeritus Directors at present who participate in meetings but do not vote. The Board does not have a policy on the number of Emeritus Directors.	• The Board in recent years has averaged 15 members. It is the sense of the Board that this size is about right. However, the Board would be willing to go to a somewhat larger size to accommodate the availability of an outstanding candidate(s).
Mix of inside and outside directors	• The Board believes that there should be a majority of independent Directors on the Board. However, the Board is willing to	• The Board believes that as a matter of policy, there should be a majority of independent Directors on the GM Board (as defined in

(Continued)

---

[34] This case was prepared for teaching purposes and does not purport to illustrate the effective or ineffective resolution of specific managerial situations.
[35] http://www.intc.com/intel/finance/corp_gov.htm
[36] http://www.gm.com/about/investor/stockholders/guidelines2.html

(*Continued*)

Board Structure

	Intel	General Motors
	have members of Management, in addition to the CEO, as Directors.	By-law 2.12). The Board is willing to have members of Management, in addition to the CEO, as Directors. But, the Board believes that Management should encourage senior managers to understand that Board membership is not necessary or a prerequisite to any higher Management position in the Company. Managers other than the Chairman and CEO and the Vice Chairman currently attend Board meetings on a regular basis even though they are not members of the Board. • On matters of corporate governance, the Board assumes decisions will be made by the independent Directors.
Definition of independence	• The Corporation complies with the Nasdaq National Market Issuer requirements for independent directors (Section 6(c) of Schedule D to the NASD Bylaws).	• GM's By-law 2.12, defining independent Directors was approved by the Board in January 1991. The Board believes there is no current relationship between any independent Director and GM that would be construed in any way to compromise any Board member being designated independent. Compliance with the By-law is reviewed annually by the Committee on Director Affairs.

(*Continued*)

(Continued)

	Board Structure	
	Intel	General Motors
Board membership criteria	• The Nominating Committee is responsible for reviewing with the Board from time to time the appropriate skills and characteristics required of Board members in the context of the current make-up of the Board. This assessment should include issues of diversity, age, skills such as understanding of manufacturing, technology, finance and marketing, and international background — all in the context of an assessment of the perceived needs of the Board at that point in time. Board members are expected to rigorously prepare for, attend, and participate in all Board and applicable Committee meetings. Each Board member is expected to ensure that other existing and planned future commitments do not materially interfere with the members service as an outstanding director.	• The Committee on Director Affairs is responsible for reviewing with the Board, on an annual basis, the appropriate skills and characteristics required of Board members in the context of the current make-up of the Board. This assessment should include issues of judgment, diversity, age, skills such as understanding of manufacturing technologies, international background, etc. — all in the context of an assessment of the perceived needs of the Board at that point in time.
Selection and orientation of new directors	• The Board should be responsible for selecting its own members. The Board delegates the screening process involved to the Nominating Committee.	• The Board itself should be responsible, in fact as well as procedure, for selecting its own members and in recommending them for election by the stockholders. The Board

(Continued)

(Continued)

	Board Structure	
	Intel	General Motors
		delegates the screening process to the Committee on Director Affairs with the direct input from the Chairman of the Board and the CEO. The Board and the Company have a complete orientation process for new Directors that include background material, meetings with senior management and visits to Company facilities. • The invitation to join the Board should be extended by the Board itself via the Chair and CEO of the Company, together with the Chairman of the Committee on Director Affairs, or the Chairman of the Executive Committee.
Former CEO's board membership	—	• The Board believes this is a matter to be decided in each individual instance. It is assumed that when the CEO resigns from that position, he/she should submit his/her resignation from the Board at the same time. Whether the individual continues to serve on the Board is a matter for discussion at that time with the new CEO and the Board. A former CEO serving on the Board will not be considered an independent

(Continued)

(*Continued*)

	Board Structure	
	Intel	General Motors
Directors who change job responsibility	• The Board does not believe that directors who retire or change from the position they held when they came on the Board should necessarily leave the Board. There should, however, be an opportunity for the Board, via the Nominating Committee, to review the continued appropriateness of Board membership under these circumstances.	Director for purposes of voting on matters of corporate governance. • It is the sense of the Board that individual Directors who change the responsibility they held when they were elected to the Board should submit a letter of resignation to the Board. • It is not the sense of the Board that in every instance the Directors who retire or change from the position they held when they came on the Board should necessarily leave the Board. There should, however, be an opportunity for the Board, via the Committee on Director Affairs, to review the continued appropriateness of Board membership under these circumstances. Independent Directors are encouraged to limit the number of other boards on which they serve taking into account potential board attendance, participation and effectiveness on these boards. Independent Directors should also advise the Chairman of the Board and the Chairman of the

(*Continued*)

(Continued)

	Board Structure	
	Intel	General Motors
		Committee on Director Affairs in advance of accepting an invitation to serve on another board.
Retirement policy	• The Board has adopted a retirement policy for officers and directors. Under the policy, inside directors, other than the CEO or former CEO, who are also employees of the Corporation retire from the Board at the same time they relinquish their corporate officer title.	• It is the sense of the Board that the current retirement age of 70 is appropriate.
Term limits	• The Board does not believe it should establish term limits. While term limits could help insure that there are fresh ideas and viewpoints available to the Board, they hold the disadvantage of losing the contribution of directors who over time have developed increasing insight into the Corporation and its operations, and therefore, provide an increasing contribution to the Board as a whole.	• The Board does not believe it should establish term limits. While term limits could help insure that there are fresh ideas and viewpoints available to the Board, they hold the disadvantage of losing the contribution of Directors who have been able to develop, over a period of time, increasing insight into the company and its operations and, therefore, provide an increasing contribution to the Board as a whole.

(Continued)

(*Continued*)

	Board Structure	
	Intel	General Motors
		• As an alternative to term limits, the Committee on Director Affairs, in conjunction with the CEO, will formally review each Director's continuation on the Board every five years. This will also allow each Director the opportunity to conveniently confirm his/her desire to continue as a member of the Board.
Board compensation review	• It is appropriate for the staff of the Corporation to report from time to time to the Compensation Committee on the status of Board compensation in relation to other large US companies. • Changes in Board compensation, if any, should come at the suggestion of the Compensation Committee, but with full discussion and concurrence by the Board.	• It is appropriate for the staff of the Company to report once a year to the Committee on Director Affairs the status of GM Board compensation in relation to other large United States companies. As part of a Director's total compensation and to create a direct linkage with corporate performance, the Board believes that a meaningful portion of a Director's compensation should be provided in common stock units. • Changes in Board compensation should come at the suggestion of the Committee on Director Affairs, but with full discussion and concurrence by the Board.

(*Continued*)

(*Continued*)

	Board Structure	
	Intel	General Motors
	Board Processes	
Scheduling and selection of agenda	• Board meetings are scheduled in advance typically every other month for a full day. Typically, the meetings are held at the Corporation's headquarters in Santa Clara, CA, but occasionally a meeting is held at another Intel facility. • The Chairman of the Board and the Secretary of the Corporation draft the agenda for each Board meeting and distribute it in advance to the Board. • Each Board member is free to suggest the inclusion of items on the agenda.	• The Chairman of the Board/CEO will establish the agenda for each Board meeting. The Chairman of the Executive Committee will act as the Board's liaison with the CEO in the development of the agendas. Each Board member is free to suggest the inclusion of item(s) on the agenda.
Distribution of meeting materials	• Information and data that is important to the Board's understanding of the business should be distributed in writing to the Board before the Board meets. • As a general rule, materials on specific subjects should be sent to the Board members in advance so that Board meeting time may be conserved and discussion time focused on questions that the Board has about the material.	• It is the sense of the Board that information and data that are important to the Board's understanding of the business be distributed in writing to the Board before the Board meets. The Management will make every attempt to see that this material is as brief as possible while still providing the desired information. • As a general rule, presentations on specific subjects should be sent to the Board members

(*Continued*)

(*Continued*)

	Board Structure	
	Intel	General Motors
	Sensitive subject matters may be discussed at the meeting without written materials being distributed in advance or at the meeting.	in advance so that Board meeting time may be conserved and discussion time focused on questions that the Board has about the material. On those occasions in which the subject matter is too sensitive to put on paper, the presentation will be discussed at the meeting.
Board presentations	• The Board encourages Management to schedule managers to present at Board Meetings who: (a) can provide additional insight into the items being discussed because of personal involvement in these areas, or (b) have future potential that Management believes should be given exposure to the Board.	• The Board welcomes the regular attendance at each Board meeting of non-Board members who are members of the President's Council. Should the CEO want to add additional people as attendees on a regular basis, it is expected that this suggestion would be made to the Board for its concurrence.
Access to employees	• The Board has complete access to any Intel employee.	• Board members have complete access to GM's Management. • It is assumed that Board members will use judgment to be sure that this contact is not distracting to the business operation of the Company and that such contact, if in writing, be copied to the CEO and the Chairman of the Executive Committee.
Access to employees		

(*Continued*)

(*Continued*)

	Board Structure	
	Intel	General Motors
		• Furthermore, the Board encourages the Management to, from time to time, bring managers into Board meetings: (a) who can provide additional insight into the items being discussed because of personal involvement in these areas, and/or (b) with future potential that the senior management believes should be given exposure to the Board.
Outside directors' discussion (executive sessions of independent directors)	• The Board's policy is to have a separate meeting time for the outside directors regularly scheduled at least twice a year during the regularly scheduled Board Meetings. The outside directors present will select the director who will assume the responsibility of chairing the regularly scheduled meetings of outside directors or other responsibilities which the outside directors as a whole might designate from time to time.	• The independent Directors of the Board will meet in Executive Session two or three times each year. Executive Sessions will be chaired by the Chairman of the Executive Committee. The format of these meetings will include a discussion with the CEO on each occasion.

(*Continued*)

(Continued)

	Board Structure	
	Intel	General Motors

Board Processes

Assessing board performance	—	• The Committee on Director Affairs is responsible to report annually to the Board an assessment of the Board's performance. This will be discussed with the full Board. This should be done following the end of each fiscal year and at the same time as the report on Board membership criteria. • This assessment should be of the Board's contribution as a whole and specifically review areas in which the Board and/or the Management believes a better contribution could be made. Its purpose is to increase the effectiveness of the Board, not to target individual Board members.

Board Committees

Succession planning and management development	• The CEO reviews succession planning and management development with the Board on an annual basis.	• There should be an annual report by the CEO to the Board on succession planning. • There should also be available, on a continuing basis, the CEO's recommendation as a successor should he/she be unexpectedly disabled.

(Continued)

(*Continued*)

	Board Structure	
	Intel	General Motors
		• There should be an annual report to the Board by the CEO on the Company's program for Management development. • This report should be given to the Board at the same time as the succession planning report noted previously.
Chairman of the executive committee	—	• The members of the Executive Committee will be the chairmen of the other standing committees of the Board of Directors and the Chairman of the Executive Committee will be a director designated by the Board of Directors. The Chairman of the Executive Committee will be an independent director and will not concurrently be the chairman of any of the standing committees of the Board of Directors but will be an ex-officio member of each standing committee of the Board. When the Chairman of the Board is an independent director, the Chairman of the Board will serve as the Chairman of the Executive Committee. • The Chairman of the Executive Committee will be responsible for developing the agenda

(*Continued*)

(Continued)

| | Board Structure | |
	Intel	General Motors
		for and chairing the regular sessions of independent directors. In addition, he/she will communicate the Board's annual evaluation of the CEO to that individual; be responsible, together with the Committee on Director Affairs, for periodic review of the Board's governance procedures (guidelines); act as the Board's liaison with the CEO in the development of the agendas for Board meetings; and such other duties as provided in these guidelines and as the Board and the CEO may feel desirable.
Performance evaluation of officers.	• The Compensation Committee conducts, and reviews with the outside directors, an evaluation annually in connection with the determination of the salary and executive bonus of all officers (including the CEO).	• The full Board (independent Directors) should make this evaluation annually, and it should be communicated to the CEO by the Chairman of the Executive Committee. • The evaluation should be based on objective criteria including performance of the business, accomplishment of long-term strategic objectives, development of Management, etc. • The evaluation will be used by the Compensation Committee in the course of its

(*Continued*)

(*Continued*)

	Board Structure	
	Intel	General Motors
		deliberations when considering the compensation of the CEO.
Committee meetings	• The Chairman of the Board, in consultation with the Secretary of the Corporation, the Committee Chairman and appropriate members of Management, will determine the frequency and length of the Committee meetings and develop the Committee's agenda. The Committee agenda and meeting minutes of the Audit & Finance Committee, Compensation Committee, Nominating Committee and Corporate Governance Committee will be shared with the full Board, and other Board members are welcome to attend Committee meetings.	• The Committee Chairman, in consultation with Committee members, will determine the frequency and length of the meetings of the Committee. • The Chairman of the Committee, in consultation with the appropriate members of Management and staff, will develop the Committee's agenda. Each Committee will issue a schedule of agenda subjects to be discussed for the ensuing year at the beginning of each year (to the degree these can be foreseen). This forward agenda will also be shared with the Board.
Assignment and term of committee members	• The Board is responsible, after consultation with the Chairman, and with consideration of the desires of individual Board members, for the assignment of Board members to various committees.	• The Committee on Director Affairs is responsible, after consultation with the Chief Executive Officer and with consideration of the desires of individual Board members, for the assignment of Board members to various Committees.

(*Continued*)

(Continued)

	Board Structure	
	Intel	General Motors
		• It is the sense of the Board that consideration should be given to rotating Committee members periodically at about a five year interval, but the Board does not feel that such a rotation should be mandated as a policy since there may be reasons at a given point in time to maintain an individual Director's Committee membership for a longer period.
Board interaction with outside stakeholders (Investors, Press, Customers, etc.)	• The Board believes that Management speaks for the Corporation. Individual Board members may, from time to time, meet or otherwise communicate with various constituencies that are involved with the Corporation, but it is expected that Board members would do this with the knowledge of Management and, in most instances, at the request of Management.	• The Board believes that the Management speaks for General Motors. Individual Board members may, from time to time at the request of the Management, meet or otherwise communicate with various constituencies that are involved with General Motors. If comments from the Board are appropriate, they should, in most circumstances, come from the Chairman.
Number of committees	• The current five Committees are Executive, Audit & Finance, Compensation, Nominating, and Corporate Governance. There will, from time to time, be occasions on which the Board may want to form a new committee or disband	• The current Committee structure of the Company seems appropriate. There will, from time to time, be occasions in which the Board may want to form a new Committee or disband a current Committee depending

(Continued)

(*Continued*)

Board Structure

Intel	General Motors
a current committee depending upon the circumstances. • The Audit & Finance Committee recommends the Corporation's certified public accountants for approval by the Board, and monitors the effectiveness of the audit effort, the Corporation's internal financial and accounting organization and controls and financial reporting. • The Nominating Committee makes recommendations to the Board regarding the size and composition of the Board, establishes procedures for the nomination process, recommends candidates for election to the Board and nominates officers for election by the Board. • The Compensation Committee administers the Corporation's stock option plans, including the review and grant of stock options to all eligible employees under the Corporation's existing stock option plans, and reviews and approves salaries and other matters relating to	upon the circumstances. The current seven Committees are Audit, Capital Stock, Director Affairs, Executive, Executive Compensation, Investment Funds, and Public Policy. Except for the Investment Funds Committee, committee membership will consist only of independent Directors as defined in By-law 2.12.

(*Continued*)

(*Continued*)

Board Structure

Intel	General Motors
compensation of the executive officers of the Corporation. • The Corporate Governance Committee reviews and reports to the Board on matters of corporate governance (that is, the relationships of the Board, the Stockholders and Management in determining the direction and performance of the Corporation) and reviews and addresses these Guidelines and recommends revisions as appropriate.	

Thinking Points

1. Compare the guidelines at Intel and GM.
2. What are notable about these guidelines?
3. In what specific areas do you think they are strong or weak?
4. With these guidelines would you feel more confident about discharging your duties? Why?
5. How easy would it be to implement such Guidelines in your company?

THE CALIFORNIA PUBLIC EMPLOYEES' RETIREMENT SYSTEM[37]

Updated February 20, 2007

CORE PRINCIPLES OF ACCOUNTABLE CORPORATE GOVERNANCE

"Everywhere shareholders are re-examining their relationships with company bosses — what is known as their system of 'corporate governance.' Every country has its own, distinct brand of corporate governance, reflecting its legal, regulatory and tax regimes... The problem of how to make bosses accountable has been around ever since the public limited company was invented in the 19th century, for the first time separating the owners of firms from the managers who run them...."

"Corporate Governance: Watching the Boss,"
The Economist 3 (Jan. 29, 1994).

I. Introduction

The California Public Employees' Retirement System (CalPERS) is the largest United States public pension fund, with assets totaling US$210 billion spanning domestic and international markets as of July 31, 2006. *Our mission is to advance the financial and health security for all who participate in the System. We will fulfill this mission by creating and maintaining an environment that produces responsiveness to all those we serve.* This statement was adopted by the CalPERS Board of Administration to guide us in serving our more than 1.4 million members and retirees.

The CalPERS Board of Administration is guided by the Board's Investment Committee, management, and more than 180 Investment Office staff who carry out the daily activities of the investment program. Our goal is to efficiently and effectively manage investments to achieve the highest possible return at an acceptable level of risk. In doing so, CalPERS has generated strong long-term returns.

CalPERS' Corporate Governance[38] Program is a product of the evolution that only experience and maturity can bring. In its infancy in 1984–1987, corporate governance at CalPERS was solely reactionary: reacting to the anti-takeover actions of corporate managers that struck a dissonant chord with one's sense — as owners of the corporate entity — of accountability and fair play. The late 1980s and early 1990s represented a period in which CalPERS learned a great deal about the "rules of the game" — how to influence corporate managers, what issues were likely to elicit fellow shareowner support, and where the traditional modes of shareowner/corporation communication were at odds with current reality.

Beginning in 1993, CalPERS turned its focus toward companies considered by virtually every measure to be "poor" financial performers.

---

[38] "Corporate Governance," at CalPERS, means the "relationship among various participants in determining the direction and performance of corporations. The primary participants are (1) shareowners, (2) management (led by the chief executive officer), and (3) the board of directors." (Robert Monks and Nell Minow, CORPORATE GOVERNANCE 1 (1995).)

By centering its attention and resources in this way, CalPERS could demonstrate to those who questioned the value of corporate governance very specific and tangible economic results.[39]

What have we learned over the years? We have learned that (a) company managers want to perform well, in both an absolute sense and as compared to their peers; (b) company managers want to adopt long-term strategies and visions, but often do not feel that their share-owners are patient enough; and (c) all companies — whether governed under a structure of full accountability or not — will inevitably experience both ascents and descents along the path of profitability.

We have also learned, and firmly embrace the belief that good corporate governance — that is, accountable corporate governance — means the difference between wallowing for long periods in the depths of the performance cycle, and responding quickly to correct the corporate course. As one commentator noted:

> *"Darwin learned that in a competitive environment an organism's chance of survival and reproduction is not simply a matter of chance. If one organism has even a tiny edge over the others, the advantage becomes amplified over time. In 'The Origin of the Species,' Darwin noted, `A grain in the balance will determine which individual shall live and which shall die.' I suggest that an independent, attentive board is the grain in the balance that leads to a corporate advantage. A performing board is most likely to respond effectively to a world where*

---

[39] See Steven L. Nesbitt, "Long-Term Rewards from Shareholder Activism: A Study of the 'CalPERS Effect'," J. of App. Corp. Fin. 75 (Winter 1994): Concluding that CalPERS' program generates approximately US$50 million, per year, in added returns. See Mark Anson, Ted White, and Ho Ho "Good Corporate Governance Works: More Evidence from CalPERS," Journal of Asset Management, Vol. 5,3 (February 204), 149–156. Also see "The Shareholder Wealth Effects of CalPERS' Focus List," *Journal of Applied Corporate Finance*, (Winter 2003), 8:17 — The authors found that between 1992 and 2002, publication of the CalPERS "Focus List" and efforts to improve the corporate governance of companies on that list generated one-year average cumulative excess returns of 59.4%. Cumulative excess return is the cumulative "return earned over and above the risk-adjusted return required for each public corporation."

*the pace of change is accelerating. An inert board is more likely to pro-
duce leadership that circles the wagons."*

Ira M. Millstein, *New York Times*, April 6, 1997,
Money & Business Section, p. 10.

II. Purpose

The Core Principles of Accountable Corporate Governance ("Core
Principles") create the framework by which CalPERS executes its proxy
voting responsibilities in addition to providing a foundation for supporting the System's corporate engagement and governance initiatives.
CalPERS implements its proxy voting responsibility and corporate governance initiatives in a manner that is consistent with the Core Principles
unless such action may result in long-term harm to the company that
outweighs all reasonably likely long-term benefit or unless such a vote is
contrary to the interests of the beneficiaries of CalPERS' system.

The execution of proxies and voting instructions is the primary
means by which shareowners can influence a company's operations
and corporate governance. It is therefore important for shareowners
to exercise their right to participate in the voting and make their decisions based on a full understanding of the information and legal documentation presented to them. CalPERS will vote in favor of or
"For", an individual or slate of director nominees up for election that
the System believes will effectively oversee CalPERS' interests as a
shareowner consistent with the Core Principles.

However, CalPERS will withhold its vote from or vote "Against"
an individual or slate of director nominees at companies that do not
effectively oversee CalPERS' interests as a shareowner consistent with
the Core Principles or in limited circumstances where a company has
consistently demonstrated long-term economic underperformance.

CalPERS believes the criteria contained in the Core Principles
are important considerations for all companies within the US market.
However, CalPERS recognizes that the adoption of the Core
Principles in its entirety may not be appropriate for every company

due to differing developmental stages, ownership structure, competitive environment, or a myriad of other distinctions. By adopting the Core Principles of Accountable Corporate Governance that follow, CalPERS strives to influence the market through advancing the corporate governance dialogue while also providing an educational forum by representing a foundation for accountability between a corporation's management and its owners.

III. Core Principles of Accountable Corporate Governance

Throughout this document, CalPERS has chosen to adopt the term "shareowner" rather than "shareholder." This is to reflect our view that equity ownership carries with it active responsibilities[40] and is not merely passively "holding" shares. The underlying tenet for CalPERS' Core Principles of Accountable Corporate Governance is that fully accountable corporate governance structures produce, over the long term, the best returns to shareowners.

CalPERS has found that there are many features that are important considerations in the continuing evolution of corporate governance best practices. Therefore, CalPERS recommends the following Core Principles:

1. Corporate governance practices should focus board attention on optimizing the company's operating performance and returns to shareowners.
2. Directors should be accountable to shareowners, and management accountable to directors. To ensure this accountability, directors must be accessible to shareowner inquiry concerning their key decisions affecting the company's strategic direction.

---

[40] "For corporate governance structures to work effectively, Shareowners must be active and prudent in the use of their rights. In this way, Shareowners must act like owners and continue to exercise the rights available to them." (2005 CFA Institute: Centre for Financial Market Integrity, The Corporate Governance of Listed Companies: A Manual for Investors.)

3. Information about companies must be readily transparent to permit accurate market comparisons; this includes disclosure and transparency of objective globally accepted minimum accounting standard.
4. All investors must be treated equitably and upon the principle of one-share/one-vote.
5. Proxy materials should be written in a manner designed to provide shareowners with the information necessary to make informed voting decisions. Similarly, proxy materials should be distributed in a manner designed to encourage shareowner participation. All shareowner votes, whether cast in person or by proxy, should be formally counted with vote outcomes formally announced.
6. Each capital market in which shares are issued and traded should adopt its own code of Best Practices; and, where such a code is adopted, companies should disclose to their shareowners whether they are in compliance.
7. Corporate directors and management should have a long-term strategic vision that, at its core, emphasizes sustained shareowner value. In turn, despite differing investment strategies and tactics, shareowners should encourage corporate management to resist short-term behavior by supporting and rewarding long-term superior returns.

A. Board independence and leadership

Independence is the cornerstone of accountability. It is now widely recognized throughout the United States that independent boards are essential to a sound governance structure. Therefore, CalPERS recommends:

1. At a minimum, a majority of the board consists of directors who are independent. Boards should strive to obtain board composition made up of a substantial majority of independent directors.
2. Independent directors meet periodically (at least once a year) alone in an executive session, without the CEO. The independent board

chair or lead (or presiding) independent director should preside over this meeting.

3. Each company should disclose in its annual proxy statement the definition of "independence" adopted or relied upon by its board. The board's definition of "independence" should address, at a minimum, those provisions set forth in Appendix A.

4. With each director nomination recommendation, the board should consider the issue of continuing director tenure and take steps as may be appropriate to ensure that the board maintains openness to new ideas and a willingness to critically re-examine the status quo.

Nearly all corporate governance commentators agree that boards should be comprised of at least a majority of "independent directors." But the definitional independence of a majority of the board may not be enough in some instances.

The **leadership** of the board must embrace independence, and it must ultimately change the way in which directors interact with management.

> *"In the past, the CEO was clearly more powerful than the board. In the future, both will share influence. In a sense, directors and the CEO will act as peers. Significant change must occur in the future if boards are to be effective monitors and stimulators of strategic change. Directors and their CEOs must develop a new kind of relationship, which is more complex than has existed in the past. . . ."*

Jay W. Lorsch, "The Board as a Change Agent,"
THE CORPORATE BOARD 1 (July/Aug, 1996).

Lastly, independence also requires a lack of conflict between the director's personal, financial, or professional interests, and the interests of shareowners.

> *"A director's greatest virtue is the independence which allows him or her to challenge management decisions and evaluate corporate perform-ance from a completely free and objective perspective. A director should not be beholden to management in any way. If an outside director*

*performs paid consulting work, he becomes a player in the management
decisions which he oversees as a representative of the shareholder...."*

Robert H. Rock, Chairman NACD, DIRECTORS &
BOARDS 5 (Summer 1996).

The National Association of Corporate Directors' (NACD's) Blue
Ribbon Commission on Director Professionalism released its report in
November 1996 (hereafter "NACD Report"). The NACD Report calls
for a "substantial majority" of a board's directors to be independent. The Business Roundtable's Principles of Corporate Governance
(November 2005, hereafter "BRT Principles") is in general accord that
a "substantial majority" of directors should be independent, both in fact
and appearance, as determined by the board (BRT Principles, p.14).
Neither the NACD, nor BRT, define "substantial."

Accordingly, to instill independent leadership, CalPERS recommends that:

5.　The board chair should be an independent director unless the company can disclose why not separating the roles of CEO and Chair is
in the best interests of shareowners. Duties of the board chair should
be disclosed to shareowners. An "Independent Chair Position Duty
Statement" (Appendix B) provides the maximum duties that should
be expected of the board chair.

6.　When the board chair also serves as the company's CEO, the
board should formally designate an independent director as a
Lead or Presiding Director who acts in a lead capacity to coordinate the other independent directors. The board should disclose how the lead or presiding director instills independent
leadership to fulfill the duties described in Appendix B.

7.　When selecting a new chief executive officer, boards should re-
examine the traditional combination of the "chief executive" and
"chair" positions.

8.　Generally, a company's retiring CEO should not continue to
serve as a director on the board and at the very least be prohibited from sitting on any of the board committees.

9. Corporate insiders are not considered independent and should therefore not constitute any more than one board seat.

10. Certain board committees consist entirely of independent directors. These include the committees who perform the aduit, director nomination, CEO evaluation, and executive compensation functions.

11. The full board is responsible for the oversight function on behalf of shareowners. Should the board decide to have other committees (e.g. executive committee) in addition to those required by law, the duties and membership of such committees should be fully disclosed.

There has been much debate concerning the wisdom, and feasibility, of an "independent chair" structure in American corporate culture. In a study of the impact within the UK market of separating, or combining, the roles of CEO and chair, the author found a "significant positive market reaction . . . followed the separation of the responsibilities of chairman and CEO." Also, companies that announced a separation subsequently performed better than their counterparts based on several accounting measures. Conversely, companies that announced combination of the positions resulted in "the largest negative market response the day after the announcement." (J. Dahya *et al.*, "The Case for Separating the Roles of Chairman and CEO: An Analysis of Stock Market and Accounting Data," 4 CORP. GOVERNANCE 71, 76 (1996).)

"Boards should consider formally designating a non-executive chairman or other independent board leader. If they do not make such a designation, they should designate, regardless of title, independent members to lead the board in its most critical functions . . . ." (*NACD Report*, pg. 4).

"What about losing the accumulated experience of the retiring CEO? That is easily solved. If the new CEO wants to tap the perceived wisdom and experience of the retired CEO, a telephone call or a quiet meeting does not require a board seat." (Former Citicorp Chairman Walter Wriston, "Resist the Desire to Stay On," DIRECTORS & BOARDS (Spring 1993) 35.)

B. Board processes & evaluation

No board can truly perform its overriding function of establishing a company's strategic direction and then monitoring management's success without a system of evaluating itself. CalPERS views this self-evaluation to have several elements, including:

1.   The board has adopted and disclosed a written statement of its own governance principles, and regularity re-evaluates them.
2.   The board has adopted and disclosed an annual board, committee, and individual director evaluation process.
3.   With each director nomination recommendation, the board considers the mix of director characteristics, experiences, diverse perspectives and skills that is most appropriate for the company. The board should address historically under-represented groups on the board, including woman and minorities.
4.   The independent directors establish performance criteria and compensation incentives for the CEO, and regularly reviews the CEO's performance against those criteria. The independent directors have access to advisers on this subject, who are independent of management. Minimally, that criteria ensure that the CEO's interests are aligned with the long-term interests of shareowners, that the CEO is evaluated against comparable peer groups, and that a portion of the CEO's total compensation is at risk.
5.   The board should have in place and disclose an effective CEO succession plan, and receive periodic reports from management on the development of other members of senior management.
6.   All directors should have access to senior management. However, the CEO, Chair, or Independent Lead Director may be designated as liaison between management and directors to ensure that the role between board oversight and management operations is respected.
7.   The board should periodically review its own size, and determine the size that is most effective toward future operations.

CalPERS does not believe that each director must possess all of the core competencies. Rather, we believe that each director should contribute some knowledge, experience or skill in at least one domain that is critical to the company.

C. Individual director characteristics

In CalPERS' view, each director should fit within the skill sets identified by the board as necessary to focus board attention on optimizing the company's operating performance and returns to shareowners. No director, however, can fulfill his or her potential as an effective board member without a personal dedication of time and energy. Corporate boards should therefore have an effective means of evaluating individual director performance.

With this in mind, CalPERS recommends that:

1. The board adopts guidelines and disclose annually in the company's proxy statement to address the competing time commitments that are faced when director candidates, especially acting CEOs, serve on multiple boards.
2. Each board should establish performance criteria not only for itself (acting as a collective body) or for the key committees; but also individual behavioral expectations for its directors. Minimally, these criteria should address the level of preparedness and participation.
3. Directors should be expected to attend at least 75% of the meetings of the boards committees on which they sit.
4. To be re-nominated, directors must satisfactorily perform based on the established criteria. Re-nomination on any other basis should neither be expected nor guaranteed.
5. The board should establish and make available to shareowners the skill sets the board seeks from director candidates. Minimally, these core competencies should address accounting or finance, international markets, business or management experience, industry knowledge, customer-base experience or perspective, crisis response, or leadership or strategic planning.

CalPers recommends that candidates who are CEOs or senior executives of public corporations be "preferred" if they hold no more than

1–2 public company directorships; other candidates who hold full-time positions be preferred if they hold no more than 3–4 public company directorships; and all other candidates be preferred if they hold no more than 5–6 other public company directorships.

"The job of being the CEO of a major corporation is one of the most challenging in the world today. Only extraordinary people are capable of performing it adequately; a small portion of these will appropriately be able to commit some energy to directorship of one other enterprise. No CEO has time for more than that." (Robert A.G. Monks, "Shareholders and Director Section", DIRECTORS & BOARDS (Autumn 1996 p.158).

D. Executive & director compensation

Compensation programs are one of the most powerful tools available to the company to attract, retain, and motivate key employees, as well as align their interests with the long-term interests of shareowners. Poorly designed compensation packages can have disastrous impacts on the company and its shareowners by incentivising short-term oriented behavior. Conversely, well-designed compensation packages can help align management with owners and drive long-term performance. Since equity owners have a strong interest in long-term performance and are the party whose interests are being diluted, CalPERS believes shareowners should provide stronger oversight of executive compensation programs.

In recognition of this, CalPERS believes that companies should formulate executive compensation policies on a periodic basis. CalPERS does not generally believe that it is optimal for shareowners to approve individual contracts at the company specific level. Rather, executive compensation policies should be comprehensive enough to provide shareowners with oversight of how the company will design and implement compensation programs, yet broad enough to permit the board of directors flexibility in implementing the policy.

Implicit in CalPERS' Core Principles related to executive compensation is the belief that the philosophy and practice of executive compensation needs to be more performance-based. Through its efforts to advocate executive compensation reform, CalPERS emphasizes the alignment of interests between executive management and shareowners, and enhanced Compensation Committee accountability for executive compensation.

1. Executive compensation programs should be designed and implemented by the board, through an independent compensation committee, to ensure alignment of interest with the long-term interests of shareowners while not restricting the company's ability to attract and retain competent executives.
2. Executive compensation should be comprised of a combination of cash and equity based compensation, and direct equity ownership should be encouraged.
3. Executive compensation policies should be transparent to shareowners. The policies should contain, at a minimum, compensation philosophy, the targeted mix of base compensation and "at risk" compensation, key methodologies for alignment of interest, and parameters for guidance of employment contract provisions, including severance packages. Appendix C sets forth the specific areas that executive compensation policies should address.
4. Companies should submit executive compensation policies to shareowners for non-binding approval.
5. Executive contracts should be fully disclosed, with adequate information to judge the "drivers" of incentive components of compensation packages.
6. Director compensation should be a combination of cash and stock in the company.

E. Audit integrity

The company should support the development of accurate audited financial statements. CalPERS believes annual audits of financial statements should be required for all companies and carried out by an independent external auditor. This audit should provide and objective opinion that the financial statements present fairly, in all material respects, the financial position of the company in conformity with applicable laws, regulations, and standards.

To ensure the integrity of audited financial statements, the corporation's interaction with the external auditor should be overseen by the Audit Committee on behalf of the shareowners. The Audit Committee should clearly disclose any non-audit services completed by the auditor and provide supporting evidence that the relationship does not affect the auditor's independence.

1. The selection of the independent external auditor should be ratified by shareowners annually.
2. The board, through its independent Audit Committee, should ensure that excessive non-audit fees are prohibited. To limit the risk of possible conflicts of interest and independence of the auditor, non-audit services and fees paid to auditors for non-audit services should both be approved in advance by the Audit Committee and disclosed in the proxy statement on an annual basis.

F. Corporate responsibility

Shareowners can be instrumental in encouraging responsible corporate citizenship. CalPERS believes that environmental, social, and corporate governance issues can affect the performance of investment portfolios (to varying degrees across companies, sectors, regions, and asset classes through time.) Therefore, CalPERS joined 19 other institutional investors from 12 countries to develop and become a signatory to The Principles for Responsible Investment.

CalPERS expects companies whose equity securities are held in the Fund's portfolio to conduct themselves with propriety and with a view toward responsible corporate conduct. If any improper practices come into being, companies should move decisively to eliminate such practices, and effect adequate controls to prevent recurrence. A level of performance above minimum adherence to the law is generally expected. To further these goals, in September 1999 the CalPERS Board adopted the Global Sullivan Principles of Corporate Social Responsibility.

CalPERS believes that boards that strive for active cooperation between corporations and stakeholders will be most likely to create wealth, employment, and sustainable economies. With adequate, accurate and timely data disclosure of environmental, social, and governance practices, shareowners are able to more effectively make investment decisions by taking into account those practices of the companies in which the Fund invests. Therefore, CalPERS recommends that:

1. Corporations adopt maximum progressive practices toward the elimination of human rights violations in all countries or environments in which the company operates. Adherence to a formal set of principles such as those exemplified in Appendix E, the Global Sullivan Principles, is recommended.
2. To ensure sustainable long-term returns, companies should provide accurate and timely disclosure of environmental risks and opportunities, such as those associated with climate change. Companies should apply the Global Framework for Climate Risk Disclosure (Appendix F) when providing such disclosure.
3. Corporations strive to measure, disclose, and be accountable to internal and external stakeholders for organizational performance toward the goal of sustainable development. It is recommended that corporations adopt the Global Reporting Initiative Sustainability Reporting Guidelines to disclose economic, environmental, and social impacts.
4. When considering reincorporation, corporations should analyze shareowner protections company economic, capital market, macro economic, and corporate governance considerations.

In accordance with the Global Reporting Initiative: Stakeholders are defined broadly as those groups or individuals: (a) that can reasonably be expected to be significantly affected by the organization's activities, products, and/or services; or (b) whose actions can reasonably be expected to affect the ability of the organization to successfully implement its strategies and achieve its objectives.

CalPERS adopted the Global Sullivan Principles of Corporate Social Responsibility in September 1999.

Additional information on the Framework and a Guide for Using the Global Framework for Climate Risk Disclosure is available on the CalPERS website: www.calpers-governance.org.

Adoption of the Guidelines will provide companies with a reporting mechanism through which to disclose, at a minimum, implementation of the Global Sullivan Principles and the Global Framework for Climate Risk Disclosure. The Guidelines along with additional information on GRI can be found at www.globalreporting.org.

G. Shareowner rights

Shareowner rights — or those structural devices that define the formal relationship between shareowners and the directors to whom they delegate corporate control — should be featured in the governance principles adopted by corporate boards. Therefore, CalPERS recommends that corporations adopt the following corporate governance principles affecting shareowner rights:

1. A majority of proxies cast should be able to amend the company's bylaws by shareowner proposal.
2. A majority of shareowners should be able to call special meetings or act by written consent.
3. In an uncontested director election, a majority of proxies cast should be required to elect a director. In a contested election, a plurality of proxies cast should be required to elect a director.
4. A majority of proxies cast should be able to remove a director with or without cause. Unless the incumbent director has earlier resigned, the term of the incumbent director should not exceed 90 days after the date on which the voting results are determined.
5. Shareowners should have the right to sponsor resolutions. A shareowner resolution that is approved by a majority of proxies cast should be implemented by the board.
6. Every company should prohibit greenmail.

7. No board should enact nor amend a poison pill except with shareowner approval.
8. Every director should elected annually.
9. Proxies should be kept confidential from the company, except at the express request of shareowners.
10. Broker non-votes should be counted for quorum purpose only.
11. Shareowners should have effective access to the director nomination process.
12. Shareowners should have the right to cumulate votes in the election of directors.

Lucian Bebchuk, Alma Cohen, and Allen Ferrell, "What matters in Corporate Governance," (2004), The John M. Olin Center for Law, Economics and Business of Harvard University: Found that portfolios of Companies with strong Shareowner-rights protections outperformed portfolios of Companies with weaker protections by 8.5% per year.

Such a right gives shareowners the ability to aggregate their votes for directors and either cast all of those votes for one candidate or distribute those votes for any number of candidates.

Definition of independent director

"Independent director" means a director who:

- Is not currently, or within the last five years has not been, employed by the Company in an executive capacity.
- Has not received more than US$50,000 in direct compensation from the company during any 12-month period in the last 3 years other than:

    (i) Director and committee fees including bona fide expense reimbursements.
    (ii) Payments arising solely from investments in the company's securities.

- Is not affiliated with a company that is an adviser or consultant to the Company or a member of the Company's senior management during any 12-month period in the last three years that has received more than US$50,000 from the Company.

- Is not a current employee of a company (customer or supplier) that has made payments to, or received payments from the Company that exceed the greater of US$200,000 or 2% of such other company's consolidated gross revenues.
- Is not affiliated with a not-for-profit entity (including charitable organizations) that receives contributions from the Company that exceed the greater of (i) 2% of consolidated gross revenues of the recipient for that year or (ii) US$200,000.
- Is not part of an interlocking directorate in which the CEO or other employee of the Company serves on the board of another company employing the director.
- Has not had any of the relationships described above with any parent or subsidiary of the Company.
- Is not a member of the immediate family of any person described in Appendix A.

Independent Chair/Lead-Director Position Duty Statement

The independent Chair is responsible for co-ordinating the activities of the Board of Directors including, but not limited to, those duties as follows:

- Co-ordinate the scheduling of board meetings and preparation of agenda material for board meetings and executive sessions of the board's independent or non-management directors.
- Lead board meetings in addition to executive sessions of the board's independent or non-management directors.
- Define the scope, quality, quantity, and timeliness of the flow of information between Company management and the board that is necessary for the board to effectively and responsibly perform their duties.
- Oversee the process of hiring, firing, evaluating, and compensating the CEO.

- Approve the retention of consultants who report directly to the board.
- Advise the independent board committee chairs in fulfilling their designated roles and responsibilities to the board.
- Interview, along with the chair of the nominating committee, all board candidates, and make recommendations to the nominating committee and the board.
- Assist the board and Company officers in assuring compliance with and implementation of the Company's Governance Principles.
- Act as principal liaison between the independent directors and the CEO on sensitive issues.
- Co-ordinate performance evaluations of the CEO, the board, and individual directors.
- Recommend to the full board the membership of the various board committees, as well as selection of the committee chairs.
- Be available for communication with shareowners.

Executive Compensation Policies

To ensure the proper alignment of executive compensation practices with shareowner interests, annual disclosure of the following provisions, at a minimum, should be addressed:

A. Structure and components of total compensation

1. Details should include reasonable ranges based on total compensation within which the company will target base salary as well as other components of total compensation. Overall targets of total compensation should also be provided.
2. Details should include how much of overall compensation is based on peer relative analysis and how much of it is based on other criteria.

Incentive Compensation

1. A significant portion of executive compensation should be comprised of "at risk" pay or tied to the attainment of achieving performance objectives.

2. The types of incentive compensation to be awarded should be disclosed.

3. Performance objectives[24] should be set before the start of a compensation period while the previous years' objectives which triggered incentive payouts should be disclosed.

4. Plan design should utilize multiple performance metrics when linking pay to performance.

5. Meaningful performance hurdles that align the interests of management with long-term shareowners should be established with incentive compensation being directly tied to the attainment and/or out-performance of such hurdles.

6. Incentive compensation should include provisions by which "at risk" compensation will not be paid if performance hurdles are not obtained.

7. Provisions for the resetting of performance hurdles in the event that incentive grants are retested should be disclosed.

8. Companies should develop and disclose a policy for recapturing incentive payments that were made to executives on the basis of having met or exceeded performance targets during this period of fraudulent activity or a material negative restatement of financial results for which executives are found personally responsible.

9. A process should be disclosed by which additional compensation for executives, which coincides with the sale or purchase of substantial company assets, can be ratified by shareowners.

C. Equity compensation

1. Equity based compensation plans should incorporate the achievement of performance-based components that provide for the vesting of equity grants, which include premium priced options, index-based options, and performance targets tied to company specific metrics that are required to achieve vesting. Time accelerated vesting is not a desirable performance-based methodology.

2. In the event of a merger, acquisition, or change in control, unvested equity should not accelerate, but should instead convert into the equity of the newly formed company.

3. Companies should develop and disclose a policy for recapturing dividend equivalent payouts on equity that does not vest.
4. Equity grants should vest over a period of at least 3 years.
5. The board's methodology and corresponding details for approving stock options for both directors and employees of the company should be highly transparent and include discloser of: (1) quantity, (2) grant date, (3) strike price, and (4) the underlying stock's market price as of grant date. The approval and granting of stock options for both directors and employees should preferably occur on a date when all corporate actions are taken by the board. The board should also require a report from the CEO stating specifically how the board's delegated authority to issue stock options to employees was used during the prior year.
6. Equity grant repricing without shareowner approval should be prohibited.
7. "Evergreen" or "Reload" provisions should be prohibited. (Evergreen provisions provide a feature that automatically increases the shares available for grant on an annual basis. Evergreen provisions include provisions for a set number of shares to be added to the plan each year, or a set percentage of outstanding shares. Reload provisions allow an optionee who exercises a stock option using stock already owned to receive a new option for the number of shares used to exercise. The intent of reload options is to make the optionee whole in cases where they use existing shares they own to pay the cost of exercising options).
8. The company's philosophy related to how equity-based compensation will be distributed within various levels of the company should be disclosed.
9. Provisions for addressing the issue of dilution, the intended life of an equity plan, and the expected yearly run rate of the equity plan should be disclosed.
10. If the company intends to repurchase equity in response to the issue of dilution, the equity plan should clearly articulate how the repurchase decision is made in relation to other capital allocation alternatives.

11. All equity-based compensation plans or material changes to existing equity-based compensation plans should be shareowner approved.
12. Reasonable ranges within which the board will target the total cost of new or material changes to existing equity-based compensation plans should be disclosed. The cost of new or material changes to existing.

D. Use and disclosure of severance agreements

1. In cases where the company will consider severance agreements, the policy should contain the overall parameters of how such agreements will be used including the specific detail regarding the positions within the company that may receive severance agreements; the maximum periods covered by the agreements; provisions by which the agreements will be reviewed and renewed; any hurdles or triggers that will affect the agreements; a clear description of what would and would not constitute termination for cause; and disclosure of where investors can view the entire text of severance agreements.
2. A definitive time frame in which the company will disclose any material amendments made to severance agreements should be disclosed.
3. Severance payments that provide benefits with a total present value exceeding market standards should be ratified by shareowners.

E. Use of "other" forms of compensation

1. Compensation policies should include guidelines by which the company will use alternative forms of compensation, and the relative weight in relation to overall compensation if "other" forms of compensation will be utilized.
2. To the degree that the company will provide other forms of compensation, it should clearly articulate its philosophy for utilizing these tools with specific treatment of how shareowners should expect to realize value from these other forms of compensation.

F. Use of retirement plans

1. Defined contribution and defined benefit retirement plans should be clearly disclosed in tabular format showing all benefits available whether from qualified or non-qualified plans and net of any offsets.

Thinking Points

1. Compare the governance guidelines set forth by CalPERS and those adopted by such companies as GM and Intel. What is notable?
2. Are there areas in the GM and Intel guidelines that do not conform with CalPERS standards?
3. Although such guidelines put out by non-government organizations do not have the force of law behind them, many pundits anticipate that they will change the way companies are governed in the new millennium. Do you agree? Why do you think this is the case?
4. Although CalPERS is a large institutional investor, they continue to be minority shareholders in many of their investee companies. In this case, how do you think CalPERS can improve the way companies are governed?

Chapter 5

Taking Back the Boardroom: Special Situations in the Boardroom

The "Costs" of an Outside Board to the Family Firm

Outside boards have real costs. They separate ownership from management. Management has the extra hassle of satisfying independent directors; management and family have to work hard to keep shareholders informed and interested rather than just putting all family shareholders on the board. Some family members feel they have sacrificed power, and those emotions need to be addressed.

[However, a]n all-family board turns business governance into a political process... and all the participants are family members. The great risk in an all-family board is that many of the goals and needs of various participants have to do with realizing or resolving family or personal emotional needs. Some family members may not feel they get enough respect or recognition for who they are. Others may feel the need for more power over family processes.

Arthur Andersen, Center for
Family Business, October 1994

So far our discussion has centered on the corporate governance problems and solutions of publicly listed corporations. However, there are many types of companies that do not fit this definition. For example, in the United States, more than 70% of the companies are privately held small and medium sized businesses. In Asia, for example, more than 30% of national economies are based on the activities of multinational subsidiaries while another third belongs to government-related corporations and their tightly held subsidiaries. In China,

205

more than two thirds of corporations are government owned while a third is composed of private entities. In Taiwan, more than 90% of the companies are family controlled and managed. Directors in these companies also have to deal with corporate governance problems and because many are not public, these directors may encounter even more difficulty in disciplining management. The purpose of this chapter is to discuss some special circumstances that require more attention from a director.

These special circumstances can be classified into two categories. In the first category, a director may find himself part of a company that is either private or closely held, family controlled or a wholly owned subsidiary of a larger corporation. In these companies, particularly those that do not have publicly traded equity, the legal duties are confined to those in the companies acts of many countries. Here, the fiduciary duty of the director is governed by the nature of the ownership of the company and special contractual arrangements such as indemnities conferred to the director by the owner.

In the second category of special circumstances, a director may experience one-off events that might overtake a company during the ordinary course of its business. Such situations include unplanned executive succession events (deaths or sudden resignations of the CEO), environmental disasters, unanticipated public relations scandals, and takeover threats. This chapter will not discuss all these situation but instead will concentrate on how directors should respond to a takeover offer because it has become one of the most commonly shared experiences by directors across the world.

The Relationship Between Ownership, Control and Board Function

The agency theory principle of corporate governance still applies in special cases, in the sense that shareholders still delegate their rights of control and therefore their responsibilities to the board. Generally, the functions of the board are governed by the ownership structure of the corporation. Thus, in the same way that the functions of the board are governed by the legal duties dictated by the relationship between the director and principal in a publicly listed corporation, the same principle applies to private companies and subsidiary companies. The critical difference is the identity of the principal.

In the case of a widely held public corporation, where the principal is a group of dispersed shareholders, the board is the ultimate decision maker. It cannot abdicate this responsibility nor can it delegate it to management. Secondly, it is also responsible for structuring the asset mix of the corporation. These two responsibilities flow from its legal status as the ultimate fiduciary of the corporation. In this context, the board's further role is to balance the interests of all shareholders, recognizing the possibility that some of these interests may sometimes conflict.

If a single shareholder effectively controls the corporation, the board plays a major role in the appointment of the top management team.[41] Because the controlling shareholder has the right to block board level decisions by voting against the board, the latter has to ensure that the corporation is run for the benefit of all shareholders and not just the controlling shareholder by putting in place a competent management team. A strong management team makes it more difficult for the controlling shareholder to expropriate the wealth of the minority shareholders for itself. Similarly, the board of a closely held corporation has a major but not ultimate role in ratifying strategic and asset allocation decisions if the controlling shareholder has not withdrawn these rights through a Shareholder's Agreement. Most importantly, the board performs these duties as the main advocate of the minority shareholders in order to countervail the power of the controlling shareholder.

In a 100% privately-owned company, the board plays an advisory role. The board's main value in this instance is to act as a source of expert advice and a foil for the owner's ideas and plans. The board is

---

[41] A subsidiary that is 51% owned by a parent is clearly controlled by the parent. However, in a public corporation with dispersed ownership, a single stockholder can exercise effective control over the board if he has enough voting shares to block a board level decision. Depending on the jurisdiction, 'effective control' has been defined as anywhere between 5–15% ownership of common voting shares.

often appointed by the owner and is often composed of his trusted associates, family members, and friends. The director plays the role of the trusted advisor whose main value is his wealth of ideas, contacts, experience, and resources.

The Family Business Board

The role of the director on the board of a wholly family controlled business is advisory in nature. He acts as a sounding board for the owner–manager and to assert the strong council of an expert. The nature of the relationship is that of a trustee without the requisite fiduciary duty. In this role, the director will find himself straddling the demands of the business-family link where political issues belonging to the dining room table are often aired on the boardroom table. Political issues inherent in the business-family link arise most prominently in three circumstances: during asset acquisition and disposal decisions, because they can severely affect the inheritance shares of family members with interests in the business; during CEO succession, because such decisions are often tied to birthrights; and during board appointments, because these will impact the allocation of resources to family members managing the business.

The key to a good family business board are the separation of business from family financial matters, and the creation of a non-family dominated board that is focused on the business decisions. Often, a family council may be constituted to focus on the family financial and political issues and such a council may have an informal link with the business board to deal with the more sensitive issues.

The effective director is one who is able to spot potential problems in the business-family link before they can erupt into crises and is willing to warn the owner of the impending problem. Such a director is one who can creatively untangle the issues in the business-family link so the needs of both constituencies can be addressed. For example, asset acquisition decisions can be separated from the family inheritance plan if proper estate plans are put in place and made known to family members. Thus, a director may find himself having to counsel the owner on such matters, even though they do not directly relate to the business of the firm. In the case of CEO succession and board appointment decisions the business-family link can be untangled if the board can convince the owner to encode the criteria for appointments in the charter and consider non-family members or non-employees for the post.

Non-executives should dominate the board of a family controlled business. For a family business to survive beyond the first stage of organic growth, it has to have in place a cadre of professional managers who may not be family members. Examples of successful family businesses that have employed this principle are Ford Motor Company and Anheuser Busch.[42] The role of senior family members who are also executive directors should be confined to that of an informational one, and they are there to provide the managerial and family perspective during board meetings. The task of the Chairperson on such a board is to ensure that lobbying by family members are kept to the minimum and to elicit the best contributions from the expert board. If the board has a committee structure, then the key standing committees should be the compensation, nomination, and audit committees, and these should be composed entirely of non-executive *and* non-family members.

The Closely Held Corporate Board

In the same way that a family business board is advisory in nature, the board of a closely held corporation also has a strongly advisory role. However, in the case of a closely held *public* corporation, the directors have an additional legal duty to the minority shareholders. The primary role of the non-executive director is to act as the liaison between the controlling shareholder and the minority shareholder. This represents an added level of complexity for the director. The non-executive directors protect minority interests by closely scrutinizing managerial proposals related party to the acquisition and disposition of assets. They have to understand the nature of the related-party transactions between the corporation and its affiliated,

---

[42] Of Budweiser fame and the largest beer brewing company in the world.

non-public companies and strive to prevent the dilution of minority interests.

In a closely held or private corporation, the director's role consists of a mix of trusteeship and control, and therefore is probably the *most* difficult role that he can play. Astute directors ask for a clarification of his responsibilities and duties from the controlling shareholder before accepting such assignments. The Chairperson of a closely held or private corporate board should always be a non-executive director and not a nominee of the controlling shareholder. His duty is to ensure that the rights of the minority shareholders are protected while remaining sensitive to the needs of the controlling shareholder.

Sometimes, a director may be a nominee of the controlling shareholder who may be a government, multinational corporation, or holding company. This places the director in a potential conflict of interest. As a director of the firm, his first legal duty is to the firm but as a nominee he also has a legal duty to the nominating party. Previously, we discussed the fact that a fiduciary relationship is essentially monogamous. Where an individual is a fiduciary to two principals, both of which have dealings with one another, that person may eventually encounter an untenable conflict and be forced to break his fiduciary to one of the principals when discharging his duty. In such countries as Canada and China, the directors of many government-linked corporations and multinational corporations are in such positions. The solution to this dilemma is for the nominee director to be indemnified by the nominating party through a legally binding agreement. In the best of situations, the controlling shareholder should resist the temptation of appointing nominee directors because of the problems that this can create for the director.

The Multinational Subsidiary Board

In the case of a wholly owned multinational subsidiary, directors are almost always nominated by the parent company. Although they may also be non-executives they still owe a fiduciary to the parent company that appointed them. If the subsidiary is also publicly listed the directors have the same legal duties as that of a public corporation. Therefore, a nominee may find himself in conflict if he comes into knowledge of plans by the parent that can hurt the subsidiary. In this instance, the directors have a duty to protect the interests of the minority and it is advisable for the parent corporation not to appoint nominee directors but instead allow the board to form a nomination committee to make independent appointments.

The director in a subsidiary is tasked with communicating industry information and the local government's policies to the parent company and educating the parent board on local business practices. In the same vein, because the subsidiary board has a direct line to the board of the parent company, it is placed well to act as a champion for the subsidiary's organizational and strategic initiatives. The board therefore acts as an advocate for the local company and its minority shareholders.

The composition of the board of a multinational subsidiary should reflect a great deal of independence. In the best of circumstances, the subsidiary board should be given the autonomy by the parent to populate itself with non-executive directors. In a wholly owned subsidiary, the parent will most likely appoint a Chairperson who is a senior executive in the parent firm. The nominee directors will most likely be home country executives while the non-executive directors will most likely be from the host country. Whatever the ownership status of the subsidiary, the principle of independence applies if an effective board is desired and therefore nominee directors should only have a minor role in the audit, compensation, and nominating committees so they will not be placed in a position of conflict when decisions have to be taken that contravene the interests of the parent corporation.

Dealing With Takeovers

Ever since the advent of the leveraged buyout in the early 1980s, no company is safe from a takeover. Since then, the methods that takeover specialists, investment bankers, and lawyers have invented to buy and dispose companies have multiplied beyond enumeration. It is during a takeover that a board of directors demonstrates its competence. While a good board will ensure that the very best price is obtained for the company's shareholders, an excellent board is one that accomplishes this without damaging the long-term prospects of the firm.

Traditionally, when faced with a tender offer or an offer to buy up the company, many boards become defensive and trigger poison pill provisions to stall the attempt. This would be a mistake because it exposes the board to a lawsuit, if the directors cannot demonstrate that they have done their due diligence before rejecting an offer. A board should not panic when it receives a tender offer but neither should it ignore the offer, particularly if it is accompanied by a high premium on the current share price. Instead it should deal with it by publicly confirming the bid and informing shareholders the steps that it intends to take to evaluate the bid and recommend a shareholder action. However, by making a public announcement, the board should also be sensitive to the possibility of creating a 'false market', defined as an artificially created demand for the firm's stock to run up its price. Thus, the board should only make a public announcement if it can determine that the bidder is determined. In short, the board contemplating a takeover offer must always act in the interests of the shareholders. This does not mean that the board has to accept any offer but that it should be prepared to do so if it cannot foresee the management improving the value of the shares to the same level as the tender offer within a reasonable period of time.

What to do during a takeover

In processing a takeover bid, it is the duty of the board to recommend an action to the shareholders. As fiduciaries, the board is responsible for the disposal of the corporation's assets, which includes the sale of the enterprise through a takeover. Therefore, the board is on the firing line for its decision and although a board member may find himself personally conflicted because a takeover will mean the lost of his position, he cannot consider his self-interests before those of the shareholders. A truly transparent and accountable board will quickly demonstrate this by its actions and the public announcements of its intentions. For example, many boards have now adopted mandatory 'go shop' provisions that encumber a board to seek additional purchasers for its assets if the company is "in play". Such provisions are important, because a tender offer or hostile takeover, for example, usually comes with a short time limit within which the board has to act. This period may be as short as a week but with a 'go shop' requirement, the board should in theory be prepared to deal with the offer by having in place a special board committee, investment banking advisors, and legal experts to evaluate the terms of the offer. At this time, if a shareholder rights plan (or poison pill) is in place, the board should consider its status and decide whether it should be triggered. A plan should only be triggered if the board feels that it needs the additional time to evaluate the merits of the offer. It should not be triggered as an ultimate defence against the bid. The board has the right to dissolve the plan by a two-thirds vote of the entire board, and it should do so the moment the board has a verdict on the valuations of its shares. The board can then recommend a course of action to the shareholders, but continue to allow the shareholders to tender their shares if they so wish. Sometimes, the board, together with management, may come up with a competing plan of action to increase shareholder value and offer this to the shareholders in place of their decision to tender their shares.

In the following mini-case example, we examine USX's shareholder's rights plan. Shareholder's right plans are very common and most listed companies in the US and Canada have such provisions. They are often points of controversy and contention between boards and institutional shareholders. Boards claim that such plans are designed to slow down the takeover process to give the board time to consider an offer and to initiate an auction if necessary. Critics claim that there are side effects. See if you can detect what these may be.

Mini Case Study[43] Example of a Shareholder Rights Plan from USX Corporation[44,45]

Section 23. **Stockholder Rights Plan** USX's Board of Directors has adopted a Stockholder Rights Plan and declared a *dividend distribution of one right for each outstanding share* of Marathon Stock and Steel Stock referred to together as "Voting Stock." Each right becomes *exercisable, at a price of US$120,* when *any person or group has acquired, obtained the right to acquire or made a tender or exchange offer for 15% or more of the total voting power* of the Voting Stock, except pursuant to a *qualifying all-cash tender offer* for all outstanding shares of Voting Stock, which is accepted with respect to shares of Voting Stock representing a majority of the voting power other than Voting Stock beneficially owned by the offeror. *Each right entitles the holder, other than the acquiring person or group, to purchase one one-hundredth of a share of Series A Junior Preferred* Stock or, upon the acquisition by any person of 15% or more of the total voting power of the Voting Stock, Marathon Stock or Steel Stock (as the case may be) or other property *having a market value of twice the exercise price.* After the rights become exercisable, if USX is acquired in a merger or other business combination where it is not the survivor, or if 50% or more of USX's assets, earnings power or cash flow are sold or transferred, *each right entitles the holder to purchase common stock of the acquiring entity having a market value of twice the exercise price.* The rights and exercise price are subject to adjustment, and the rights expire on October 9, 1999, or may be redeemed by USX for one cent per right at any time prior to the point they become exercisable. Under certain circumstances, the *Board of Directors has the option to exchange one share of the respective class of Voting Stock for each exercisable right.*

During the tender offer phase, it is the duty of the board to recommend a course of action to the firm's shareholders. This may be to

---

[43] This example is cited for teaching purposes and does not purport to illustrate the effective or ineffective resolution of specific managerial situations.

[44] From USX 10-K SEC Filing on 1999-2003-2008.

[45] The Plan expired on October 9, 1999.

advise rejecting the offer, accepting the offer, or accepting it with provisions such as the removing of any freeze-out or preferential treatment provisions for late or early bidders, respectively. If the board elects
to recommend a rejection, it has to state why the management should
be given a chance to improve the value of the firm's stock and how it
proposes to do so. Thus, in assessing the merits of the offer, the board
must also take proposals from the management for improving the
firm's stock price. The board should also indicate how long its shareholders should wait. Usually, the board has to make a recommendation within one week of the offer so that if a board is not prepared for
the eventuality of a takeover, it will not be able to make an accurate
assessment and a sensible recommendation to the shareholders.

Finally, the board should initiate an auction if the sale of the company appears inevitable. In the US, auctions are now *de rigueur* whenever a takeover offer is received. In many companies, particularly
those engaged in management buyouts, 'go shop' requirements have
been adopted by boards of directors to ensure that the firm's assets
fetch the best price in the market for corporate control. It is the best
defence that a board has against charges of breach of fiduciary.
Auctions expose the firm to the full forces of the marketplace, and
therefore the eventual sale price will reflect the best that the market
has to offer. There are procedures to initiate an auction and these will
vary by jurisdiction. In the US, for example, an acquirer has to
announce its intention to takeover the firm if it accumulates 15% of
the stock within a short period of time. This announcement will itself
trigger an auction, which takes the process out of the hands of the
board. In other cases, a board that sees the intention of a determined
acquirer may announce that the company is for sale, thus triggering
an auction before the 15% limit is reached.

In Asia and Europe, where stock markets are thinner, the board
has to be careful not to create a 'false market'. False markets are more
easily created when thin trading volumes can dramatically drive up the
price of the stock because of rumors and hearsay. This is a particularly
sensitive issue for stock market regulators in these regions. Thus, a
board that is contemplating an auction of its shares must do so transparently and with the approval of the relevant authorities. The auction

process has to be managed carefully to ensure that bidders have full access to information and are given every opportunity to participate on equal footing with the firm's majority or block shareholders.

After the takeover

In a hostile takeover, a board may be asked to step down immediately by the successful acquirer, particularly if the process was acrimonious. However, the interests of the corporation are best served if the target board has handled the takeover in such a way as to reduce conflict with the acquirer and to prepare the company for transition in the post-takeover process. Research has demonstrated unequivocally that most acquisitions do not realize the full value of their stated goals. This is because asset valuations often cannot accurately predict the costs of disruptions to operations, lowered employee morale, organization cultural incompatibilities, and even employee sabotage during the post-takeover period.

Thus, it is the duty of the board to plan for the smooth transition of the firm and they do so by working closely with the acquirer's management team during the due diligence phase of the takeover negotiations. The target board should also direct the top management team to prepare the firm for transition by dealing with the uncertainty over employees' job securities. Most large corporations include the costs of outplacement and layoffs in the sale price of the firm so that the morale of the *remaining* employees can be protected.

If the bid was unsuccessful, the board has a duty to explain what improvements to the firm's value the shareholders should expect. The board should immediately initiate an internal strategic and financial audit of the firm to understand the causes for the low price of its shares. This audit must include a strategic assessment of the firm's prospects and ascertain the net present market value of its current strategy. If the actual market value is lower than that of the assessed value, then the board will have to take steps to either make their plans more transparent to the market or to put its assets to more productive uses.

Finally, a board must be prepared to step down if it loses the confidence of the firm's major shareholders. A good sign that the board has lost credibility is when a shareholder advocacy group or institutional shareholder initiates a proxy battle to replace the board. In such situations, the board should engage in some serious self-reflection, take steps to gain back the lost confidence or be prepared to resign and make a place for a new board. Although resigning is contrary to the self-interests of the directors and perhaps even hurt the shareholders in the short run, a board that has lost the trust of the stockholders can no longer be effective because its pronouncements cannot be believed, exposing the firm to further takeover attempts.

Preventing takeovers

It is the duty of every board to ensure that the firm is fully maximizing the potential of its assets. Maximizing return on assets and ensuring that the market fairly values the firm's prospects are two ways that a board protects the company from a takeover. While the use of poison pills is popular in most large corporations, they should never be employed to thwart a takeover. They can be useful tools for slowing down the process to allow the board more time to contemplate the offer. Still, many boards are accused of using poison pills to shield management from the forces of the takeover market.

The board should not always think that takeovers *per se* are bad things. A board may, in the course of its strategic plans, realize that the firm can only maximize the use of its assets by being part of another organization. Such friendly mergers are common and they allow a firm to leverage its competencies by combining them with those of another firm to create new opportunities. Furthermore, takeover offers can be construed as opportunities for a board to evaluate the job that management is doing. A shock to the organization is often necessary to gain a different perspective. Even boards can become myopic and unless there are policies such as term limits and formal director nominations, only the threat of takeover can trigger self-renewal in the boardroom.

In the final analysis, the only safe defense from a takeover is a well-run company with high market valuation. Regardless of how well the board runs the company, it cannot prevent anyone from mounting a takeover bid and a well-prepared board is one that is cognizant of that eventuality. However, just because a bid is launched does not mean that it will be consummated because as long as directors keep the interests of their shareholders a priority they will have fulfilled their legal and moral duties.

The following case on Jeremiah Brown Electric Wire and Cable illustrates some of the issues covered in this chapter. In particular, it demonstrates the problems that can arise when a family board is composed entirely of the Chairman's appointees and is not allowed to act independently. It also shows what a board can expect when confronted with a takeover bid and is not prepared to deal with it. As you read the case, ask yourself if your family business' board is like Jeremiah Brown's, and how you can use the principles in this chapter to deal with the problems that such a board raises.

The Jeremiah Brown Electric Wire and Cable[46]

Mark McGough, a board member of Brown Electric Wire and Cable Corporation, stared at the memo in front of him. It was a notice from Gerald Brown, part owner-manager and large shareholder that he intended to sell all his shares of Brown to LTR CORP., an American auto parts manufacturer that was in the process of making a bid for the family firm. The memo was sent to all board members as a courtesy gesture in advance of a more formal notice from Gerald's business lawyer.

Mark was deeply distressed because Henry Brown, Chairman and Chief Executive Officer, had convinced the board that there was little likelihood of an unfriendly takeover. However, on the outside chance that one might occur, the company had retained a team of lawyers and bankers, for a very handsome fee, to advise them on the matter. The experts had unanimously concluded that the company was safe from takeover, given the anti-takeover provisions in the constitution and large block of stock controlled by the family.

In their analysis of the situation, none of the advisers and certainly none of the Board, had ever anticipated that a member of the family might sell voting shares. Mark was now deeply concerned because it seemed to him that the fact one of the family was willing to do so indicated that personal preferences and egos could now be getting in the way of sound decision making. A drawn-out battle for control, let alone a family battle, could have dire financial consequences for the company.

Mark was uncertain as to what he should, as a director, do. He knew that Henry, the Chair and CEO, was an autocratic leader and was used to getting whatever he wanted from the board. And yet he felt, as a director, he had a major responsibility in giving advice as to what to

---

[46] This case was prepared by Professor Phillip Phan and does not purport to illustrate the effective or ineffective resolution of specific managerial situations.

do. At the same time, he had no desire to be dragged into a messy family feud and be exposed to a possible lawsuit if things turned really nasty. There was always the option of resigning, but before he took this drastic step, he felt he should find out Henry's reaction to this latest development. He picked up the phone and dialled Henry's office number.

The company

Brown Electric Cable and Wire Corp. is a Hamilton-based manufacturer of cable and wire harnesses for the automotive industry in Ontario. The company was founded as a private business in 1928 by Jeremiah Brown, an engineer from Scotland who arrived in Montreal to pursue his dream of commercializing a new internal combustion engine design for the new horse-less carriage that was all the rage in North America. Armed with nothing more than a design, a strong back, and a supportive family, Mr. Brown eventually became a moderately successful manufacturer of engine pistons. He had quickly realized that his engine proved too expensive to build but in attempting to do so, came up with an efficient way of precision milling pistons that won him several years of contract work with the Ford Motor Company and later, with the Buick Division of General Motors. The Company was incorporated as Jeremiah Brown Precision Milling in 1932.

The depression years of the early 1930s almost wiped out Jeremiah Brown Precision Milling. In his bid to expand the company to exploit what he saw as a tremendous growing opportunity, old man Brown took on large amounts of debt. But with the drastic slow down in sales, cash flows were not enough to cover the interest obligations and the bankers, spooked by the ever-increasing spate of business failures, threatened to foreclose and seize his assets. It was an up and coming young financier, Jonathon MacMillan, who saw the potential for growth in the automobile industry and by extension for the suppliers to that industry, that saved Brown Precision Milling. Through massive restructuring, the installation of a professional management system, and the aid of Jonathon's small list of contacts in the financial community, he and Jeremiah managed to convince the bankers to leave the loans in place. With the advent of World War II in 1939 the company entered a period of great growth precision milling the pistons for much of the industry that was now turning out tanks and military vehicles.

As a result of those prosperous years by the early 1950s the company was back on an even keel and had begun diversifying production into automotive parts such as cables, wire harnesses, brakes, and joints. Jonathon, who had become very close to Jeremiah, married the patriarch's daughter, Mary, some 15 years his junior, and became President of the company. By then, unfortunately, Jeremiah was in ill health, and he soon retired, naming Jonathon MacMillan Chairman and Chief Executive of the Brown Precision Milling.

When Jeremiah Brown died in 1968, he left most of his estate, some 75% of the company, to his two sons, Henry and Gerald, dividing it equally between them. Mary received the family's vacation home in Georgian Bay and a sum of money, which she used to establish a cancer research centre in the Faculty of Medicine at McGill University.

Jeremiah had hoped that the two boys would someday co-lead the company. However, he knew that sibling rivalry had a way of sometimes spoiling the best laid plans and thus stipulated in his will that Henry, the older brother, become CEO of the company upon the voluntary retirement of Jonathon MacMillan. Both of Mr. MacMillan's sons had entered the medical profession and had moved to British Columbia. Seeing that there was no interest by his family in the company, Mr. MacMillan sold his 25% ownership interest in the company to a Canadian syndicate of private investors and retired to Florida.

The company experienced a grave financial crisis in the early 1970s. The slow down in the automobile business, caused by the oil shocks of the early 1970s, alone would have been sufficient to put the company in financial jeopardy; but at the same time, engine manufacturers perfected a new casting technology which made the use of the Brown piston milling process obsolete. As a result, the company lost most of its core business and survived only by restructuring its operations and specialising in the manufacture of a few specific automobile parts — particularly those associated with wire and cable. At the end of the process Brown Precision Milling emerged as Brown Electric Cable and Wire Corporation.

Table 1.   Brown Wire and Cable Corp. Key Financial data (C$ millions)

	1996	1995	1994	1993	1991	1990	1989	1988	1987	1986	1985
Revenues*											
Cable and Wire	118	101	83	90	130	122	88	75	65	46	47
Other	35	0	0	0	0	0	0	0	0	0	0
Total	153	101	83	90	130	122	88	75	65	46	47
Net earnings	0.24	0.20	0.16	0.68	0.56	0.56	0.40	0.64	-0.76	0.70	0.64
Shareholders' Equity	127	156	132	148	155	156	146	126	59	45	36
Total Assets	388	339	318	379	402	364	331	270	138	82	58
Earnings per share	0.12	0.10	0.08	0.34	0.28	0.28	0.20	0.32	0.38	0.35	0.32
Dividends per share	0.06	0.05	0.03	0.10	0.10	0.11	0.12	0.11	0.11	0.07	0.05
Common shares (mil)	2	2	2	2	2	2	2	2	2	2	2

*Restated to include the acquisition of Ontario Prototyping.

Once the restructuring was complete, Henry moved the Company's operations to Hamilton, Ontario — a more competitive site from which to serve the "Big Three". It was a wise move for when the demand for auto-parts once again began to grow in the mid-1980s and early 1990s, because of the growing concentration of Japanese automakers in Southern Ontario, Brown Electric Wire and Cable was in a strong position to capitalise on the growth and profits returned. Indeed, the growth in sales was so strong that Henry felt justified in establishing a small research and development department that worked with manufacturers and major systems assembly suppliers to custom engineer cables and wires to their exact specifications and needs.

At this time, Brown employed over 800 workers, mostly in production, in three plants in Southern Ontario. The corporate structure was simple. The company consisted of four divisions: sales and marketing, research and development, production, and accounting and finance. Gerald Brown was the Vice President in charge of production, and reported directly to Henry Brown. Catherine Brown, Henry's wife whom he met in the MBA program at York, was Vice-President in charge of accounting and finance, while Franklin "Franky" Cole, an engineer Henry hired from General Electric, was VP of R&D. Currently, there was no one in charge of sales and marketing; Henry filled that position himself.

Until 1985, the company was privately owned. In that year, however, in order to raise funds to finance expansion the company went public through the sale of Class A (voting) shares which over the years traded in the range of US$5–US$8. In 1990, facing the need for more capital, the company issued Class B (non-voting) shares. These shares provided an opportunity for interested investors to participate in the gains (and losses) of the company without diluting the control position of the Browns. Dividends were declared regularly and there were no complaints from the shareholders.

Currently the company is capitalised with 2,000,000 Class A common shares, representing about 60% of the equity, and 5,000,000 Class B common non-voting shares representing the remaining 40%. The Brown family control 55% of the voting shares and the investment syndicate to whom Jonathon MacMillan sold his stake owned

30%. The remaining shares were held by a relatively large number of individuals with smallholdings and were traded on the Ontario Over-the-Counter exchange. Eighty percent of the non-voting stock was publicly traded and the company, as part of an employees stock option plan, held the remainder. The shares were normally thinly traded but lately there had been more transactions as the stock market in general became more active and as rumors of a possible takeover of the company began to circulate.

In spite of the growth in the past decade, and even though Toyota, Ford, and Honda were among its major customers the Company was still only one of over 15 large cable and wire manufacturers in Ontario. It had to compete for business against such large manufacturers as Noma, General Electric, Magna, and Loral Corp. By any definition, it was a tough business in which to make a good profit.

Not only was competition for market share strong but the structure of the industry was also changing. In their search for lower costs manufacturers were beginning to out-source more and more of the engineering and design aspects of various parts to parts-manufacturers. To stay in the business, therefore, a parts-supplier had to have more and more engineering and design capabilities. To meet this need and to stay competitive Henry decided to increase the company's expertise in auto parts R&D by acquiring Ontario Prototyping, for US$15 million, a laser prototyping and specialty parts production operation, located in Concord, a small town north of Toronto.

Ontario Prototyping employed 650 people, most of them engineers and highly skilled production workers. It operated two plants, both in Southern Ontario, and was considering expanding into Mexico to follow the Big Three in their moves to take advantage of the North American Free Trade Agreement (NAFTA). The company was organized with three departments — research and development, administration, and production. The merger was a friendly one and the CEO of Prototyping, Frank Hillhouse, stayed on to manage the division.

Henry was unsure how he should organise the new division, whether to absorb it into the existing R&D and manufacturing operation at Brown or to leave it standing alone. There were advantages and disadvantages to both options: the chief advantage from integration was that Brown would be seen to have a larger and more visible R&D department. On the other hand, if the new acquisition was totally absorbed, there could be a clash of cultures, which might result in wiping out any gains to be had from integration. After considerable consideration, Henry decided to have the newly acquired company operated as a separate, wholly owned, division of Brown Electric Wire and Cable.

The industry

The wire and cable industry, of which the manufacture of wiring harnesses is one component, comprises manufacturers of bare and insulated conductors for the transmission and distribution of electrical energy as well as manufacturers of telephone cables, coaxial and fiber optical cables for telecommunications applications. Figure 1 shows some examples of wiring harnesses for automotive applications.

Sales of the wire and harness industry in North America were about US$7 billion in 1990. In Canada, total shipments were under C$2 billion. Exports accounted for about 12.8% of total shipments in Canada, with 74% of these going to the United States, 8% to the European Community and 18% to newly industrialised countries (NICs). Imports captured 16.6% of the Canadian market in 1990 with 87% of these coming from the United States Imports of wiring harnesses into

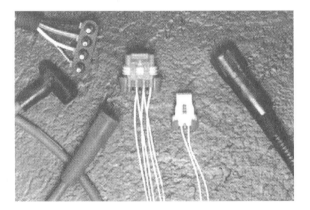

Figure 1. Wire harnesses for automobiles.

Canada are generally of types not manufactured in Canada, either because they are new products or are required in volumes too small to manufacture domestically on an economically efficient scale. Worldwide, the industry is generally oriented toward domestic markets since the low value to weight ratio of these products make transportation expensive and tends to keep production facilities close to major markets.

In 1991, the wire and harness industry in North America consisted of about 560 establishments, ranging in size from less than US$ 5 million to more than US$1 billion in sales. Companies in the industry can be roughly classified into five size segments — less than US$5 million, US$5–7 million, US$7–11 million, US$12–25 million, and US$12 million – $1.1 billion in sales. The composition of the segments has been relatively stable over the last 15 years. The industry is quite labor intensive and because there are so many manufacturers there is a good deal of price competition in the industry.

The key factors necessary for the success of a firm in the industry appear to be location relatively close to customers, a relatively large supply of unskilled labor and the ability to deliver a reliable product. While being close to the market provides some protection for Canadian firms against foreign competitors the reality is that productivity differences can give the offshore producer an occasional price advantage. Consequently to be successful a firm has to constantly innovate and invest to keep its technology close to that of other producers.

Companies within the business are classified into tiers. Brown was a second tier player. First tier players are those with more than US$1 billion in revenues, second tier players have sales of US$100–1000 million annually, and are basically specialty suppliers, focusing on filling niches in the market. Companies in the third, fourth, and fifth tiers tend to supply very specialized products to specific users for specific purposes. They normally operate with very low margins. While some second tier level companies augmented their activities by diversifying by supplying consumer and household product manufacturers, Brown chose to concentrate solely on selling to the automotive sector, believing that by doing so, it could become known as the industry's preferred supplier.

By the early 1990s, many parts suppliers began entering into long-term, often open-ended, contracts with parts suppliers and sub-system assemblers. In effect, these suppliers became the out-sourced departments of these automakers, allowing the latter to reduce overheads while giving the former the security or reasonably long-term contract. As a result of these changes it became unnecessary for the automakers to work with a large number of suppliers so that in the early 1990s there was fierce competition among auto parts manufacturers to become a preferred supplier. Those that did not become so designated simply had to go out of business. Brown survived this fierce round of competition by dramatically cutting prices and reducing margins. Henry felt that by doing so he guaranteed the company's long-term survival and, of course, the hope was that over time prices would improve.

Governance and the board of directors

In 1996, there were six people on the board of directors of Brown Electric Wire and Cable. The chairman of the board was 56 year-old Henry Brown. He had a mechanical engineering degree from Queen's University and a Masters of Business Administration degree from York. As a boy, he spent his summers in the family firm, tinkering with factory equipment, asking questions about the business and generally making himself a nuisance on the factory floor when he was not reading his father's engineering books or designing cars in his doodle pad. After graduating with his Masters, he worked as General Manager for Production under Jonathon MacMillan for a few years before moving into the executive suite. He was 38 years old when he became the Chairman and CEO of the company.

Like his father, Henry was known by friends and business associates as a serious, no nonsense, honest businessman who exerted iron-willed control over every aspect of the business. His family life was well-ordered and relatively uneventful. He met his wife Kate while at university and she remembers their courtship as one that was short and "efficient". He had two children, Kate and Rudi, who "lived in awe" of their father. They lived in a rustic, large ranch style home on a 50 acre farm near Orangeville, north of Toronto where Henry raised horses — an indulgence he allowed himself.

Other members of the board included Gerald, his brother, who graduated from McGill with a degree in industrial art and design. Gerald, who was 10 years younger than Henry, although unmarried, was very well known in Toronto's social circles. In his own words, he preferred to "keep his options open". He lived in a penthouse on the Toronto waterfront. His hobby was sailing and he spent most of his weekends in the summer cruising the Great Lakes and in the winters the Caribbean and the Atlantic eastern seacoast.

Gerald joined the company as an R&D engineer when he was 26. Henry did not believe in nepotism so Gerald had to make his mark on the company before he could move into a major management position. Gerry, as he is often called, eventually became VP of Production at Brown, reporting directly to Henry. In that position, he is in-charge of inventory control, production scheduling, and quality management to ISO:9002 standards. He is, however, not involved in the taking of strategic decisions and, therefore, had little input into the decision to acquire Ontario Prototyping. After the acquisition, Gerry was convinced that the company had excess capacity in R&D and also believed that solving the problem, primarily by reducing the staff at Ontario Prototype would be very difficult because of the manner in which the merger was completed.

Although he owned as many shares as Henry he had little interest in administration and was content to leave the day-to-day decisions to his brother. As a shareholder, he was an investor — not an operator. The company faced few decisions in which the shareholders were required to vote; it had declared steady, although somewhat unimpressive, dividends over the years and thus issues of corporate governance that required Gerald's attention seldom came up.

By the end of 1996, however, Gerald was becoming dissatisfied with the returns from his holdings. Conversations with friends in the investment banking community persuaded him that the company was grossly undervalued. He was led to believe that if there was a market for his stock, he could sell it for a sum, which would realize him a much greater return from investments than he was getting at the present time. He needed money because he had a rich life-style and came to the conclusion that Henry's conservative and overbearing management style was not maximizing shareholders' value.

In 1995, in an effort to broaden the input into major decisions about the company, Henry invited Mark McGough, to join the board. Mark was Gerald's sailing buddy and was identified as a potential board member by Henry because he ran an appliance assembly operation for Generic Electric Canada. Although Brown Wire and Cable did not supply to the appliance industry, Henry felt that having a connection with the industry would be wise. Moreover, the appliance and automotive industries were similar in structure — both were cyclical, large ticket purchase items, and capital intensive. In addition, both industries made extensive use of electrical wires and cables, making Mark's expertise valuable. Mark had initially agreed to join because it seemed like a glamorous thing to do. He did not know anything about boards or about being a board member, but was assured by Henry that he would learn very quickly. He did, and found nothing he did not like in the four board meetings that he attended. Henry knew how to treat his board members, flying them to expensive resorts once a year for a strategic planning retreat and always making sure that they were fully informed of what was going on with the company.

Eric Naughton was the company lawyer and the fourth board member. He also acted as company secretary. He kept the board minutes and ensured the timely filing of documentation with the appropriate stock exchange and governmental bodies. He was also responsible for ensuring that the company discharged its statutory obligations, and that the company's directors and officers insurance was kept current. He was hired by Henry to replace the former company lawyer who retired with Jonathon MacMillan. Eric, a happy-go-lucky free spirit who came from an old Montreal family, met Henry at college and they became good friends. After a few years working in the family law firm and leading a wide-ranging social life Eric settled down with a local actress he met in an after hours bar. When Henry offered him the job at Brown he immediately accepted, delighted to be united once again with his old college friend.

William Lam, the fifth member of the board, represented the syndicate that purchased 25% of the company from Jonathon MacMillan.

He was the fourth such representative and had been on the board for about 5 years. He usually attended every board meeting, asked intelligent questions but did little else. He saw his role as the conduit for information between the company and his bosses and, therefore, was diligent in reading the pre-meeting materials, and company reports he received regularly. Normally, the syndicate largely ignored its investment in Brown Electric Cable and Wire Corporation because it represented a very small portion of their entire holdings. However, the recent run up in PE ratios in the stock market led them to look more closely at all their holdings, with the aim of reconfiguring their portfolios to capitalize on the strong market. Lam was convinced that Brown would be a much more attractive investment as a public company if it were traded more widely.

The final member on the board of Brown, Dr. Paul Broward, an Associate Professor of Engineering at the University of Waterloo, was invited onto the board by Henry to provide expertise in the area of R&D and engineering. He was brought in when the company went public in 1985, and was instrumental in evaluating the R&D capabilities and technology of Ontario Prototyping during the due diligence phase of the acquisition. Dr. Broward and Henry met during an auto parts manufacturers convention in Detroit where the professor was giving a paper on flexible manufacturing technology and Henry, fascinated by his ideas, had sought him out in the lobby after the presentation. A short conversation about Brown Electric Cable and Wire and a site visit by Broward convinced him to accept Henry's invitation to join the company's board of directors.

There were three board committees — executive, audit, and compensation. The executive committee was comprised of Henry, who served as chair, William and Eric and basically looked after board operations and made routine decisions for the board when it was impossible to bring the entire group together. The audit committee consisted of William, who acted as chair, Paul and Mark. The committee was responsible for dealing with the auditors and settling any problems that might arise with the manner in which the company's financial statements were prepared. The third committee — the compensation committee — was chaired by Eric and had Henry and William as members. The committee was in charge of assessing management performance and determining the bonus and incentive plans for the company. It also administered the company's employee bonus plan and stock option plan.

The board has not fundamentally changed in structure or practice since it went public. It continues to meet four times a year unless there are special circumstances that require extra attention. The evening before each meeting there is a dinner, at which time the executive committee convenes to set the agenda for the following day. The meetings are almost always confined to the morning, and they invariable end with a round of golf at the Lionhead Country Club in Brampton, Ontario. If a board member has to be flown in from an out-of-town location, Henry always ensures that the member travels business class. Henry felt that it was important for board members to be alert during meetings as the board was so small. Each member of the board receives a US$15,000 yearly retainer plus US$1,200 for each board meeting and committee meeting attended. There is currently no stock option plan for the board but Henry was considering implementing one when the announcement of LTR's tender offer arrived at his desk.

Mark, as the newest member on the board, initially felt a little guilty for the lack of work they did at these meetings. It always seemed that the decisions were already taken, as was the case with the Ontario Prototyping acquisition, and the board meetings were merely information sessions to which each member put his signature of approval. Lately, however, he has begun to adapt to the board culture, arguing that his level of involvement is appropriate. After all, he thought to himself, that is why management is paid so much — to make those tough decisions.

Current situation

Henry Brown, Chairman and CEO of Jeremiah Brown Electric Cable and Wire Corporation, picked up the phone. He was not surprised to hear Mark on the other end of the line. He was the newest member of the board and thus most likely to panic. Henry briefly described the genesis of the current situation.

In the Spring of 1997, the chair of the Brown board was officially informed by its lawyers that the company was the subject of a takeover bid by LTR, an American auto parts manufacturer. LTR had been shopping for a major Ontario auto parts maker for sometime and had learned that Brown might be obtainable. The investment syndicate was offering to sell its holdings in Brown for a rumoured 60% premium. Consequently it was clear that the company was, as they say, "in play". Henry had no warning that the syndicate wanted to sell its shares or he would have recommended to the board that the company buy the shares back from the syndicate. Unfortunately, the recent acquisition had left the company cash poor and the company would have had to borrow substantially to pay a 60% premium for the shares.

"So what do you want to do now?" Mark asked. "I am concerned that this does not distract us from the business of making and selling wire. Besides, with the acquisition of Ontario Prototype, we can't really afford an extended battle with LTR. As I recall, the acquisition was completed on the premise that the company will be able to sell more product, so it can pay down the loan. This fight could really hurt our cash position and put us in danger of not being able to meet our statutory obligations". Mark was particularly concerned with the last point because directors were personally liable for such obligations. There was no legal defence or insurance against them.

Henry thought about Mark's comments. As far as Henry was concerned the investment syndicate's action was now irrelevant. In fact the company was in play and if he wanted to maintain control he had very little time to act. Given the fact that the family owned over 50% of the voting shares, he had always assumed the company to be safe from such attacks, Now that Gerald was threatening to sell his part of the company he could well lose control. He had never thought this situation would arise so he hardly knew where to start in preparing his defence. He was sufficiently acquainted with the industry to know that there could be a number of strong buyers for Brown now that the company was in play.

Henry knew a good deal about LTR and why it was making such a strong offer for his company. He knew that the board of LTR had decided that if it were to become a preferred supplier to the auto industry their company (LTR) had to have a significant presence in the Ontario manufacturing hinterland because of the large number of assembly plants located in the area. It could buy or build a plant but building would take time and it was costly to build an operation from scratch. Therefore, LTR had decided to buy an existing operation. On advise of their investment bankers they put out the word that they were on the hunt for a suitable target. Once that decision had been made it was inevitable, Henry knew, that he would get an offer for Brown.

Assuring Mark that Gerald was merely grandstanding Henry replied, "I am going to call Gerald and tell him to call off this silly game. We cannot afford it and it is the wrong time to air out the family's skeletons! I shall let you know what he says".

As Henry waited for Gerald to pick up his phone, he mused that he should really convene a board meeting to deal with the situation but if he could talk Gerald out of selling his shares, he could solve this problem in one stroke without involving the entire board. Without Gerald's shares, he was sure LTR would go away. They would simply not have enough shares to gain control.

After Mark hung up the phone, he became more concerned. He had thought Henry would immediately call a board meeting but he had appeared too stubborn (or proud) to admit that he had lost control over the family business. As a board member, Mark had learnt this much: Even if the family retained control of its shares, the board ignored any takeover attempt to its peril because a shareholder could always sue for oppression. Beyond the takeover issue, Mark had a nagging feeling that the board had been remiss in its duties. He surmised that if the board had been doing its job, such a situation would not have occurred in the first place. What he could not decide was whether the fault, if any, was with the board, the business or Henry, and how he would, if he could, go about trying to change things. I suppose I *can* always quit, he mused.

Thinking Points

1. What are the key issues facing JBC?
2. Comment on the strengths and weaknesses of the board
3. If JBC had followed the guidance principles set forth in the CalPERS Guidelines do you think they would still be in trouble?

4. If you were McGough, what do you think your responsibilities are at this stage of the game?
5. What should you do if you were McGough? Do you think you can do it?

Conclusion

Taking back the boardroom!
Thriving as a 21st century director

Corporate governance continues to hold the interests of politicians, academics, and practitioners. With the fallout from the Enron crisis of 2001 and the subsequent reaction from the United State Congress, corporate governance has garnered even greater prominence and leading to the evolution of other mechanisms for achieving board independence. For example, highly diversified corporations often invest the powers of CEO and Chair in the same person as this improves communication. However, to maintain director independence, it is becoming more common for boards to appoint lead non-executive directors who are tasked with organizing the non-executives for influence. In Asia, the widespread use of nominee directors in public corporations is an attempt by block shareholders to assert sovereignty in the boardroom. However, because it exposes directors to a great deal of risk due to the inherent conflicts of interests, this practice is declining with time. Large institutional funds such as CalPERS and LENS are leading the way by making it a policy not to use nominees even though they have the right to do so. Institutional investors are also lobbying for such fundamental reforms as the elimination of poison pills, the imposition of directorship term limits, and the use of performance-based compensation for directors and officers. In short, they are attempting to create a higher level of accountability by reducing the incentives for directors to engage in nest feathering.

There is an increasing concern by policymakers worldwide over the rights of the minority stockholders, as cross border mergers, global product, and capital markets become realities in today's competitive landscape. The Hollinger case is a good illustration of how controlling shareholders, using related party transactions, can expropriate from minority shareholders. In the past, priority was given to the claims made by stakeholders such as family shareholders and controlling shareholder in business networks in order to cement trading relationships but this often meant the subordination of minority shareholder interests. Corporate directors could ignore this problem as long as equity markets remained localized and small with weak laws and weaker enforcement regimes. However, as foreign investors increase their holdings globally, the ability for boards to ignore the minority shareholders, many of whom are now powerful institutional investors, has decreased. These institutional investors bring with them a brand of activism heretofore only seen in the US and UK. For example, in Asia and South America and the emerging economies of Central Europe, the traditional business systems that relied on personal networks and relationships are giving way to arms length contracting. Where in the past, communal values of duty, loyalty and obligation to stakeholders reigned supreme, today only the mantra of "maximizing shareholder value", encouraged and supported by lawmakers, can be heard in the boardrooms of Japan, Korea, Canada, Russia, and Chile.

In the US, more attention is being paid to stakeholder concerns, notably those of employees and communities affected by the impact of globalized product markets. The relentless drive toward shareholder value and success in global competition has caused a great deal of community hardship between the late 1980s to 2000s, characterized by restructurings and plant closings leading to employee layoffs, the lost of pension security, and the collapse of local townships such as those in upper New England that depended on such industries as textiles, forestry, and high-skilled manufacturing. This has led to a reaction by elected officials to slow down the drive toward shareholder friendly but stakeholder hostile corporate practices. In Continental Europe, where the role of the corporation includes a stronger social dimension, community awareness is already encoded in many laws governing the composition of boards. For example in Germany, the co-determination doctrine ensures labor representation on the supervisory boards of the country's largest corporations. Yet, as German companies such as DaimlerChrysler, Volkswagen, and Siemens face their own competitive pressures from the global marketplace, such governance practices have made it more difficult for them to restructure. Across the Atlantic, taking their cues from the Europeans, American state legislators have successfully introduced community laws. These community laws aim to hold corporations and boards responsible for business decisions that adversely impact broad sections of the community in which they operate. These laws are particularly salient in the small company towns that dot the Midwest. For example, the State of Pennsylvania adopted special legislation to block the sale of Hershey Foods, a Pennsylvanian icon, to Dutch food conglomerate, Nestle. Other laws related to environmental protection, wage, and labor protection, and taxes hold directors criminally responsible for violations.

The developments in Europe, Asia and the US signal a new phenomenon, known as convergence, in corporate governance. The convergence in standards of performance, driven by globalization and an increasing dispersion of foreign share ownership in previously closely held firms result in clearer, if not higher, standards of corporate governance. Foreign institutional shareholders have no humor for managerial incompetence, particularly when they own large blocks of equity, which they cannot easily dump on the stock market. In Asia, as mutual funds and unit trusts gain popularity and become larger, we will see more involvement and pressure at the board level to monitor and hold management accountable. The shareholder activism of the previous decade in the US and UK has escalated and spilled over into Continental Europe, even as the Americans and the British are struggling with the social fallout of this movement. As the multibillion-dollar mutual and pension funds increase their investments in these parts of the world, they will bring with them their strong and unequivocal message of shareholder sovereignty. Companies who want to take part in the global capital markets should take note.

Some have argued that boards of directors are useless to corporate governance. The same observers also suggest that it is the pressure resulting from the threat of takeover that ensures managers do not stray too far from shareholder value maximization. Certainly, the less-than-stellar record of corporate performance in the last half a century, and the stories of boardroom excess and incompetence lend much credence to this view. However, the operational costs of takeovers, the economic leakage leading up to a takeover attempt, and the costs of failed attempts mean that it is a resource intensive and messy process. In addition, the corporation often has to undergo a period of post-takeover transition in which productivity is lost and the opportunity costs of capital not fully employed can be high. The board, when properly configured and managed, is a more efficient and fine grained tool for governance. The key is to ensure that the board is sensitive to the subtle competitive pressures of the product and input markets that may be ignored by the management until the deterioration in shareholder value triggers a takeover attempt.

In the final analysis, whether a company survives intact, without becoming a victim of a takeover attempt or the bankruptcy court, depends solely on whether it is able to maximize shareholder value. It is all about leadership and as case after case in this book has made clear, at the center of a well-led company is a disciplined and professionally organized board of directors, led by a visionary Chairperson, who can act independently of political pressure from special and personal interests.

References and Further Readings

Abetti, P, and Phillip H. P. (2003). Zobele chemical industries: The evolution of a family company from Flyerpaper to Globalization (1919–2001). *Journal of Business Venturing*, Vol. 19, 589–600.

Agrawal, A. and Gershon N. M. (1992). Shark repellants and the role of institutional investors in corporate governance, *Managerial and Decision Economics*, 13, 15–22.

Alchain, A. and Harold D. (1972). Production, information costs, and economic organization, *American Economic Review*, 62, 777–795.

Allen, M. P. (1974). The structure of interorganizational elite cooptation: interlocking directorates, *American Sociological Review*, 39, 393–406.

Andrews, K. R. (1989). Ethics in practice, *Harvard Business Review*, Sept–Oct, 2–7.

Band, D. (1992). Corporate governance: Why agency theory is not enough? *European Management Journal*, Vol. 10, 453–459.

Bathala, C.T. and Ramesh P. R. (1995). The determinants of board composition: An agency theory perspective, *Managerial and Decision Economics*, 16, 59–69.

Berglof, E. and Enrico P. (1994). The governance structure of the Japanese financial keiretsu, *Journal of Financial Economics*, 36, 259–285.

Berle, A. and Gardiner M. (1934). The modern corporation and private property, Macmillan: New York, USA.

Bhide, A. and Howard H. S. (1990). Why be honest if honesty doesn't pay, *Harvard Business Review*, Sep–Oct, 2–9.

Bonn, I., Toru Y. and Phillip H. P. (2004). Effects of board structure on firm performance: A comparison between Japan and Australia, *Asian Business & Management*, Vol. 3, 105–126.

Booth, J. R. and Daniel N. D. (1996). Factors affecting the number of outside directorships held by CEOs, *Journal of Financial Economics*, 40, 81–105.

Buckley, W. (1967). *Sociology and Modern Systems Theory*, Prentice Hall: Englewood Cliffs, USA.

Burrough, B. and John H. (1990). *Barbarians at the Gate: The Fall of RJR Nabisco*, Harper and Row: New York, USA.

Business Sector Advisory Group on Corporate Governance (Chairman: Ira M. Millstein), (1998). *Improving Competitiveness and Access to Foreign Markets*, April, OECD Publications: Paris, France.

Butler, J. E., Phan, P. H., Saxberg, B. O. and Lee, S. H. (2001). "Entrepreneurial succession, firm growth and performance", *Journal of Enterprising Culture*, 9, 407–436.

Cadbury, Adrian (Chairman) Committee on the Financial Aspects of Corporate Governance, 1992, *Report of the Committee on the Financial Aspects of Corporate Governance*, Gee & Co: London, UK.

Coase, R. (1937). The nature of the firm, *Economica*, 4, 386–405.

Cochran, P. L. and Robert A. W. (1984). Corporate social responsibility and financial performance, *Academy of Management Journal*, 27, 42–56.

Coffee, J. C., Louis L. and Susan R.-A. (1988). *Knights, Raiders, and Targets*, Oxford University Press: New York, USA.

Corporate Finance Committee (1998). Consultative paper on the securities market, *SES Journal*, June, 15–22.

Daily, C. M., and Charles S. (1996). Chief Executive Officers, top management team, and boards of directors: congruent or countervailing forces? *Journal of Management*, 22, 185–208.

Daily, C. M., Jonathan L. J. and Dan R. D. On the measurements of board composition: poor consistency and a serious mismatch of theory and operationalization, *Decision Sciences*, 30, 83–106.

Demsetz, H. (1983). The structure of ownership and theory of the firm, *Journal of Law and Economics*, 26, 387–389.

Demsetz, H. and Kenneth L. (1985). The structure of corporate ownership: theory and consequences, *Journal of Political Economics*, 93, 11–55.

Dey, P. (Chairman) (1994). The Toronto Stock Exchange Committee on Corporate Governance in Canada, *Where were the Directors? Guidelines for Improved Corporate Governance in Canada*, Toronto Stock Exchange Publications: Toronto, Canada.

Ding, H. and Phillip H. P. (2005). Family member employment and the formation of family business networks, *Journal of Business and Entrepreneurship*, 17, 24–38.

Donaldson, T. (1996). Values in tension: ethics away from home, *Harvard Business Review*, Sep–Oct, pp. 4–12.

Dulewicz, V., Keith M. and Peter H. (1995). Appraising and developing the effectiveness of boards and their directors, *Journal of General Management*, 20, 1–19.

Eisenhardt, K. M. (1989). Agency theory: An assessment and review, *Academy Management Review*, 14, 57–70.

Evans, J. and Charlie W. (1995). Decision processes, monitoring, incentives and large firm performance in the UK, *Management Decision*, 33, 32–38.

Fama, E. F. and Michael C. J. (1983). Separation of ownership and control, *Journal of Law and Economics*, 26, 301–325.

Forker, J. J. (1992). Corporate governance and disclosure quality, *Accounting and Business Research*, 22, 111–124.

Garrat, B. (1999). Developing effective directors and building dynamic boards, *Long Range Planning*, 32, 28–35.

Geeraerts, G. (1984). The effect of ownership on the organization structure of small firms, *Administrative Science Quarterly*, 29, 232–237.

Ghemawat, P. (1991). *Commitment: The Dynamic of Strategy*, Free Press: New York, USA.

Gillies, J. (1992). *Boardroom Renaissance: Power, Morality and Performance in the Modern Corporation*, McGraw Hill-Ryerson: Toronto, Canada.

Goleman, D. (1998). What makes a leader? *Harvard Business Review*, Nov–Dec, pp. 93–102.

Goodwin, J. and Seow J. L. (1998). Disclosure relating to board members: shedding light to build investors' confidence, *SES Journal*, August, 6–12.

Hardaker, M. and Bryan K. W. (1987). How to make a team work, *Harvard Business Review*, Nov–Dec, 2–7.

Harvard Business School (1993). Conflicting Responsibilities, *Harvard Business School Case 9-392-002*, Harvard Business School: Cambridge, MA.

Herman, E. S. (1981). *Corporate Control, Corporate Power*, Cambridge University Press: New York, USA.

Hill, C. W. L. and Scott A. S. (1989). Effects of ownership and control on corporate productivity, *Academy of Management Journal*, 32, 25–46.

Hill, C. W. L. and Phan, P. H. (1991). CEO tenure as a determinant of CEO Pay, *Academy of Management Journal*, 34, 707–717.

Hofer, C. W., and Dan S. (1978). *Strategy Formulation: Analytical Concepts*, West Publishing: St. Paul, USA.

Howard, R. (1990). Values make the company: an interview with Robert Haas, *Harvard Business Review*, Sept–Oct, 134–143.

Jensen, M. C. and Robert S. R. (1983). The market for corporate control: the scientific evidence, *Journal of Financial Economics*, 11, 5–50.

Jensen, M. C. and William H. M. (1976). Theory of the firm: managerial behavior, agency costs and ownership structure, *Journal of Financial Economics*, 3, 305–360.

Jensen, M. C. (1989). Eclipse of the public corporation, *Harvard Business Review*, Sep–Oct, 67, 61–74.

Jensen, M. C. (1993). The modern industrial revolution, exit, and the failure of internal control systems, *The Journal of Finance*, 47, 831–880.

Jensen, M. C. (1986). Agency costs of free cash flow, corporate finance and takeovers, *American Economic Review*, 76, 323–329.

Judge, W. Q., Jr., and Gregory H. D. (1995). Antecedents and effectives of outside director's awareness of CEO decision Style, *Journal of Management*, 21, 43–64.

Juran, J. M. and Keith Louden, J. (1966). *The Corporate Director*, American Management Association: New York, USA.

Kaplan, S. N. and Bernadette A. M. (1994). Appointments of outsiders to Japanese boards: determinants and implications for management, *Journal of Financial Economics*, 36, 225–258.

Kester, W. C. and Richard W. L. (1992). Note on Corporate Governance Systems: The United States, Japan and Germany, *HBS Note 9-292-012*, Harvard Business School Press: Boston, USA.

Khan, H. A. (1999). The Problem of Transition from Family-Based Corporate Governance in East Asia, *Asia Development Bank Institute Working Paper*, ADBI: Tokyo, Japan.

Kim, W. C. and Renee M. (1997). Fair process: managing in the knowledge economy, *Harvard Business Review*, Jul–Aug, 65–75.

Kotz, D. M. (1978). *Bank Control of Large Corporations in the United States*, University of California Press: Berkeley, USA.

La Porta, R., Florencio L. S., Andrei S. and Robert W. V. (1998). Agency Problems and Dividend Policies Around the World, *National Bureau of Economic Research Working Paper 6594*, NBER: Washington DC, USA.

La Porta, R., Florencio L. S., Andrei S. and Robert W. V. (1997). Legal determinants of external finance, *Journal of Finance*, **52**, 1131–1150.

La Porta, R., Florencio L. S, Andrei S, and Robert W. V. (1996). Law and finance, *National Bureau of Economic Research Working Paper 5661*, NBER: Washington DC, USA.

Lease, R. C., Wilbur G. L. and Gary G. S. (1974). The individual investor: attributes and attitudes, *Journal of Finance*, 29, 413–433.

Lee, S-H. and Phillip H. P. (2000). Competencies of directors in global firms: requirements for recruitment and evaluation. *Corporate Governance: An International Review*, 8, 204–214.

Leech, D. (1987). Ownership concentration and the theory of the firm: a simple game theoretic approach, *Journal of Industrial Economics*, 35, 225–240.

Leighton, D. S. R. and Donald H. T. (1997). *Making Boards Work: What Directors Must Do To Make Canadian Boards Effective*, McGraw-Hill Ryerson: Toronto, Canada.

Li, J. (1994). Ownership structure and board composition: a multi-country test of agency theory predictions, *Managerial and Decision Economics*, **15**, 359–368.

Lim, G. H. (1997). Guaranteeing local control, dual listing, foreign share premiums, and tranche merger, *National University of Singapore FBA Working Paper*, NUS: Singapore.

Mace, M. L. (1971). *Directors: Myth and Reality*, Harvard University Press: Boston, USA.

Mace, M. L. (1976). Designing a plan for the ideal board, *Harvard Business Review*, 54, 20–36.

Mallette, P. and Raymond L. H., (1995). Board composition, stock ownership and the exemption of directors from liability, *Journal of Management*, 21, 861–878.

Mangel, R. and Harbir S. (1993). Ownership structure, board relationships and CEO compensation in large US corporations, *Accounting and Business Research*, 23, 339–350.

Marris, R. (1964) *The Economic Theory of Managerial Capitalism*, Free Press: Glencoe, USA.

Melman, S. (1956). *Dynamic Factors in Industrial Productivity*, Basil Blackwell: Oxford, UK.

Mileham, P. (1995). Corporate leadership: how well do non-executives influence boards? *Journal of General Management*, 21, 1–20.

Mizruchi, M. S. (1983). Who controls whom? an examination of the relation between management and board of directors in large American corporations, *Academy of Management Review*, 8, 426–435.

Molz, R. (1995). The theory of pluralism in corporate governance: a conceptual framework and empirical test, *Journal of Business Ethics*, 14, 789–804.

Monks, R. A. G. (1999). What will be the impact of active shareholders? a practical recipe for constructive change, *Long Range Planning*, 32, 20–27.

North-South Institute (The), 1998, *Canadian Corporations and Social Responsibility: Overview*, June, Renouf Publishing, Toronto: Canada.

Parker, H. (1990). The company chairman–his role and responsibilities, *Long Range Planning*, 23, 35–43.

Pfeffer, J. (1972). Size and composition of corporate boards of directors, *Administrative Science Quarterly*, 17, 221–228.

Phan, P. H. and Soo Hoon L. (1995). Human capital or social networks: What constrains CEO dismissals? *Academy of Management Journal*, Special Volume/Issue: Best Papers Proceedings, 37–42.

Phan, P. H. (1998). Effective corporate governance in Singapore: another look, *Singapore Management Review*, 20, 43–62.

Phan, P. H. (1998). Relevancy of the boards of directors: a Canadian perspective and some suggestions for further investigation. *Business and the Contemporary World*, 9, 1–14.

Phan, P. H. (2001). Corporate governance in the newly emerging economies. *Asia Pacific Journal of Management*, 18, 131–136.

Phan, P. H. and Hill, C. W. L. (1995). Leveraged buyouts: An ex-post study, *Academy of Management Journal*, 38, 704–739.

Phan, P. H. and Mark Y. T. (1999). Corporate Governance in Singapore: towards the 21st century, *Banker's Journal*, 109, 56–70.

Phan, P. H. and Mark Y. T. (1998). "An exploratory study of corporate Governance in Singapore", *Malaysian Journal of Economic Studies*, 35, 199–230.

Phan, P. H. and Yoshikawa, T. (1998). Effects of capital market exposure on firm strategy and performance: an analysis of Japanese firms, *Journal of Business Research*, 20, 101–115.

Phan, P. H., Soo Hoon L. and Siang Chi L. (2003). The performance impact of interlocking directorates: the case of Singapore. *Journal of Managerial Issues*, 15, 338–352.

Porter, M. E. (1980). *Competitive Strategy: Techniques for Analyzing Industries and Competitors*, Free Press: New York, USA.

Prahalad, C. K. and Richard A. B. (1986). The dominant logic: a new linkage between diversity and performance, *Strategic Management Journal*, 6, 485–501.

Price Waterhouse (1998). Standards of corporate Governance in Singapore, *SES Journal*, May, 6,8,12,13,16.

Prince, G. M. (1969). How to be a better meeting chairman, *Harvard Business Review*, Jan–Feb, 98–107.

Prowse, S. (1998) Corporate Governance in East Asia: a framework for analysis, *Federal Reserve Bank of Dallas Working Paper*, Dallas, TX.

Rappaport, A. (1981). Selecting strategic that create shareholder value, *Harvard Business Review*, May–Jun, 139–149.

Rappaport, A. (1990). The staying power of the public corporation, *Harvard Business Review*, Jan–Feb, 68, 96–104.

Ravenscraft, D. J. and Federic M. S. (1987). *Mergers, Sells-offs, and Economic Efficiency*, Brookings Institution: Washington, DC, USA.

Regan, P. J. (1984). Management responsibility in attempted takeovers, *Financial Analysts Journal*, Sep–Oct, 40, 16–17, 56.

Roberts, J. and Philip S. (1999). The relationship between Chairmen and Chief Executives: competitive or complementary roles? *Long Range Planning*, 32, 36–48.

Roll, R. (1986). The Hubris hypothesis of corporate takeovers, *Journal of Business*, 59, 197–216.

Scherer, F. M. (1984). *Innovation and Growth: Schumperterian Perspectives*, MIT Press: Cambridge, USA.

Schumpeter, J. A. (1934). *The Theory of Economic Development*, Harvard University Press: Cambridge, USA.

Shleifer, A. and Robert W. V. (1997). A survey of corporate governance. *Journal of Finance*, 52, 737–783.

Singh, K. and Siah H. A. (1998). The Strategies and Success of government Linked Corporations in Singapore, *National University of Singapore Working Paper RPS #98-06*, Singapore.

Sonnenfield, S. (1995). When the CEO can't let go, *Harvard Business Review*, Sept–Oct, 2–12.

Teece, D. J. (1981). Internal organization and economic performance: an empirical analysis of the profitability principle of firms, *Journal of Industrial Economics*, 30, 173–199.

Teen, M. Y. and Phillip H. P. (2000). Corporate Governance in Singapore: recent developments for the next millennium. *Philippine Review of Economics*, **37** 68–91.

Torabzadeh, K. M. and William J. B. (1987). Leveraged buyouts and shareholder returns, *Journal of Financial Research*, 10, 313–319.

Vance, S. C. (1968). *The Corporate Director*, Irwin: Homewood, USA.

Vance, S. C. (1983). *Corporate Leadership: Boards, Directors and Strategy*, McGraw Hill: New York, USA.

Varaiya, NP. (1988). The winner's curse hypothesis and corporate takeover, *Managerial and Decision Economics*, 9, 209–219.

Westphal, J. D. and Edward J. Z. (1995). Who shall govern? CEO/board power, demographic similarity, and new director selection, *Administrative Science Quarterly*, 40, 60–83.

Williamson, OE. (1985). *The Economic Institutions of Capitalism: Firms, Markets, Relational Contracting*, Free Press: New York, USA.

Yoshikawa, T. and Phillip H. P. (2005). The effects of ownership and capital structure on board composition and strategic diversification in Japanese corporations. *Corporate Governance: An International Review*, 13, 303–312.

Yoshikawa, T. and Phillip H. P. (2001). Alternative corporate governance systems in Japanese firms: implications for a shift to stockholder-centered corporate governance. *Asia Pacific Journal of Management*, 18, 183–206.

Yoshikawa, T., Phillip H. P. (2003). The performance implications of ownership-driven governance reform. *European Management Journal*, 21, 698–706.

Yoshikawa, T., Phillip H. P. and Jonathon L. (2004). The relationship between governance structure and strategy choice in Japanese venture capital firms, *Journal of Business Venturing*, 19, 831–849.

Yoshikawa, T., Phillip H. P. and Parthiban D. (2005). The impact of ownership structure on wage intensity in Japanese corporations. *Journal of Management*, 31, 278–300.

Zajac, E. J. and James D. W. (1996). Director reputation, CEO-board power and the dynamics of board interlocks, *Administrative Science Quarterly*, 41, 507–529.

Zajac, E. J. and James D. W. (1996). Who shall succeed? How CEO/board preferences and power affect the choice of new CEOs, *Academy of Management Journal*, 31, 64–90.

Appendix:
Abstracted Codes of Conduct

Directorate For Financial, Fiscal And Enterprise Affairs

Ad Hoc Task Force on Corporate Governance

OECD Principles of Corporate Governance
For Official Use

SG/CG(99)5 Or. Eng.

For any further information, please contact Mr. R. Frederick Tel. 33 1 45 24 18 02, e-mail: richard.frederick@oecd.org 76775

Document complet disponible sur OLIS dans son format d'origine

Complete document available on OLIS in its original format

OECD Principles of Corporate Governance

The OECD Council, meeting at Ministerial level on 27–28 April 1998, called upon the OECD to develop, in conjunction with national governments, other relevant international organizations and the private sector, a set of corporate governance standards and guidelines. In order to fulfil this objective, the OECD established the *Ad-Hoc* Task Force on Corporate Governance to develop a set of non-binding principles that embody the views of Member countries on this issue.

The Principles contained in this document build upon experiences from national initiatives in Member countries and previous work carried out within the OECD, including that of the OECD Business Sector Advisory Group on Corporate Governance. During their preparation, a number of OECD committees also were involved: the Committee on Financial Markets, the Committee on International Investment and Multinational Enterprises, the Industry Committee, and the Environment Policy Committee. They also benefited from broad exposure to input from non-OECD countries, the World Bank, the International Monetary Fund, the business sector, investors, trade unions, and other interested parties.

Preamble

The Principles are intended to assist Member and non-Member governments in their efforts to evaluate and improve the legal, institutional, and regulatory framework for corporate governance in their countries, and to provide guidance and suggestions for stock exchanges, investors, corporations, and other parties that have a role in the process of developing good corporate governance. The Principles focus on publicly traded companies. However, to the extent they are deemed applicable, they might also be a useful tool to improve corporate governance in non-traded companies, for example, privately held and state-owned enterprises. The Principles represent a common basis that OECD Member countries consider essential for the development of good governance practice. They are intended to be concise, understandable and accessible to the international community. They are not intended to substitute for private sector initiatives to develop more detailed "best practice" in governance.

Increasingly, the OECD and its Member governments have recognized the synergy between macroeconomic and structural policies. One key element in improving economic efficiency is corporate governance, which involves a set of relationships between a company's management, its board, its shareholders and other stakeholders. Corporate governance also provides the structure through which the objectives of the company are set, and the means of attaining those objectives and monitoring performance are determined. Good corporate governance should provide proper incentives for the board and management to pursue objectives that are in the interests of the company and shareholders and should facilitate effective monitoring, thereby encouraging firms to use resources more efficiently.

Corporate governance is only part of the larger economic context in which firms operate, which includes, for example, macroeconomic policies and the degree of competition in product and factor markets. The corporate governance framework also depends on the legal, regulatory, and institutional environment. In addition, factors such as business ethics and corporate awareness of the environmental and societal interests of the communities in which it operates can also have an impact on the reputation and the long-term success of a company.

While a multiplicity of factors affect the governance and decision-making processes of firms, and are important to their long-term success, the Principles focus on governance problems that result from the separation of ownership and control. Some of the other issues relevant to a company's decision-making processes, such as environmental or ethical concerns, are taken into account but are treated more explicitly in a number of other OECD instruments (including the Guidelines for Multinational Enterprises and the Convention and Recommendation on Bribery) and the instruments of other international organizations.

The degree to which corporations observe basic principles of good corporate governance is an increasingly important factor for investment decisions. Of particular relevance is the relation between corporate governance practices and the increasingly international character of investment. International flows of capital enable companies to access financing from a much larger pool of investors. If countries are to reap the full benefits of the global capital market, and if they are to attract long-term "patient" capital, corporate governance arrangements must be credible and well-understood across borders. Even if corporations do not rely primarily on foreign sources of capital, adherence to good corporate governance practices will help improve the confidence of domestic investors, may reduce the cost of capital, and ultimately induce more stable sources of financing.

Corporate governance is affected by the relationships among participants in the governance system. Controlling shareholders, which may be individuals, family holdings, bloc alliances, or other corporations acting through a holding company or cross shareholdings, can significantly influence corporate behaviour. As owners of equity, institutional investors are increasingly demanding a voice in corporate governance in some markets. Individual shareholders usually do not seek to exercise governance rights but may be highly concerned about obtaining fair treatment from controlling shareholders and management. Creditors play an important role in some governance systems and have the potential to serve as external monitors over corporate performance. Employees and other stakeholders play an important role in contributing to the long-term success and performance of the corporation, while governments establish the overall institutional and legal framework for corporate governance. The role of each of these participants and their interactions vary widely among OECD countries and among non-Members as well. These relationships are subject, in part, to law and regulation and, in part, to voluntary adaptation and market forces.

There is no single model of good corporate governance. At the same time, work carried out in Member countries and within the OECD has identified some common elements that underlie good corporate governance. The Principles build on these common elements and are formulated to embrace the different models that exist. For example, they do not advocate any particular board structure and the term "board" as used in this document is meant to embrace the different national models of board structures found in OECD countries.

In the typical two-tier system, found in some countries, "board" as used in the Principles refers to the "supervisory board" while "key executives" refers to the "management board". In systems where the unitary board is overseen by an internal auditor's board, the term "board" includes both.

The Principles are non-binding and do not aim at detailed prescriptions for national legislation. Their purpose is to serve as a reference point. They can be used by policy makers, as they examine and develop their legal and regulatory frameworks for corporate governance that reflect their own economic, social, legal and cultural circumstances, and by market participants as they develop their own practices.

The Principles are evolutionary in nature and should be reviewed in light of significant changes in circumstances. To remain competitive in a changing world, corporations must innovate and adapt their corporate governance practices so that they can meet new demands and grasp new opportunities. Similarly, governments have an important responsibility for shaping an effective regulatory framework that provides for sufficient flexibility to allow markets to function effectively and to respond to expectations of shareholders and other stakeholders. It is up to governments and market participants to decide how to apply these Principles in developing their own frameworks for corporate governance, taking into account the costs and benefits of regulation.

The following document is divided into two parts. The Principles presented in the first part of the document cover five areas: i) The rights of shareholders; ii) The equitable treatment of shareholders; iii) The role of stakeholders; iv) Disclosure and transparency; and v) The responsibilities of the board. Each of the sections is headed by a single Principle that appears in bold italics and is followed by a number of supporting recommendations. In the second part of the document, the Principles are supplemented by annotations that contain commentary on the Principles and are intended to help readers understand their rationale. The annotations may also contain descriptions of dominant trends and offer alternatives and examples that may be useful in making the Principles operational.

I. *The rights of shareholders*

The corporate governance framework should protect shareholders' rights.

A.   Basic shareholder rights include the right to: (1) secure methods of ownership registration; (2) convey or transfer shares; (3) obtain relevant information on the corporation on a timely and regular basis; (4) participate and vote in general shareholder meetings; (5) elect members of the board; and (6) share in the profits of the corporation.

B.   Shareholders have the right to participate in, and to be sufficiently informed on, decisions concerning fundamental corporate changes such as: (1) amendments to the statutes, or articles of incorporation or similar governing documents of the company; (2) the authorisation of additional shares; and (3) extraordinary transactions that in effect result in the sale of the company.

C.   Shareholders should have the opportunity to participate effectively and vote in general shareholder meetings and should be informed of the rules, including voting procedures, that govern general shareholder meetings:

1.   Shareholders should be furnished with sufficient and timely information concerning the date, location and agenda of general meetings, as well as full and timely information regarding the issues to be decided at the meeting.

2.   Opportunity should be provided for shareholders to ask questions of the board and to place items on the agenda at general meetings, subject to reasonable limitations.

3.   Shareholders should be able to vote in person or in absentia, and equal effect should be given to votes whether cast in person or in absentia.

D.   Capital structures and arrangements that enable certain shareholders to obtain a degree of control disproportionate to their equity ownership should be disclosed.

E.   Markets for corporate control should be allowed to function in an efficient and transparent manner.

1. The rules and procedures governing the acquisition of corporate control in the capital markets, and extraordinary transactions such as mergers, and sales of substantial portions of corporate assets, should be clearly articulated and disclosed so that investors understand their rights and recourse. Transactions should occur at transparent prices and under fair conditions that protect the rights of all shareholders according to their class.
2. Anti-take-over devices should not be used to shield management from accountability.

F. Shareholders, including institutional investors, should consider the costs and benefits of exercising their voting rights.

II. The equitable treatment of shareholders

The corporate governance framework should ensure the equitable treatment of all shareholders, including minority and foreign shareholders. All shareholders should have the opportunity to obtain effective redress for violation of their rights.

A. All shareholders of the same class should be treated equally.

1. Within any class, all shareholders should have the same voting rights. All investors should be able to obtain information about the voting rights attached to all classes of shares before they purchase. Any changes in voting rights should be subject to shareholder vote.
2. Votes should be cast by custodians or nominees in a manner agreed upon with the beneficial owner of the shares.
3. Processes and procedures for general shareholder meetings should allow for equitable treatment of all shareholders. Company procedures should not make it unduly difficult or expensive to cast votes.

B. Insider trading and abusive self-dealing should be prohibited.
C. Members of the board and managers should be required to disclose any material interests in transactions or matters affecting the corporation.

254 *Phillip H. Phan*

III. The role of stakeholders in corporate governance

The corporate governance framework should recognize the rights of stakeholders as established by law and encourage active co-operation between corporations and stakeholders in creating wealth, jobs, and the sustainability of financially sound enterprises.

A. The corporate governance framework should assure that the rights of stakeholders that are protected by law are respected.
B. Where stakeholder interests are protected by law, stakeholders should have the opportunity to obtain effective redress for violation of their rights.
C. The corporate governance framework should permit performance-enhancing mechanisms for stakeholder participation.
D. Where stakeholders participate in the corporate governance process, they should have access to relevant information.

IV. Disclosure and transparency

The corporate governance framework should ensure that timely and accurate disclosure is made on all material matters regarding the corporation, including the financial situation, performance, ownership, and governance of the company.

A. Disclosure should include, but not be limited to, material information on:
    1. The financial and operating results of the company
    2. Company objectives
    3. Major share ownership and voting rights
    4. Members of the board and key executives, and their remuneration
    5. Material foreseeable risk factors
    6. Material issues regarding employees and other stakeholders
    7. Governance structures and policies.
B. Information should be prepared, audited, and disclosed in accordance with high quality standards of accounting, financial and non-financial disclosure, and audit.

C. An annual audit should be conducted by an independent auditor in order to provide an external and objective assurance on the way in which financial statements have been prepared and presented.
D. Channels for disseminating information should provide for fair, timely and cost-efficient access to relevant information by users.

V. The responsibilities of the board

The corporate governance framework should ensure the strategic guidance of the company, the effective monitoring of management by the board, and the board's accountability to the company and the shareholders.

A. Board members should act on a fully informed basis, in good faith, with due diligence and care, and in the best interest of the company and the shareholders.
B. Where board decisions may affect different shareholder groups differently, the board should treat all shareholders fairly.
C. The board should ensure compliance with applicable law and take into account the interests of stakeholders.
D. The board should fulfil certain key functions, including:

   1. Reviewing and guiding corporate strategy, major plans of action, risk policy, annual budgets and business plans; setting performance objectives; monitoring implementation and corporate performance; and overseeing major capital expenditures, acquisitions, and divestitures.
   2. Selecting, compensating, monitoring and, when necessary, replacing key executives and overseeing succession planning.
   3. Reviewing key executive and board remuneration, and ensuring a formal and transparent board nomination process.
   4. Monitoring and managing potential conflicts of interest of management, board members and shareholders, including misuse of corporate assets and abuse in related party transactions.
   5. Ensuring the integrity of the corporation's accounting and financial reporting systems, including the independent audit,

and that appropriate systems of control are in place, in particular, systems for monitoring risk, financial control, and compliance with the law.
    6. Monitoring the effectiveness of the governance practices under
       which it operates and making changes as needed.
    7. Overseeing the process of disclosure and communications.

E. The board should be able to exercise objective judgment on
    corporate affairs independent, in particular, from management.

    1. Boards should consider assigning a sufficient number of non-
       executive board members capable of exercising independent
       judgment to tasks where there is a potential for conflict of
       interest. Examples of such key responsibilities are financial
       reporting, nomination and executive and board remuneration.
    2. Board members should devote sufficient time to their respon-
       sibilities.

F. In order to fulfil their responsibilities, board members should have
    access to accurate, relevant and timely information.

Annotations to the OECD
Principles of Corporate Governance

I. The rights of shareholders

The corporate governance framework should protect shareholders'
rights. Equity investors have certain property rights. For example, an
equity share can be bought, sold, or transferred. An equity share also
entitles the investor to participate in the profits of the corporation,
with liability limited to the amount of the investment. In addition,
ownership of an equity share provides a right to information about
the corporation and a right to influence the corporation, primarily by
participation in general shareholder meetings and by voting.

    As a practical matter, however, the corporation cannot be managed
by shareholder referendum. The shareholding body is made up of individuals and institutions whose interests, goals, investment horizons

and capabilities vary. Moreover, the corporation's management must be able to take business decisions rapidly. In light of these realities and the complexity of managing the corporation's affairs in fast moving and ever changing markets, shareholders are not expected to assume responsibility for managing corporate activities. The responsibility for corporate strategy and operations is typically placed in the hands of the board and a management team that is selected, motivated and, when necessary, replaced by the board.

Shareholders' rights to influence the corporation center on certain fundamental issues, such as the election of board members, or other means of influencing the composition of the board, amendments to the company's organic documents, approval of extraordinary transactions, and other basic issues as specified in company law and internal company statutes. This Section can be seen as a statement of the most basic rights of shareholders, which are recognised by law in virtually all OECD countries. Additional rights such as the approval or election of auditors, direct nomination of board members, the ability to pledge shares, the approval of distributions of profits, etc., can be found in various jurisdictions.

A. Basic shareholder rights include the right to: (1) secure methods of ownership registration; (2) convey or transfer shares; (3) obtain relevant information on the corporation on a timely and regular basis; (4) participate and vote in general shareholder meetings; (5) elect members of the board; and (6) share in the profits of the corporation.

B. Shareholders have the right to participate in, and to be sufficiently informed on, decisions concerning fundamental corporate changes such as: (1) amendments to the statutes, or articles of incorporation or similar governing documents of the company; (2) the authorization of additional shares; and (3) extraordinary transactions that in effect result in the sale of the company.

C. Shareholders should have the opportunity to participate effectively and vote in general shareholder meetings and should be informed of the rules, including voting procedures, that govern general shareholder meetings: (1) Shareholders should be furnished with sufficient and timely information concerning the date, location and agenda of general meetings, as well as full and timely information regarding the issues to be decided at the meeting. (2) Opportunity should be provided for shareholders to ask questions of the board and to place items on the agenda at general meetings, subject to reasonable limitations.

In order to enlarge the ability of investors to participate in general meetings, some companies have increased the ability of shareholders to place items on the agenda by simplifying the process of filing amendments and resolutions. The ability of shareholders to submit questions in advance and to obtain replies from management and board members has also been increased. Companies are justified in assuring that frivolous or disruptive attempts to place items on the agenda do not occur. It is reasonable, for example, to require that in order for shareholder-proposed resolutions to be placed on the agenda, they need to be supported by those holding a specified number of shares.

3. Shareholders should be able to vote in person or in absentia, and equal effect should be given to votes whether cast in person or in absentia.

The Principles recommend that voting by proxy be generally accepted. Moreover, the objective of broadening shareholder participation suggests that companies consider favourably the enlarged use of technology in voting, including telephone and electronic voting. The increased importance of foreign shareholders suggests that on balance companies ought to make every effort to enable shareholders to participate through means which make use of modern technology. Effective participation of shareholders in general meetings can be enhanced by developing secure electronic means of communication and allowing shareholders to communicate with each other without having to comply with the formalities of proxy solicitation. As a matter of transparency, meeting procedures should ensure that votes are properly counted and recorded, and that a timely announcement of the outcome be made.

D. Capital structures and arrangements that enable certain share-holders to obtain a degree of control disproportionate to their equity ownership should be disclosed.

Some capital structures allow a shareholder to exercise a degree of control over the corporation disproportionate to the shareholders' equity ownership in the company. Pyramid structures and cross shareholdings can be used to diminish the capability of non-controlling shareholders to influence corporate policy.

In addition to ownership relations, other devices can affect control over the corporation. Shareholder agreements are a common means for groups of shareholders, who individually may hold relatively small shares of total equity, to act in concert so as to constitute an effective majority, or at least the largest single block of shareholders. Shareholder agreements usually give those participating in the agreements preferential rights to purchase shares if other parties to the agreement wish to sell. These agreements can also contain provisions that require those accepting the agreement not to sell their shares for a specified time. Shareholder agreements can cover issues such as how the board or the Chairman will be selected. The agreements can also oblige those in the agreement to vote as a block.

Voting caps limit the number of votes that a shareholder may cast, regardless of the number of shares the shareholder may actually possess. Voting caps therefore redistribute control and may affect the incentives for shareholder participation in shareholder meetings. Given the capacity of these mechanisms to redistribute the influence of shareholders on company policy, shareholders can reasonably expect that all such capital structures and arrangements be disclosed.

E. Markets for corporate control should be allowed to function in an efficient and transparent manner.

1. The rules and procedures governing the acquisition of corporate control in the capital markets, and extraordinary transactions such as mergers, and sales of substantial portions of

corporate assets, should be clearly articulated and disclosed so that investors understand their rights and recourse. Transactions should occur at transparent prices and under fair conditions that protect the rights of all shareholders according to their class.

2. Anti-take-over devices should not be used to shield management from accountability. In some countries, companies employ anti-take-over devices. However, both investors and stock exchanges have expressed concern over the possibility that widespread use of anti-take-over devices may be a serious impediment to the functioning of the market for corporate control. In some instances, take-over defences can simply be devices to shield the management from shareholder monitoring.

F.   Shareholders, including institutional investors, should consider the costs and benefits of exercising their voting rights.

The Principles do not advocate any particular investment strategy for investors and do not seek to prescribe the optimal degree of investor activism. Nevertheless, many investors have concluded that positive financial returns can be obtained by undertaking a reasonable amount of analysis, and by exercising their voting rights. Some institutional investors also disclose their own policies with respect to the companies in which they invest.

II. The equitable treatment of shareholders

The corporate governance framework should ensure the equitable treatment of all shareholders, including minority and foreign shareholders. All shareholders should have the opportunity to obtain effective redress for violation of their rights. Investors' confidence that the capital they provide will be protected from misuse or misappropriation by corporate managers, board members or controlling shareholders is an important factor in the capital markets. Corporate boards, managers, and controlling shareholders may have the opportunity to engage in activities that may advance their own interests at the expense of non-controlling shareholders. The Principles support equal treatment for foreign and domestic shareholders in corporate governance. They do not address government policies to regulate foreign direct investment.

One of the ways in which shareholders can enforce their rights is to be able to initiate legal and administrative proceedings against management and board members. Experience has shown that an important determinant of the degree to which shareholder rights are protected is whether effective methods exist to obtain redress for grievances at a reasonable cost and without excessive delay. The confidence of minority investors is enhanced when the legal system provides mechanisms for minority shareholders to bring lawsuits, when they have reasonable grounds to believe that their rights have been violated.

There is some risk that a legal system, which enables any investor to challenge corporate activity in the courts, can become prone to excessive litigation. Thus, many legal systems have introduced provisions to protect management and board members against litigation abuse in the form of tests for the sufficiency of shareholder complaints, so-called safe harbours for management and board member actions (such as the business judgment rule) as well as safe harbours for the disclosure of information. In the end, a balance must be struck between allowing investors to seek remedies for infringement of ownership rights and avoiding excessive litigation. Many countries have found that alternative adjudication procedures, such as administrative hearings or arbitration procedures organised by the securities regulators or other regulatory bodies, are an efficient method for dispute settlement, at least at the first instance level.

A.   All shareholders of the same class should be treated equally.

 1. Within any class, all shareholders should have the same voting rights. All investors should be able to obtain information about the voting rights attached to all classes of shares before they purchase. Any changes in voting rights should be subject to shareholder vote.

 The optimal capital structure of the firm is best decided by the management and the board, subject to the approval of the shareholders. Some companies issue preferred (or preference) shares which have a preference in respect of receipt of the profits of the firm but which normally have no voting rights. Companies may also issue participation certificates or shares without voting rights, which would presumably trade at different prices than shares with voting rights. All of these structures may be effective in distributing risk and reward in ways that are thought to be in the best interest of the company and to cost-efficient financing. The Principles do not take a position on the concept of "one share one vote". However, many institutional investors and shareholder associations support this concept.

Investors can expect to be informed regarding their voting rights before they invest. Once they have invested, their rights should not be changed unless those holding voting shares have had the opportunity to participate in the decision. Proposals to change the voting rights of different classes of shares are normally submitted for approval at general shareholders meetings by a specified majority of voting shares in the affected categories.

2. Votes should be cast by custodians or nominees in a manner agreed upon with the beneficial owner of the shares.

In some OECD countries, it was customary for financial institutions, which held shares in custody for investors to cast the votes of those shares. Custodians such as banks and brokerage firms holding securities as nominees for customers were sometimes required to vote in support of management unless specifically instructed by the shareholder to do otherwise.

The trend in OECD countries is to remove provisions that automatically enable custodian institutions to cast the votes of shareholders. Rules in some countries have recently been revised to require custodian institutions to provide shareholders with information concerning their options in the use of their voting rights.

Shareholders may elect to delegate all voting rights to custodians. Alternatively, shareholders may choose to be informed of all upcoming shareholder votes and may decide to cast some votes while delegating some voting rights to the custodian. It is necessary to draw a reasonable balance between assuring that shareholder votes are not cast by custodians without regard for the wishes of shareholders, and not imposing excessive burdens on custodians to secure shareholder approval before casting votes. It is sufficient to disclose to the shareholders that, if no instruction to the contrary is received, the custodian will vote the shares in the way he deems consistent with shareholder interest.

It should be noted that this item does not apply to the exercise of voting rights by trustees or other persons acting under a special legal mandate (such as, for example, bankruptcy receivers, and estate executors).

3. Processes and procedures for general shareholder meetings should allow for equitable treatment of all shareholders. Company procedures should not make it unduly difficult or expensive to cast votes.

   In Section I of the Principles, the right to participate in general shareholder meetings was identified as a shareholder right. Management and controlling investors have at times sought to discourage non-controlling or foreign investors from trying to influence the direction of the company. Some companies charged fees for voting.

   Other impediments included prohibitions on proxy voting and the requirement of personal attendance at general shareholder meetings to vote. Still other procedures may make it practically impossible to exercise ownership rights. Proxy materials may be sent too close to the time of general shareholder meetings to allow investors adequate time for reflection and consultation. Many companies in OECD countries are seeking to develop better channels of communication and decision-making with shareholders. Efforts by companies to remove artificial barriers to participation in general meetings are encouraged.

B.   Insider trading and abusive self-dealing should be prohibited.

Abusive self-dealing occurs when persons having close relationships to the company exploit those relationships to the detriment
of the company and investors. Since insider trading entails manipulation of the capital markets, it is prohibited by securities regulations, company law and/or criminal law in most OECD countries.
However, not all jurisdictions prohibit such practices, and in some
cases enforcement is not vigorous. These practices can be seen as
constituting a breach of good corporate governance inasmuch as
they violate the principle of equitable treatment of shareholders.

The Principles reaffirm that it is reasonable for investors to
expect that the abuse of insider power be prohibited. In cases
where such abuses are not specifically forbidden by legislation or
where enforcement is not effective, it will be important for governments to take measures to remove any such gaps.

C.   Members of the board and managers should be required to disclose any material interests in transactions or matters affecting
the corporation.

This item refers to situations where members of the board and
managers have a business, family or other special relationship to
the company that could affect their judgment with respect to a
transaction.

III. *The role of stakeholders in corporate governance*

The corporate governance framework should recognise the rights of
stakeholders as established by law and encourage active co-operation
between corporations and stakeholders in creating wealth, jobs, and
the sustainability of financially sound enterprises.

A key aspect of corporate governance is concerned with ensuring
the flow of external capital to firms. Corporate governance is also concerned with finding ways to encourage the various stakeholders in the
firm to undertake socially efficient levels of investment in firm-specific
human and physical capital. The competitiveness and ultimate success

of a corporation is the result of teamwork that embodies contributions from a range of different resource providers including investors, employees, creditors, and suppliers. Corporations should recognise that the contributions of stakeholders constitute a valuable resource for building competitive and profitable companies. It is, therefore, in the long-term interest of corporations to foster wealth-creating co-operation among stakeholders. The governance framework should recognize that the interests of the corporation are served by recognizing the interests of stakeholders and their contribution to the long-term success of the corporation.

A. The corporate governance framework should assure that the rights of stakeholders that are protected by law are respected.

In all OECD countries stakeholder rights are established by law, such as labour law, business law, contract law, and insolvency law. Even in areas where stakeholder interests are not legislated, many firms make additional commitments to stakeholders, and concern over corporate reputation and corporate performance often require the recognition of broader interests.

B. Where stakeholder interests are protected by law, stakeholders should have the opportunity to obtain effective redress for violation of their rights.

The legal framework and process should be transparent and not impede the ability of stakeholders to communicate and to obtain redress for the violation of rights.

C. The corporate governance framework should permit performance-enhancing mechanisms for stakeholder participation.

Corporate governance frameworks will provide for different roles for stakeholders. The degree to which stakeholders participate in corporate governance depends on national laws and practices, and may vary from company to company as well. Examples of mechanisms for stakeholder participation include: employee representation on boards; employee stock ownership plans or other profit sharing mechanisms or governance processes that consider stakeholder viewpoints in certain key decisions. They may, in addition, include creditor involvement in governance in the context of insolvency proceedings.

D.   Where stakeholders participate in the corporate governance process, they should have access to relevant information.

Where laws and practice of corporate governance systems provide for participation by stakeholders, it is important that stakeholders have access to information necessary to fulfil their responsibilities.

IV. Disclosure and transparency

The corporate governance framework should ensure that timely and accurate disclosure is made on all material matters regarding the corporation, including the financial situation, performance, ownership, and governance of the company.

In most OECD countries, a large amount of information, both mandatory and voluntary, is compiled in publicly traded and large unlisted enterprises, and subsequently disseminated to a broad range of users. Public disclosure is typically required, at a minimum, on an annual basis though some countries require periodic disclosure on a semi-annual or quarterly basis, or even more frequently in the case of material developments affecting the company. Companies often make voluntary disclosure that goes beyond minimum disclosure requirements in response to market demand.

A strong disclosure regime is a pivotal feature of market-based monitoring of companies and is central to shareholders' ability to exercise their voting rights. Experience in countries with large and active equity markets shows that disclosure can also be a powerful tool for influencing the behavior of companies and for protecting investors. A strong disclosure regime can help to attract capital and maintain confidence in the capital markets. Shareholders and potential investors require access to regular, reliable, and comparable information in sufficient detail for them to assess the stewardship of management, and make informed decisions about the valuation, ownership and voting of shares. Insufficient or unclear information may hamper the ability of the markets to function, may increase the cost of capital and result in a poor allocation of resources.

Disclosure also helps to improve public understanding of the structure and activities of enterprises, corporate policies and performance with respect to environmental and ethical standards, and companies' relationships with the communities in which they operate. The OECD Guidelines for Multinational Enterprises are relevant in this context.

Disclosure requirements are not expected to place unreasonable administrative or cost burdens on enterprises. Nor are companies expected to disclose information that may endanger their competitive position unless disclosure is necessary to fully inform the investment decision and to avoid misleading the investor. In order to determine what information should be disclosed at a minimum, many countries apply the concept of materiality. Material information can be defined as information whose omission or misstatement could influence the economic decisions taken by users of information.

The Principles support timely disclosure of all material developments that arise between regular reports. They also support simultaneous reporting of information to all shareholders in order to ensure their equitable treatment.

A.   Disclosure should include, but not be limited to, material information on:

1. The financial and operating results of the company

Audited financial statements showing the financial performance and the financial situation of the company (most typically including the balance sheet, the profit and loss statement, the cash flow statement and notes to the financial statements) are the most widely used source of information on companies. In their current form, the two principal goals of financial statements are to enable appropriate monitoring to take place and to provide the basis to value securities. Management's discussion and analysis of operations is typically included in annual reports. This discussion is most useful when read in conjunction with the accompanying financial statements.

Investors are particularly interested in information that may shed light on the future performance of the enterprise. It is important that transactions relating to an entire group be disclosed. Arguably, failures of governance can often be linked to the failure to disclose the "whole picture", particularly where off-balance sheet items are used to provide guarantees or similar commitments between related companies.

2. Company objectives

In addition to their commercial objectives, companies are encouraged to disclose policies relating to business ethics, the environment and other public policy commitments. Such information may be important for investors and other users of information to better evaluate the relationship between companies and the communities in which they operate and the steps that companies have taken to implement their objectives.

3. Major share ownership and voting rights

One of the basic rights of investors is to be informed about the ownership structure of the enterprise and their rights vis-à-vis the rights of other owners. Countries often require disclosure of ownership data once certain thresholds of ownership are passed. Such disclosure might include data on major shareholders and others that control or may control the company, including information on special voting rights, shareholder agreements, the ownership of controlling or large blocks of shares, significant cross shareholding relationships and cross guarantees. (See Section I.D)

Companies are also expected to provide information on related party transactions.

4. Members of the board and key executives, and their remuneration

Investors require information on individual board members and key executives in order to evaluate their experience and qualifications and assess any potential conflicts of interest that might affect their judgement.

Board and executive remuneration are also of concern to shareholders. Companies are generally expected to disclose sufficient information on the remuneration of board members and key executives (either individually or in the aggregate) for investors to properly assess the costs and benefits of remuneration plans and the contribution of incentive schemes, such as stock option schemes, to performance.

5. Material foreseeable risk factors

Users of financial information and market participants need information on reasonably foreseeable material risks that may include: risks that are specific to the industry or geographical areas; dependence on commodities; financial market risk including interest rate or currency risk; risk related to derivatives and off-balance sheet transactions; and risks related to environmental liabilities.

The Principles do not envision the disclosure of information in greater detail than is necessary to fully inform investors of the material and foreseeable risks of the enterprise. Disclosure of risk is most effective when it is tailored to the particular industry in question. Disclosure of whether or not companies have put systems for monitoring risk in place is also useful.

6. Material issues regarding employees and other stakeholders

Companies are encouraged to provide information on key issues relevant to employees and other stakeholders that may materially affect the performance of the company. Disclosure may include management/employee relations, and relations with other stakeholders, such as creditors, suppliers, and local communities.

Some countries require extensive disclosure of information on human resources. Human resource policies, such as programmes for human resource development or employee share ownership plans, can communicate important information on the competitive strengths of companies to market participants.

7. Governance structures and policies

Companies are encouraged to report on how they apply relevant corporate governance principles in practice. Disclosure of the governance structures and policies of the company, in particular the division of authority between shareholders, management and board members is important for the assessment of a company's governance

B.   Information should be prepared, audited, and disclosed in accordance with high quality standards of accounting, financial and non-financial disclosure, and audit.

The application of high quality standards is expected to significantly improve the ability of investors to monitor the company by providing increased reliability and comparability of reporting, and improved insight into company performance. The quality of information depends on the standards under which it is compiled and disclosed. The Principles support the development of high quality internationally recognized standards, which can serve to improve the comparability of information between countries.

C.   An annual audit should be conducted by an independent auditor in order to provide an external and objective assurance on the way in which financial statements have been prepared and presented.

Many countries have considered measures to improve the independence of auditors and their accountability to shareholders. It is widely felt that the application of high quality audit standards and codes of ethics is one of the best methods for increasing independence and strengthening the standing of the profession. Further measures include strengthening of board audit committees and increasing the board's responsibility in the auditor selection process.

Other proposals have been considered by OECD countries. Some countries apply limitations on the percentage of non-audit income that the auditor can receive from a particular client. Other countries require companies to disclose the level of fees paid to auditors for non-audit services. In addition, there may be limitations on the total percentage of auditor income that can come from one client. Examples of other proposals include quality reviews of auditors by another auditor, prohibitions on the provision of non-audit services, mandatory rotation of auditors and the direct appointment of auditors by shareholders.

D.   Channels for disseminating information should provide for fair, timely and cost-efficient access to relevant information by users.

Channels for the dissemination of information can be as important as the content of the information itself. While the disclosure of information is often provided for by legislation, filing and access to information can be cumbersome and costly. Filing of statutory reports has been greatly enhanced in some countries by electronic filing and data retrieval systems. The Internet and other information technologies also provide the opportunity for improving information dissemination.

V. The responsibilities of the board

The corporate governance framework should ensure the strategic guidance of the company, the effective monitoring of management by the board, and the board's accountability to the company and the shareholders.

Board structures and procedures vary both within and among OECD countries. Some countries have two-tier boards that separate the supervisory function and the management function into different bodies. Such systems typically have a "supervisory board" composed of non-executive board members and a "management board" composed entirely of executives. Other countries have "unitary" boards, which bring together executive and non-executive board members. The Principles are intended to be sufficiently general to apply to whatever board structure is charged with the functions of governing the enterprise and monitoring management.

Together with guiding corporate strategy, the board is chiefly responsible for monitoring managerial performance and achieving an adequate return for shareholders, while preventing conflicts of interest and balancing competing demands on the corporation. In order for boards to effectively fulfil their responsibilities they must have some degree of independence from management. Another important board responsibility is to implement systems designed to ensure that the corporation obeys applicable laws, including tax, competition, labor, environmental, equal opportunity, health, and safety laws. In addition, boards are expected to take due regard of, and deal fairly with, other stakeholder interests including those of employees, creditors, customers, suppliers, and local communities. Observance of environmental and social standards is relevant in this context.

A. Board members should act on a fully informed basis, in good faith, with due diligence and care, and in the best interest of the company and the shareholders.

In some countries, the board is legally required to act in the interest of the company, taking into account the interests of shareholders, employees, and the public good. Acting in the best interest of the company should not permit management to become entrenched.

B. Where board decisions may affect different shareholder groups differently, the board should treat all shareholders fairly.

C. The board should ensure compliance with applicable law and take into account the interests of stakeholders.

D. The board should fulfill certain key functions, including:

1. Reviewing and guiding corporate strategy, major plans of action, risk policy, annual budgets, and business plans; setting performance objectives; monitoring implementation and corporate performance; and overseeing major capital expenditures, acquisitions and divestitures.

2. Selecting, compensating, monitoring and, when necessary, replacing key executives and overseeing succession planning.

3. Reviewing key executive and board remuneration, and ensuring a formal and transparent board nomination process.

4. Monitoring and managing potential conflicts of interest of management, board members and shareholders, including misuse of corporate assets and abuse in related party transactions.

5. Ensuring the integrity of the corporation's accounting and financial reporting systems, including the independent audit, and that appropriate systems of control are in place, in particular, systems for monitoring risk, financial control, and compliance with the law.

6. Monitoring the effectiveness of the governance practices under which it operates and making changes as needed.

7. Overseeing the process of disclosure and communications.

The specific functions of board members may differ according to the articles of company law in each jurisdiction and according to the statutes of each company. The above-noted elements are, however, considered essential for purposes of corporate governance.

E. The board should be able to exercise objective judgement on corporate affairs independent, in particular, from management.

The variety of board structures and practices in different countries will require different approaches to the issue of independent board members. Board independence usually requires that a sufficient number of board members not be employed by the company and not be closely related to the company or its management through significant economic, family or other ties. This does not prevent shareholders from being board members. Independent board members can contribute significantly to the decision-making of the board. They can bring an objective view to the evaluation of the performance of the board and management. In addition, they can play an important role in areas where the interests of management, the company and shareholders may diverge such as executive remuneration, succession planning, changes of corporate control, take-over defences, large acquisitions and the audit function.

The Chairman as the head of the board can play a central role in ensuring the effective governance of the enterprise and is responsible for the board's effective function. The Chairman may in some countries, be supported by the company secretary. In unitary board systems, the separation of the roles of the Chief Executive and Chairman is often proposed as a method of ensuring an appropriate balance of power, increasing accountability and increasing the capacity of the board for independent decision making.

1. Boards should consider assigning a sufficient number of non-executive board members capable of exercising independent judgement to tasks where there is a potential for conflict of interest. Examples of such key responsibilities are financial reporting, nomination and executive and board remuneration.

    While the responsibility for financial reporting, remuneration and nomination are those of the board as a whole, independent non-executive board members can provide additional assurance to market participants that their interests are defended.

    Boards may also consider establishing specific committees to consider questions where there is a potential for conflict of interest. These committees may require a minimum number or be composed entirely of non-executive members.

2. Board members should devote sufficient time to their responsibilities.

    It is widely held that service on too many boards can interfere with the performance of board members. Companies may wish to consider whether excessive board service interferes with board performance. Some countries have limited the number of board positions that can be held. Specific limitations may be less important than ensuring that members of the board enjoy legitimacy and confidence in the eyes of shareholders.

    In order to improve board practices and the performance of its members, some companies have found it useful to engage in training and voluntary self-evaluation that meets the needs of the individual company. This might include that board members acquire appropriate skills upon appointment, and thereafter remain abreast of relevant new laws, regulations, and changing commercial risks.

F. In order to fulfill their responsibilities, board members should have access to accurate, relevant and timely information.

Board members require relevant information on a timely basis in order to support their decision-making. Non-executive board members do not typically have the same access to information as key managers within the company. The contributions of non-executive board members to the company can be enhanced by providing access to certain key managers within the company such as, for example, the company secretary and the internal auditor, and recourse to independent external advice at the expense of the company. In order to fulfil their responsibilities, board members should ensure that they obtain accurate, relevant and timely information.

Abstracted Cadbury Code

REPORT OF THE COMMITTEE ON
THE
FINANCIAL ASPECTS
OF
CORPORATE GOVERNANCE

1 December 1992

Preface

When our Committee was formed just over 18 months ago, neither our title nor our work programme seemed framed to catch the headlines. In the event, the Committee has become the focus of far more attention than I ever envisaged when I accepted the invitation to become its chairman. The harsh economic climate is partly responsible, since it has exposed company reports and accounts to unusually close scrutiny. It is, however, the continuing concern about standards of financial reporting and accountability, heightened by BCCI, Maxwell and the controversy over directors' pay, which has kept corporate governance in the public eye.

Unexpected though this attention may have been, it reflects a climate of opinion which accepts that changes are needed and it presents an opportunity to raise standards of which we should take full advantage. Our draft proposals have been thoroughly aired and have attracted a considerable weight of informed comment from a wide range of individuals and bodies with an interest in matters of corporate governance. While it has not been uncritical, the great majority of our respondents have supported the Committee's approach and it is this consensus which gives us a mandate to proceed. The Committee is being looked to for a lead, which we have a duty to provide.

I wish to thank the members of the Committee for their diligence and above all our Secretary, whose single-minded commitment to the Committee's progress has enabled us to complete the task we were set in May of last year. The report represents a shared view of the action which needs to be taken in the field of financial reporting and accountability and it is one to which every member of the Committee has contributed. The Committee has benefited from the breadth of its representation, which has included members of those bodies best placed to support the implementation of its recommendations.

I would also like on behalf of the Committee to express our gratitude to everyone who has contributed to our work either by submitting evidence to us directly, or through the press or by providing platforms for debates on governance issues. Acceptance of the report's findings will mark an important advance in the process of establishing corporate standards. Our recommendations will however, have to be reviewed as circumstances change and as the broader debate on governance develops. We will continue in existence as a Committee until a successor body is appointed, to act as a source of authority on our recommendations and to review their implementation.

Adrian Cadbury
Chairman
1 December 1992

The Setting for the Report

1.1   The country's economy depends on the drive and efficiency of its companies. Thus the effectiveness with which their boards discharge their responsibilities determines Britain's competitive position. They must be free to drive their companies forward, but exercise that freedom within a framework of effective accountability. This is the essence of any system of good corporate governance.

1.2   The Committee's recommendations are focused on the control and reporting functions of boards, and on the role of auditors. This reflects the Committee's purpose, which was to review those aspects of corporate governance specifically related to financial reporting and accountability. Our proposals do, however, seek to contribute positively to the promotion of good corporate governance as a whole.

1.3   At the heart of the Committee's recommendations is a Code of Best Practice designed to achieve the necessary high standards of corporate behavior. The London Stock Exchange intend to require all listed companies registered in the United Kingdom, as a continuing obligation of listing, to state whether they are complying with the Code and to give reasons for any areas of non-compliance. This requirement will enable share-holders to know where the companies in which they have invested stand in relation to the Code. The obligation will be enforced in the same way as all other listing obligations. This may include, in appropriate cases, the publication of a formal statement of censure.

1.4   The Committee will remain responsible for reviewing the implementation of its proposals until a successor body is appointed in two years' time, to examine progress and to continue the ongoing governance review. It will be for our sponsors to agree the remit of the new body and to establish the basis of its support. In the meantime, a programme of research will be undertaken to assist the future monitoring of the Code.

1.5   By adhering to the Code, listed companies will strengthen both their control over their businesses and their public accountability. In so doing. they will be striking the right balance between meeting the standards of corporate governance now expected of them and retaining the essential spirit of enterprise.

1.6   Bringing greater clarity to the respective responsibilities of directors, shareholders, and auditors will also strengthen trust in the corporate system. Companies whose standards of corporate governance are high are the more likely to gain the confidence of investors and support for the development of their businesses.

1.7   The basic system of corporate governance in Britain is sound. The principles are well-known and widely followed. Indeed the Code closely reflects existing best practice. This sets the standard which all listed companies need to match.

1.8   Our proposals aim to strengthen the unitary board system and increase its effectiveness, not to replace it. In law, all directors are responsible for the stewardship of the company's assets. All directors, therefore, whether or not they have executive responsibilities, have a monitoring role and are responsible for ensuring that the necessary controls over the activities of their companies are in place — and working.

1.9   Had a Code such as ours been in existence in the past, we believe that a number of the recent examples of unexpected company failures and cases of fraud would have received attention earlier. It must, however, be recognized that no system of control can eliminate the risk of fraud without so shackling companies as to impede their ability to compete in the market place.

1.10   We believe that our approach, based on compliance with a voluntary code coupled with disclosure, will prove more effective than a statutory code. It is directed at establishing best practice, at encouraging pressure from shareholders to hasten its widespread adoption, and at allowing some flexibility in implementation. We recognize, however, that if companies do not back our recommendations. it is probable that legislation and external regulation will be sought to deal with some of the underlying problems which the report identifies. Statutory measures would impose a minimum standard and there would be a greater risk of boards complying with the letter, rather than with the spirit, of their requirements.

1.11   The Committee is clear that action by boards of directors and auditors on the financial aspects of corporate governance is expected and necessary. We are encouraged by the degree to which boards are already reviewing their structures and systems in the light of our draft recommendations. The adoption of our recommendations will mark an important step forward in the continuing process of raising standards in corporate governance.

Introduction

Corporate governance

2.5   Corporate governance is the system by which companies are directed and controlled. Boards of directors are responsible for the governance of their companies. The shareholders' role in governance is to appoint the directors and the auditors and to satisfy themselves that an appropriate governance structure is in place. The responsibilities of the board include setting the company's strategic aims, providing the leadership to put them into effect, supervising the management of the business and reporting to shareholders on their stewardship. The board's actions are subject to laws, regulations, and the shareholders in general meeting.

2.6 Within that overall framework, the specifically financial aspects of corporate governance (the Committee's remit) are the way in which boards set financial policy and oversee its implementation, including the use of financial controls, and the process whereby they report on the activities and progress of the company to the shareholders.

2.7 The role of the auditors is to provide the shareholders with an external and objective check on the directors' financial statements which form the basis of that reporting system. Although the reports of the directors are addressed to the shareholders, they are important to a wider audience, not least to employees whose interests boards have a statutory duty to take into account.

2.8 The Committee's objective is to help to raise the standards of corporate governance and the level of confidence in financial reporting and auditing by setting out clearly what it sees as the respective responsibilities of those involved and what it believes is expected of them.

Report content

2.9 The report begins by reviewing the structure and responsibilities of boards of directors; here we have summarized our recommendations in a Code of Best Practice. Next, we consider the role of auditors and address a number of recommendations to the accountancy profession. We then deal with the rights and responsibilities of shareholders. The report concludes with several appendices, including at Appendix 2 notes on the roles of some of the bodies referred to in the report.

Companies to whom directed

3.1 The Code of Best Practice (on pages 58–60) is directed to the boards of directors of all listed companies registered in the UK, but we would encourage as many other companies as possible to aim at meeting its requirements.

Code principles

3.2 The principles on which the Code is based are those of openness, integrity and accountability. They go together. Openness on the part of companies, within the limits set by their competitive position, is the basis for the confidence which needs to exist between business and all those who have a stake in its success. An open approach to the disclosure of information contributes to the efficient working of the market economy, prompts boards to take effective action and allows shareholders and others to scrutinize companies more thoroughly.

3.3 Integrity means both straightforward dealing and completeness. What is required of financial reporting is that it should be honest and that it should present a balanced picture of the state of the company's affairs. The integrity of reports depends on the integrity of those who prepare and present them.

3.4 Boards of directors are accountable to their shareholders and both have to play their part in making that accountability effective. Boards of directors need to do so through the quality of the information, which they provide, to shareholders, and shareholders through their willingness to exercise their responsibilities as owners.

3.5 The arguments for adhering to the Code are two-fold. First, a clear understanding of 'responsibilities and an open approach to the way in which they have been discharged will assist boards of directors in framing and winning support for their strategies. It will also assist the efficient operation of capital markets and increase confidence in boards, auditors, and financial reporting and hence the general level of confidence in business.

3.6 Second, if standards of financial reporting and of business conduct more generally are not seen to be raised, a greater reliance on regulation may be inevitable. Any further degree of regulation would, in any event, be more likely to be well directed, if it were to enforce what has already been shown to be workable and effective by those setting the standard.

Statement of compliance

3.7   We recommend that listed companies reporting in respect of years ending after 30 June 1993 should state in the report and accounts whether they comply with the Code and identify and give reasons for any areas of non-compliance. The London Stock Exchange intends to require such a statement as one of its continuing listing obligations.

3.8   We envisage, however, that many companies will wish to go beyond the strict terms of the London Stock Exchange rule and make a general statement about the corporate governance of their enterprises as some leading companies have already done. We welcome such statements and leave it to boards to decide the terms in which they make their statement of compliance. Boards are not expected to comment separately on each item of the Code with which they are complying, but areas of non-compliance will have to be dealt individually.

3.9   The continuing obligations laid down by the London Stock Exchange should require companies' statements of compliance to have been the subject of review by the auditors before publication. The review should cover only those parts of the compliance statement, which relate to provisions of the Code where compliance can be objectively verified (see footnote to the Code). The auditors should not be required to report formally a satisfactory conclusion to their review, but if they identify an area of non-compliance, which is not properly disclosed, they should draw attention to it in their report on the financial statements. We recommend that the Auditing Practices Board should consider guidance for auditors accordingly.

3.10 The Code is to be followed by individuals and companies in the light of their own particular circumstances. They are responsible for ensuring that their actions meet the spirit of the Code and in interpreting it they should give precedence to substance over form.

Keeping the code up to date

3.11   We have addressed those issues, which appeared from the evidence before us to require the most immediate attention. The situation, however, is developing. The Accounting Standards Board has in hand a programme of work on the basis of financial reporting. Revised accounting standards and improved methods of financial presentation will result. At the same time, views on best boardroom practice will evolve in the light of experience, and European Community directives and regulations may give rise to new issues. It is essential, therefore, that the Code, in addition to being monitored, is kept up to date.

3.12   We recommend that our sponsors, convened by the Financial Reporting Council, should appoint a new Committee by the end of June 1995 to examine how far compliance with the Code has progressed, how far our other recommendations have been implemented, and whether the Code needs updating in line with emerging issues. Our sponsors should also determine whether the sponsorship of the new Committee should be broadened, and whether wider matters of corporate governance should be included in its brief. In the meantime, the present Committee will remain responsible for reviewing the implementation of its proposals and for identifying further issues, which its successor body might usefully consider. These steps will establish a continuing process of governance review.

Compliance

3.13   Raising standards of corporate governance cannot be achieved by structures and rules alone. They are important because they provide a framework, which will encourage and support good governance, but what counts is the way in which they are put to use.

3.14   The responsibility for putting the Code into practice lies directly with the boards of directors of listed companies to whom it is addressed. Compliance itself, however, is a matter for everyone concerned with corporate governance. We look to the financial institutions and the wide range of bodies backing our work to encourage the adoption of our recommendations by companies in which they have an interest. The media also have a part to play in drawing attention to governance issues of public or shareholder concern. It is vital to seize the opportunity presented by a climate of opinion, which accepts that changes are needed and which is expecting the Committee to give the necessary lead.

3.15 The Committee recognizes that smaller listed companies may initially have difficult in complying with some aspects of the Code, and we have given careful consideration to the responses to the draft report which addressed this point. The boards of smaller listed companies who cannot, for the time being, comply with parts of the Code should note that they may instead give their reasons for non-compliance. We believe, however, that full compliance will bring benefits to the boards of such companies, and it should be their objective to ensure that the benefits achieved. In particular, the appointment of appropriate non-executive directors should make a positive contribution to the development of their businesses. Any practical issues, which may arise in respect of smatter listed companies wilt be thoroughly reviewed by the Committee and its successor.

3.16 The Committee notes that companies will not be able to comply with items 4.5 and 4.6 in the Code until the necessary guidance for companies has been developed.

Board effectiveness

4.1 Every public company should be headed by an effective board which can both lead and control the business. Within the context of the UK unitary board system, this means a board made up of a combination of executive directors, with their intimate knowledge of the business, and of outside, non-executive directors, who can bring a broader view to the company's activities, under a chairman who accepts the duties and responsibilities which the post entails.

4.2 Tests of board effectiveness include the way in which the members of the board as a whole work together under the chairman, whose roles in corporate governance is fundamental, and their collective ability to provide both the leadership and the checks and balances which effective governance demands. Shareholders are responsible for electing board members, and it is in their interests to see that the boards of their companies are properly constituted and not dominated by any one individual.

4.3 All directors are equally responsible in law for the board's actions and decisions. Certain directors may have particular responsibilities, as executive or non-executive directors, for which they are accountable to the board. Regardless of specific duties undertaken by individual directors, however, it is for the board collectively to ensure that it is meeting its obligations.

4.4 Whilst it is the board as a whole, which is the final authority, executive, and non-executive directors are likely to contribute in different ways to its work. Non-executive directors have two particularly important contributions to make to the governance process as a consequence of their independence from executive responsibility. Neither is in conflict with the unitary nature of the board.

4.5 The first is in reviewing the performance of the board and of the executive. Non-executive directors should address this aspect of their responsibilities carefully and should ensure that the chairman is aware of their views. If the chairman is also the chief executive, board members should look to a senior non-executive director, who might be the deputy chairman, as the person to whom they should address any concerns about the combined office of chairman/chief executive and its consequences for the effectiveness of the board. A number of companies have recognized that role, and some have done so formally in their Articles.

4.6 The second is in taking the lead where potential conflicts of interest arise. An important aspect of effective corporate governance is the recognition that the specific interests of the executive management and the wider interests of the company may at times diverge, for example, over takeovers, boardroom succession, or directors' pay. Independent non-executive directors, whose interests are less directly affected, are well-placed to help to resolve such situations.

The chairman

4.7 The chairman's role in securing good corporate governance is crucial. Chairmen are primarily responsible for the working of the board, for its balance of membership subject to board and shareholders' approval, for ensuring that all relevant issues are on the agenda, and for ensuring that all directors, executive and non-executive alike, are enabled and encouraged to play their full part in its activities. Chairmen should be able to stand sufficiently back from the day-to-day running of the business to ensure that their boards are in full control of the company's affairs and alert to their obligations to their shareholders.

4.8 It is for chairmen to make certain that their non-executive directors receive timely, relevant information tailored to their needs, that they are properly briefed on the issues arising at board meetings, and that they make an effective contribution as board members in practice. It is equally for chairmen to ensure that executive directors look beyond their executive duties and accept their full share of the responsibilities of governance.

4.9 Given the importance and particular nature of the chairman's role, it should in principle be separate from that of the chief executive. If the two roles are combined in one person, it represents a considerable concentration of power. We recommend, therefore, that there should be a clearly accepted division of responsibilities at the head of a company, which will ensure a balance of power and authority, such that no one individual has unfettered powers of decision. Where the chairman is also the chief executive, it is essential that there should be a strong and independent element on the board.

Non-executive directors

4.10 The Committee believes that the calibre of the non-executive members of the board is of special importance in setting and maintaining standards of corporate governance. The emphasis in this report on the control function of non-executive directors is a consequence of our remit and should not in any way detract from the primary and positive contribution, which they are expected to make, as equal board members, to the leadership of the company.

4.11 Non-executive directors should bring an independent judgment to bear on issues of strategy, performance, resources, including key appointments, and standards of conduct. We recommend that the calibre and number of non-executive directors on a board should be such that their views will carry significant weight in the board's decisions. The meet our recommendations on the composition of sub-committees of the board, all boards will require a minimum of three non-executive directors, one of whom may be the chairman of the company provided he or she is not also its executive head. Additionally, two of the three should be independent in the terms set out in the next paragraph.

4.12 An essential quality, which non-executive directors should bring to the board's deliberations is that of independence of judgment. We recommend that the majority of non-executives on a board should be independent of the company. This means that apart from their directors' fees and shareholdings, of the management and free from any business or other relationship which could materially interfere with the exercise of their independent judgment. It is for the board to decide in particular cases whether this definition is met. Information about the relevant interests of directors should be disclosed in the Directors' Report.

4.13 On fees, there is a balance to be struck between recognizing the value of the contribution made by non-executive directors and not undermining their independence. The demands which are now being made on conscientious non-executive directors are significant and their fees should reflect the time which they devote to the company's affairs. There is, therefore, a case for paying for additional responsibilities taken on, for example, by chairmen of board committees. In order to safeguard their independent position, we regard it as good practice for non-executive directors not to participate in share option schemes and for their service as non-executive directors not to be pensionable by the company.

4.14 Non-executive directors lack the inside knowledge of the company of the executive directors, but have the same right of access to information as they do. Their effectiveness turns to a considerable extent on the quality of the information, which they receive and on the use, which they make of it. Boards should regularly review the form and the extent of the information, which is provided to all directors.

4.15 Given the importance of their distinctive contribution, non-executive directors should be selected with the same impartiality and care as senior executives. We recommend that their appointment should be a matter for the board as a whole and that there should be a formal selection process, which will reinforce the independence of non-executive directors and make it evident that they have been appointed on merit and not through any form of patronage. We regard it as good practice for a nomination committee (dealt with below) to carry out the selection process and to make proposals to the board.

4.16 Companies have to be able to bring about changes in the composition of their boards to maintain their vitality. Non-executive directors may lose something of their independent edge, if they remain on a board too long. Furthermore, the make-up of a board needs to change in line with new challenges. We recommend, therefore, that non-executive directors should be appointed for specified terms. Their Letter of Appointment should set out their duties, term of office, remuneration and its review. Reappointment should not be automatic, but a conscious decision by the board and the director concerned.

4.17 Our emphasis on the qualities to be looked for in non-executive directors, combined with the greater demands now being made on them, raises the question of whether the supply of non-executive directors will be adequate to meet the demand.

When companies encourage their executive directors to accept appointments on the hoards of other companies, the companies and the individuals concerned all gain. A policy of promoting this kind of appointment will increase the pool of potential non-executive directors, particularly if the divisional directors of larger companies are considered for non-executive posts, as well as their main board colleagues.

Professional advice

4.18 Occasions may arise when directors have to seek legal or financial advice in the furtherance of their duties. They should always be able to consult the company's advisers. If, however, they consider it necessary to take independent professional advice, we recommend that they should be entitled to do so at the company's expense, through an agreed procedure laid down formally, for example, in a Board Resolution, in the Articles, or in the Letter of Appointment.

Directors' training

4.19 The weight of responsibility carried by all directors and the increasing commitment, which their duties require emphasize the importance of the way in which they prepare themselves for their posts. Given the varying backgrounds, qualifications and experience of directors, it is highly desirable that they should all undertake some form of internal or external training; this is particularly important for directors, whether executive or non-executive, with no previous board experience. Newly appointed board members are also entitled to expect a proper process of induction into the company's affairs. It is then up to individual directors to keep abreast of their legislative and broader responsibilities.

4.20 There are already courses for newly appointed directors run by the Institute of Directors and business schools. With the support of the Bank of England, the Confederation of British Industry, the Institute of Directors, and PRONED, a new course covering the full range of board responsibilities will be open to directors shortly. The training and development of directors is of importance to good governance, and it is one of the issues which we suggest our successor body should keep under review.

Board structures and procedures

4.21 The effectiveness of a board is buttressed by its structure and procedures. One aspect of structure is the appointment of committees of the board, such as the audit, remuneration and nomination committees, referred to later in the report.

4.22 Another is that boards should recognize the importance of the finance function bymaking the designated responsibility of a main board director, who should be a signatory to the accounts on behalf of the board, and should have the right of access to the Audit Committee.

4.23 The basic procedural requirements are that the board should meet regularly, with due notice of the issues to be discussed supported by the necessary paperwork, and should record its conclusions. We recommend that boards should have a formal schedule of matters specifically reserved to them for their collective decision, to ensure that the direction and control of the company remains firmly in their hands and as a safeguard against misjudgments and possible illegal practices. A schedule of these matters should be given to directors on appointment and should be kept up to date.

4.24 We envisage that such a schedule would at least include:

   (a) acquisition and disposal of assets of the company or its subsidiaries that are material to the company;
   (b) investments, capital projects, authority levels, treasury policies, and risk management policies.

Boards should lay down rules to determine materiality for any transaction and should establish clearly which transactions require multiple board signatures. Boards should also agree the procedures to be followed when, exceptionally, decisions are required between board meetings.

The company secretary

4.25 The company secretary has a key role to play in ensuring that board procedures are both followed and regularly reviewed. The chairman and the board will look to the company secretary for guidance on what their responsibilities are under the rules and regulations to which they are subject and on how those responsibilities should be discharged. All directors should have access to the advice and services of the company secretary and should recognise that the chairman is entitled to the strong and positive support of the company secretary in ensuring the effective functioning of the board. It should be standard practice for the company secretary to administer, attend, and prepare minutes of board proceedings.

4.26 Under the Companies Act the directors have a duty to appoint as secretary someone who is capable of carrying out the duties which the post entails. The responsibility for ensuring that the secretary remains capable, and any question of the secretary's removal, should be a matter for the board as a whole.

4.27 The Committee expects that the company secretary will be a source of advice to the chairman and to the board on the implementation of the Code of Best Practice.

Directors' responsibilities

4.28 So that shareholders are clear where the boundaries between the duties of directors and auditors lie, we recommend that a brief statement of directors' responsibilities for the accounts should appear in the report and accounts, as a counterpart to a statement by the auditors about their reporting responsibilities. The ground which would need to be covered by the directors' statement is set out in Appendix 3. The appropriate position for the directors' statement is immediately before the auditors' report, which in future will include a statement of auditors' responsibilities. The two statements will thus. complement each other.

Standards of conduct

4.29 It is important that all employees should know what standards of conduct are expected of them. We regard it as good practice for boards of directors to draw up codes of ethics or statements of business practice and to publish them both internally and externally.

Nomination committees

4.30 One approach to making board appointments. which makes clear how these appointments are made and assists boards in making them, is through the setting up of a nomination committee, with the responsibility of proposing to the board, in the first instance, any new appointments, whether of executive or of non-executive directors. A nomination committee should have a majority of non-executive directors on it and be chaired either by the chairman or a non-executive director.

Internal controls

4.31 Directors are responsible under section 221 of the Companies Act 1985 for maintaining adequate accounting records. To meet these responsibilities directors need in practice to maintain a system of internal control over the financial management of the company, including procedures designed to minimize the risk of fraud. There is, therefore, already an implicit requirement on directors to ensure that a proper system of internal control is in place.

4.32 Since an effective internal control system is a key aspect of the efficient management of a company, we recommend that the directors should make a statement in the report and accounts on the effectiveness of their system of internal control and that the auditors should report thereon. The criteria for assessing effectiveness and the detailed guidance for auditors will need to be established and our recommendation to this effect is in paragraph 5.16.

Audit committees

4.33 Since 1978, the New York Stock Exchange has required all listed companies to have audit committees composed solely of independent directors, and the 1987 report of the American Treadway Commission concluded that audit committees had a critical role to play in ensuring the integrity of US Company financial reports. While experience of audit committees in this country is shorter, it is encouraging, and around two-thirds of the top 250 UK listed companies now have them in place.

4.34 Experience in the US has shown that, even where audit committees might have been set up mainly to meet listing requirements, they have proved their worth and developed into essential committees of the board. Similarly, recently published research in the UK concludes that the majority of companies with audit committees are enthusiastic about their value to their businesses. They offer added assurance to the shareholders that the auditors, who act on their behalf, are in a position to safeguard their interests.

4.35 The Committee, therefore, recommends that all listed companies should establish an audit committee. Our further recommendations on audit committees are as follows:

(a) Audit committees should be formally constituted to ensure that they have a clear relationship with the boards to whom they are answerable and to whom they should report regularly. They should be given written terms of reference which deal adequately with their membership, authority and duties, and they should normally meet at least twice a year.

(b) There should be a minimum of three members. Membership should be confined to the non-executive directors of the company and a majority of the non-executives serving on the committee should be independent, as defined in paragraph 4.12 above. Membership of the committee should be disclosed in the annual report.

(c) The external auditor should normally attend audit committee meetings, as should the finance director. As the board as a whole is responsible for the financial statements, other board members should also have the right to attend. The committee should have a discussion with the external auditors, at least once a year, without executive board members present, to ensure that there are no unresolved issues of concern.

(d) The audit committee should have explicit authority to investigate any matters within its terms of reference, the resources which it needs to do so, and full access to information. The committee should be able to obtain external professional advice and to invite outsiders with relevant experience to attend if necessary.

4.37 The Committee, therefore, regards the appointment of properly constituted audit committees as an important step in raising standard of corporate governance. Their effectiveness depends on their having a strong chairman who has the confidence of the board and of the auditors, and on the quality of the non-executive directors. Membership of an audit committee is a demanding task requiring commitment, training and skill. The directors concerned need to have sufficient understanding of the issues to be dealt with by the committee to take an active part in its proceedings. This is why committees should, if it is appropriate and within their authority, be able to invite outsiders with relevant experience to attend meetings.

4.38 The external auditors should be present at the board meeting when the annual report and accounts are approved and preferably when the half-yearly report is considered as well.

Internal audit

4.39 The function of the internal auditors is complementary to, but different from, that of the outside auditors. We regard it as good practice for companies to establish internal audit functions to undertake regular monitoring of key controls and procedures. Such regular monitoring is an integral part of a company's system of internal control and helps to ensure its effectiveness. An internal audit function is well placed to undertake investigations on behalf of the audit committee and to follow up any suspicion of fraud. It is essential that the heads of internal audit should have unrestricted access to the chairman of the audit committee in order to ensure the independence of their position.

Board remuneration

4.40 The over-riding principle in respect of board remuneration is that of openness. Shareholders are entitled to a full and clear statement of directors' present and future benefits, and of how they have been determined. We recommend that in disclosing directors' total emoluments and those of the chairman and highest-paid UK director, separate figures should be given for their salary and performance-related elements and that the criteria on which performance is measured should be explained. Relevant information about stock options, stock appreciation rights, and pension contributions should also be given.

4.41 In addition, we recommend that future service contracts should not exceed 3 years without shareholders' approval, and that the Companies Act should be amended in line with this recommendation. This would strengthen shareholder control over levels of compensation for loss of office.

4.42 We also recommend that boards should appoint remuneration committees, consisting wholly or mainly of non-executive directors and chaired by a non-executive director, to recommend to the board the remuneration of the executive directors in all its forms, drawing on outside advice as necessary. Executive directors should play no part in decisions on their own remuneration. Membership of the remuneration committee should appear in the Directors' Report. Best practice in this field is set out in PRONED's Remuneration Committee guidelines, published in 1992.

4.43 The Committee has received proposal for giving shareholders the opportunity to determine matters, such as directors' pay at general meetings, but does not see how these suggestions could be made workable. A director's remuneration is not a matter which can be sensibly reduced to a vote for or against; were the vote to go against a particular remuneration package, the board would still have to determine the remuneration of the director concerned. In addition, there are such practical considerations as the need to agree directors' remuneration on appointment.

4.44 Shareholders require that the remuneration of directors should be both fair and competitive. Striking this balance involves detailed consideration of the kind which a remuneration committee, whose members have no personal interest in the outcome, can give to the matter. Remuneration committees need to have the interests of the company and the shareholders always in mind in coming to their decisions and the chairman of the committee should be available to respond to any concerns of shareholders at the Annual General Meeting.

4.45 The Annual General Meeting provides the opportunity for shareholder to make their views on such matters as director's benefits known to their boards. It is the Committee's view that shareholder can play a more practical governance role by aiming to influence board policies in this way, than by seeking to make the detail of board decisions subject to their vote.

4.46 Further change to the rules for disclosure, such as lengthening the list of directors whose remuneration is individually identified, and the role which shareholders could play, either in vioting on particular aspects of remuneration or in tabling advisory resolutions along lines now developing in the USA, will need to be reviewed in the light of experience. Directors' contracts and pay are aspects of board accountability which the Committee will continue to monitor in the expectation that they will be on the agenda of our successor body.

Financial reports

4.47   A basic weakness in the current system of financial reporting is the possibility of different accounting treatments being applied to, essentially the same facts, with the consequence that different results or financial positions could be reported, each apparently complying with the over riding requirement to show a true and fair view. Regardless of how far the market can understand the implications of alternative accounting treatments or see through presentation techniques designed to show a company's figures in the most flattering light, there are advantages to investors, analysts, other accounts users and ultimately to the company itself in financial reporting rules which limit the scope for uncertainty and manipulation.

4.48   The lifeblood of markets is information and barriers to the flow of relevant information represent imperfections in the market. The need to sift and correct the information put out by companies adds cost and uncertainty to the market's pricing function. The more the activities of companies are transparent, the more accurately will their securities be valued.

4.49   In addition, the wider the scope for alternative treatments, the less useful financial reports become in terms of comparability — over time and between companies.

4.50   What shareholders (and others) need from the report and accounts is a coherent narrative, supported by the figures, of the company's performance and prospects. We recommend that boards should pay particular attention to their duty to present a balance, and understandable assessment of their company's position. Balance requires that setbacks should be dealt with as well as successes, while the need for the report to be readily understood emphasizes that words are as important as figures.

4.51 The cardinal principle of financial reporting is that the view presented should be true and fair. Further principles are that boards should aim for the highest level of disclosure consonant with presenting reports, which are understandable and with avoiding damage to their competitive position. They should also aim to ensure the integrity and consistency of their reports, and they should meet the spirit as well as the letter of reporting standards.

4.52 The Committee wholeheartedly endorses the objectives of the Financial Reporting Council and the Accounting Standards Board in setting reporting standards. It also welcomes the action being taken by the Financial Reporting Review Panel over companies whose accounts fall below accepted reporting standards.

4.53 The Committee recognizes the advantage to users of reports and accounts of some explanation of the factors likely to influence their company's future progress. The inclusion of an essentially forward-looking Operating and Financial Review, along the lines developed by the Accounting Standards Board for consultation, would serve this purpose.

Reporting practice

4.54 Listed companies publish full financial statements annually and half-yearly reports in the interim. In between these major announcements, board may need to keep shareholders and the market in touch with their company's progress. The guiding principle once again is openness and boards should aim for any intervening statements to be widely circulated, in fairness to individual shareholders and to minimize the possibility of insider trading.

4.55 If companies reported quarterly, the need for more informal methods of keeping investors informed would be diminished.

Quarterly reporting would, however, involve additional costs for companies and ultimately for their shareholders and has not been recommended to us by shareholder bodies, who accept the present pattern of reporting by boards.

4.56   We consider that interim reports should be expanded in order to increase their value to users. We recommend that:

(a)   balance sheet information should be included with the interim report. There should not be a requirement for a full audit, but the interim report should be reviewed by the auditors, who should discuss their findings with the audit committee;

(b)   the continuing obligations laid down by the London Stock Exchange on UK companies admitted to listing should be amended to that effect and the Auditing Practices Board should develop appropriate review guidance;

(c)   the Accounting Standards Board in conjunction with the London Stock Exchange should clarify. The accounting principles which companies should follow in preparing interim reports;

(d)   a requirement for inclusion of cash flow information in interim reports should be considered by our successor body.

4.57   Research has shown that the most widely read part of company reports is the opening statement, normally by the chairman. It is therefore of special importance that it should provide a balanced and readable summary of the company's performance and prospects and that it should represent the collective view of the board.

4.58   The demand for an ever-increasing amount of detail in reports and accounts has to be weighed against the need for them to be understandable by the reasonably informed shareholder. Simplified forms of report, including the shortened version of the accounts, allow boards to address shareholders who would prefer such a statement, but make the need for the assessment to be balanced even more exacting.

4.59   Although a company's published reports and its Annual General Meeting are its primary channels of communication with shareholders, companies, and their major shareholders may need to be in touch more frequently. The Institutional Shareholders' Committee's Statement on the Responsibilities of Institutional Shareholders gives practical guidance on how shareholders can best exercise their responsibilities as owners in this regard. We fully endorse their recommendation that there should be regular contact between companies and their majority institutional shareholders at senior level and that such matters as board strategy and structure should be kept under review.

Abstracts from Title III and Title IV of the Sarbanes-Oxley Act of 2002

Public Law 107–204 — July 30, 2002
107th Congress

An Act

To protect investors by improving the accuracy and reliability of corporate disclosures made pursuant to the securities laws, and for other purposes. Be it enacted by the Senate and House of Representatives of the United States of America in Congress assembled,

Section 1. Short title
Table of contents.

(a) Short title — This Act may be cited as the "Sarbanes-Oxley Act of 2002"

(b) Table of contents — The table of contents for this Act is as follows:
Sec.1. Short title; Table of contents
Sec.2. Definitions

Title III — Corporate Responsibility

Sec.301 Public company audit committees
Sec.302 Corporate responsibility for financial reports
Sec.303 Improper influence on conduct of audits
Sec.304 Forfeiture of certain bonuses and profits
Sec.305 Officer and director bars and penalties
Sec.306 Insider trades during pension fund blackout periods
Sec.307 Rules of professional responsibility for attorneys
Sec.308 Fair funds for investors

Title IV — Enhanced Financial Disclosures

Sec. 2. Definitions

(a) In General — In this Act, the following definitions shall apply:

(1) Appropriate state regulatory authority — The term "appropriate State regulatory authority" means the State agency or other authority responsible for the licensure or other regulation of the practice of accounting in the State or States having jurisdiction over a registered public accounting firm or associated person thereof, with respect to the matter in question.

(2) Audit — The term "audit" means an examination of the financial statements of any issuer by an independent public accounting firm in accordance with the rules of the Board or the Commission (or, for the period preceding the adoption of applicable rules of the Board under Section 103, in accordance with then-applicable generally accepted auditing and related standards for such purposes), for the purpose of expressing an opinion on such statements.

(3) Audit committee — The term "audit committee" means —

(A) a committee (or equivalent body) established by and amongst the board of directors of an issuer for the purpose of overseeing the accounting and financial reporting processes of the issuer and audits of the financial statements of the issuer; and

(B) if no such committee exists with respect to an issuer, the entire board of directors of the issuer.

(4) Audit report — The term "audit report" means a document or other record —

(A) prepared following an audit performed for purposes of compliance by an issuer with the requirements of the securities laws; and
(B) in which a public accounting firm either —

(i) sets forth the opinion of that firm regarding a financial statement, report, or other document; or
(ii) asserts that no such opinion can be expressed.

(5) Board — The term "Board" means the Public Company Accounting Oversight Board established under Section 101.
(6) Commission — The term "Commission" means the Securities and Exchange Commission.
(7) Issuer — The term "issuer" means an issuer (as defined in Section 3 of the Securities Exchange Act of 1934 (15 U.S.C. 78c)), the securities of which are registered under section 12of that Act (15 U.S.C. 78l), or that is required to file reports under section 15(d) (15 U.S.C. 78o(d)), or that files or has filed a registration statement that has not yet become effective under the Securities Act of 1933 (15 U.S.C. 77a et seq.), and that it has not withdrawn.
(8) Non-audit services — The term "non-audit services" means any professional services provided to an issuer by a registered public accounting firm, other than those provided to an issuer in connection with an audit or a review of the financial statements of an issuer.
(9) Person associated with a public accounting firm —

(A) In General — The terms "person associated with a public accounting firm" (or with a "registered public accounting firm") and "associated person of a public accounting firm" (or of a "registered public accounting firm") mean any individual proprietor, partner, shareholder, principal, accountant, or other professional employee of a public accounting firm, or any other independent contractor or entity that, in connection with the preparation or issuance of any audit report —

(i) shares in the profits of, or receives compensation in any other form from, that firm; or
(ii) participates as agent or otherwise on behalf of such accounting firm in any activity of that firm.

(B) Exemption authority — The Board may, by rule, exempt persons engaged only in ministerial tasks from the definition in subparagraph (A), to the extent that the Board determines that any such exemption is consistent with the purposes of this Act, the public interest, or the protection of investors.

(10) Professional standards — The term "professional standards" means —

(A) accounting principles that are —

(i) established by the standard setting body described in Section 19(b) of the Securities Act of 1933, as amended by this Act, or prescribed by the Commission under section 19(a) of that Act (15 U.S.C. 17a(s)) or section 13(b) of the Securities Exchange Act of 1934(15 U.S.C. 78a(m)); and
(ii) relevant to audit reports for particular issuers, or dealt with in the quality control system of a particular registered public accounting firm; and

(B) auditing standards, standards for attestation engagements, quality control policies and procedures, ethical and competency standards, and independence standards (including rules implementing title II) that the Board or the Commission determines —

(i) relate to the preparation or issuance of audit reports for issuers; and

(ii) are established or adopted by the Board undersection 103(a), or are promulgated as rules of the Commission.

(11) Public accounting firm — The term "public accounting firm" means —

(A) a proprietorship, partnership, incorporated association, corporation, limited liability company, limited liability partnership, or other legal entity that is engaged in the practice of public accounting or preparing or issuing audit reports; and
(B) to the extent so designated by the rules of the Board, any associated person of any entity described in subparagraph (A).

(12) Registered public accounting firm — The term "registered public accounting firm" means a public accounting firm registered with the Board in accordance with this Act.

(13) Rules of the board — The term "rules of the Board" means the bylaws and rules of the Board (as submitted to, and approved, modified, or amended by the Commission, in accordance with Section 107), and those stated policies, practices, and interpretations of the Board that the Commission, by rule, may deem to be rules of the Board, as necessary or appropriate in the public interest or for the protection of investors.

(14) Security — The term "security" has the same meaning as in Section 3(a) of the Securities Exchange Act of 1934 (15 U.S.C. 78c(a)).

(15) Securities laws — The term "securities laws" means the provisions of law referred to in section 3(a)(47) of the Securities Exchange Act of 1934 (15 U.S.C. 78c(a)(47)), as amended by this Act, and includes the rules, regulations, and orders issued by the Commission thereunder.

(16) State — The term "State" means any State of the United States, the District of Columbia, Puerto Rico, the Virgin Islands, or any other territory or possession of the United States.

(b) Conforming amendment — Section 3(a)(47) of the Securities Exchange Act of 1934 (15 U.S.C. 78c(a)(47)) is amended by inserting "the Sarbanes-Oxley Act of 2002," before "the Public".

[Titles I–II Are omitted in this abstract]

Title III — Corporate responsibilitys

Sec. 301. Public company audit committees

Section 10A of the Securities Exchange Act of 1934 (15 U.S.C.78f) is amended by adding at the end the following:

"(m) Standards relating to audit committees—

"(1) Commission rules —

"(A) In general — Effective not later than 270 days after the date of enactment of this subsection, the Commission shall, by rule, direct the national securities exchanges and national securities associations to prohibit the listing of any security of an issuer that is not in compliance with the requirements of any portion of paragraphs (2) through (6).

"(B) Opportunity to cure defects — The rules of the Commission under subparagraph (A) shall provide for appropriate procedures for an issuer to have an opportunity to cure any defects that would be the basis for a prohibition under subparagraph (A), before the imposition of such prohibition.

"(2) Responsibilities relating to registered public accounting firms — The audit committee of each issuer, in its capacity as a committee of the board of directors, shall be directly responsible for the appointment, compensation, and oversight of the work of any registered public accounting firm employed by that issuer (including resolution of disagreements between management and the auditor regarding financial reporting) for the purpose of preparing or issuing an audit report or related work, and each such registered public accounting firm shall report directly to the audit committee.

"(3) Independence —

"(A) In general — Each member of the audit committee of the issuer shall be a member of the board of directors of the issuer, and shall otherwise be independent.

"(B) Criteria — In order to be considered to be independent for purposes of this paragraph, a member of an audit committee of an issuer may not, other than in his or her capacity as a member of the audit committee, the board of directors, or any other board committee —

"(i) accept any consulting, advisory, or other compensatory fee from the issuer; or

"(ii) be an affiliated person of the issuer or any subsidiary thereof.

"(C) Exemption authority — The Commission may exempt from the requirements of subparagraph (B) a particular relationship with respect to audit committee members, as the Commission determines appropriate in light of the circumstances.

"(4) Complaints — Each audit committee shall establish procedures for —

"(A) the receipt, retention, and treatment of complaints received by the issuer regarding accounting, internal accounting controls, or auditing matters; and

"(B) the confidential, anonymous submission by employees of the issuer of concerns regarding questionable accounting or auditing matters.

"(5) Authority to engage advisers — Each audit committee shall have the authority to engage independent counsel and other advisers, as it determines necessary to carry out its duties.

"(6) Funding — Each issuer shall provide for appropriate funding, as determined by the audit committee, in its capacity as a committee of the board of directors, for payment of compensation —

"(A) to the registered public accounting firm employed by the issuer for the purpose of rendering or issuing an audit report; and

"(B) to any advisers employed by the audit committee under paragraph (5)."

Sec. 302. Corporate responsibility for financial reports.

(a) Regulations required — The Commission shall, by rule, require, for each company filing periodic reports under Section 13(a) or 15(d) of the Securities Exchange Act of 1934 (15 U.S.C. 78m, 78o(d)), that the principal executive officer or officers and the principal financial officer or officers, or persons performing similar functions, certify in each annual or quarterly report filed or sub-mitted under either such section of such Act that —

(1) the signing officer has reviewed the report;
(2) based on the officer's knowledge, the report does not contain any untrue statement of a material fact or omit to state a material fact necessary in order to make the statements made, in light of the circumstances under which such statements were made, not misleading;
(3) based on such officer's knowledge, the financial statements, and other financial information included in the report, fairly present in all material respects the financial condition and results of operations of the issuer as of, and for, the periods presented in the report;
(4) the signing officers —

(A) are responsible for establishing and maintaining internal controls;
(B) have designed such internal controls to ensure that material information relating to the issuer and its consolidated subsidiaries is made known to such officers by others within those entities, particularly during the period in which the periodic reports are being prepared;
(C) have evaluated the effectiveness of the issuer's internal controls as of a date within 90 days prior to the report; and
(D) have presented in the report their conclusions about the effectiveness of their internal controls based on their evaluation as of that date;

(5) the signing officers have disclosed to the issuer's auditors and the audit committee of the board of directors (or persons fulfilling the equivalent function) —

> (A) all significant deficiencies in the design or operation of internal controls which could adversely affect the issuer's ability to record, process, summarize, and report financial data and have identified for the issuer's auditors any material weaknesses in internal controls; and
> (B) any fraud, whether or not material, that involves management or other employees who have a significant role in the issuer's internal controls; and

(6) the signing officers have indicated in the report whether or not there were significant changes in internal controls or in other factors that could significantly affect internal controls subsequent to the date of their evaluation, including any corrective actions with regard to significant deficiencies and material weaknesses.

(b) Foreign reincorporations have no effect — Nothing in this Section 302 shall be interpreted or applied in any way to allow any issuer to lessen the legal force of the statement required under this Section 302, by an issuer having reincorporated or having engaged in any other transaction that resulted in the transfer of the corporate domicile or offices of the issuer from inside the United States to outside of the United States.
(c) Deadline — The rules required by subsection (a) shall be effective not later than 30 days after the date of enactment of this Act.

Sec. 303. Improper influence on conduct of audits

(a) Rules to prohibit — It shall be unlawful, in contravention of such rules or regulations as the Commission shall prescribe as necessary and appropriate in the public interest or for the protection of investors, for any officer or director of an issuer, or any other person acting under the direction thereof, to take any action to fraudulently influence, coerce, manipulate, or mislead any independent public or certified accountant engaged in the performance of an audit of the financial statements of that issuer for the purpose of rendering such financial statements materially misleading.

(b) Enforcement — In any civil proceeding, the Commission shall have exclusive authority to enforce this section and any rule or regulation issued under this section.

(c) No preemption of other law — The provisions of Sub section (a) shall be in addition to, and shall not supersede or preempt, any other provision of law or any rule or regulation issued thereunder.

(d) Deadline for rulemaking — The Commission shall —

(1) propose the rules or regulations required by this section, not later than 90 days after the date of enactment of this Act; and

(2) issue final rules or regulations required by this section, not later than 270 days after that date of enactment.

Sec. 304. Forfeiture of certain bonuses and profits.

(a) Additional compensation prior to noncompliance with commission financial reporting requirements — If an issuer is required to prepare an accounting restatement due to the material noncompliance of the issuer, as a result of misconduct, with any financial reporting requirement under the securities laws, the chief executive officer and chief financial officer of the issuer shall reimburse the issuer for —

(1) any bonus or other incentive-based or equity-based compensation received by that person from the issuer during the 12-month period following the first public issuance or filing with the Commission (whichever first occurs) of the financial document embodying such financial reporting requirement; and

(2) any profits realized from the sale of securities of the issuer during that 12-month period.

(b) Commission exemption authority — The Commission may exempt any person from the application of Subsection (a), as it deems necessary and appropriate.

Sec. 305. Officer and director bars and penalties

(a) Unfitness standard —

(1) Securities exchange act of 1934 — Section 21(d)(2) of the Securities Exchange Act of 1934 (15 U.S.C. 78u(d)(2)) is amended by striking "substantial unfitness" and inserting "unfitness".

(2) Securities act of 1933 — Section 20(e) of the Securities Act of 1933 (15 U.S.C. 77t(e)) is amended by striking "substantial unfitness" and inserting "unfitness".

(b) Equitable relief — Section 21(d) of the Securities Exchange Act of 1934 (15 U.S.C. 78u(d)) is amended by adding at the end the following:"

(5) Equitable relief — In any action or proceeding brought or instituted by the Commission under any provision of the securities laws, the Commission may seek, and any Federal court may grant, any equitable relief that may be appropriate or necessary for the benefit of investors".

Sec. 306. Insider trades during pension fund blackout periods.

(a) Prohibition of insider trading during pension fund blackout periods —

(1) In general — Except to the extent otherwise provided by rule of the Commission pursuant to paragraph (3), it shall be unlawful for any director or executive officer of an issuer of any equity security (other than an exempted security), directly or indirectly, to purchase, sell, or otherwise acquire or transfer any equity security of the issuer (other than an exempted security) during any blackout period with respect to such equity security if such director or officer acquires such equity security in connection with his or her service or employment as a director or executive officer.

(2) Remedy —

(A) In general — Any profit realized by a director or executive officer referred to in paragraph (1) from any purchase, sale, or other acquisition or transfer in violation of this subsection shall insure to and be recoverable by the issuer, irrespective of any intention on the part of such director or executive officer in entering into the transaction.

(B) Actions to recover profits — An action to recover profits in accordance with this subsection may be instituted by law or in equity in any court of competent jurisdiction by the issuer, or by the owner of any security of the issuer in the name and in behalf of the issuer if the issuer fails or refuses to bring such action within 60 days after the date of request, or fails diligently to prosecute the action thereafter, except that no such suit shall be brought more than 2 years after the date on which such profit was realized.

(3) Rulemaking authorized — The Commission shall, in consultation with the Secretary of Labor, issue rules to clarify the application of this subsection and to prevent evasion thereof. Such rules shall provide for the application of the requirements of paragraph (1) with respect to entities treated as a single employer with respect to an issuer under section 414(b), (c), (m), or (o) of the Internal Revenue Code of 1986 to the extent necessary to clarify the application of such requirements and to prevent evasion thereof. Such rules may also provide for appropriate exceptions from the requirements of this sub-section, including exceptions for purchases pursuant to an automatic dividend reinvestment program or purchases or sales made pursuant to an advance election.

(4) Blackout period — For purposes of this subsection, the term "blackout period", with respect to the equity securities of any issuer—

(A) means any period of more than three consecutive business days during which the ability of not fewer than 50% of the participants or beneficiaries under all individual account plans maintained by the issuer to purchase, sell, or otherwise acquire or transfer an interest in any equity of such issuer held in such an individual account plan is temporarily suspended by the issuer or by a fiduciary of the plan; and

(B) does not include, under regulations which shall be prescribed by the Commission —

(i) a regularly scheduled period in which the participants and beneficiaries may not purchase, sell, or otherwise acquire or transfer an interest in any equity of such issuer, if such period is —

(I) incorporated into the individual account plan; and
(II) timely disclosed to employees before becoming participants under the individual account plan or as a subsequent amendment to the plan; or

(ii) any suspension described in subparagraph (A) that is imposed solely in connection with persons becoming participants or beneficiaries, or ceasing to be participants or beneficiaries, in an individual account plan by reason of a corporate merger, acquisition, divestiture, or similar transaction involving the plan or plan sponsor.

(5) Individual account plan — For purposes of this sub-section, the term "individual account plan" has the meaning provided in Section 3(34) of the Employee Retirement Income Security Act of 1974 (29 U.S.C. 1002(34), except that such term shall not include a one-participant retirement plan (within the meaning of Section 101(i)(8)(B) of such Act (29 U.S.C. 1021(i)(8)(B))).

(6) Notice to directors, executive officers, and the commission — In any case in which a director or executive officer is subject to the requirements of this subsection in connection with a blackout period (as defined in paragraph(4)) with respect to any equity securities, the issuer of such equity securities shall timely notify such director or officer and the Securities and Exchange Commission of such blackout period.

(b) Notice requirements to participants and beneficiaries under erisa —

(1) In general — Section 101 of the Employee Retirement Income Security Act of 1974 (29 U.S.C. 1021) is amended by

redesignating the second Subsection (h) as Subsection (j), and by inserting after the first Subsection (h) the following new subsection:

"(i) Notice of blackout periods to participant or beneficiary under individual account plan —

"(1) Duties of plan administrator — In advance of the commencement of any blackout period with respect to an individual account plan, the plan administrator shall notify the plan participants and beneficiaries who are affected by such action in accordance with this subsection.

"(2) Notice requirements —

"(A) In general — The notices described in paragraph (1) shall be written in a manner calculated to be understood by the average plan participant and shall include —

"(i) the reasons for the blackout period,

"(ii) an identification of the investments and other rights affected,

"(iii) the expected beginning date and length of the blackout period,

"(iv) in the case of investments affected, a statement that the participant or beneficiary should evaluate the appropriateness of their current investment decisions in light of their inability to direct or diversify assets credited to their accounts during the blackout period, and

"(v) such other matters as the Secretary may require by regulation.

"(B) Notice to participants and beneficiaries — Except as otherwise provided in this subsection, notices described in paragraph (1) shall be furnished to all participants and beneficiaries under the plan to whom the black-out period applies at least 30 days in advance of the black-out period.

"(C) Exception to 30-day notice requirement — In any case in which —

"(i) a deferral of the blackout period would violate the requirements of subparagraph (A) or (B) of Section

404(a)(1), and a fiduciary of the plan reasonably so determines in writing, or

"(ii) the inability to provide the 30-day advance notice is
due to events that were unforeseeable or circumstances
beyond the reasonable control of the plan administrator,
and a fiduciary of the plan reasonably so determines in writing, subparagraph (B) shall not apply, and the notice shall
be furnished to all participants and beneficiaries under the
plan to whom the blackout period applies as soon as reasonably possible under the circumstances unless such a
notice in advance of the termination of the blackout period
is impracticable.

"(D) Written notice — The notice required to be provided under
this subsection shall be in writing, except that such notice may be
in electronic or other form to the extent that such form is reasonably accessible to the recipient.

"(E) Notice to issuers of employer securities subject to blackout
period — In the case of any blackout period in connection with an
individual account plan, the plan administrator shall provide timely
notice of such blackout period to the issuer of any employer securities subject to such blackout period.

"(3) Exception for blackout periods with limited applicability — In any
case in which the blackout period applies only to one or more participants or beneficiaries in connection with a merger, acquisition,
divestiture, or similar transaction involving the plan or plan sponsor
and occurs solely in connection with becoming or ceasing to be a participant or beneficiary under the plan by reason of such merger, acquisition, divestiture, or transaction, the requirement of this sub-section
that the notice be provided to all participants and beneficiaries shall
be treated as met if the notice required under paragraph (1) is provided to such participants or beneficiaries to whom the blackout
period applies as soon as reasonably practicable.

"(4) Changes in length of blackout period — If, following the fur-
nishing of the notice pursuant to this subsection, there is a change in
the beginning date or length of the blackout period (specified in
such notice pursuant to paragraph (2)(A)(iii)), the administrator shall

provide affected participants and beneficiaries notice of the change as soon as reasonably practicable. In relation to the extended blackout period, such notice shall meet the requirements of paragraph (2)(D) and shall specify any material change in the matters referred to in clauses (i) through (v) of paragraph (2)(A).

"(5) Regulatory exceptions — The Secretary may provide by regulation for additional exceptions to the requirements of this subsection which the Secretary determines are in the interests of participants and beneficiaries.

"(6) Guidance and model notices — The Secretary shall issue guidance and model notices which meet the requirements of this subsection.

"(7) Blackout period — For purposes of this subsection —

"(A) In general — The term 'blackout period' means, in connection with an individual account plan, any period for which any ability of participants or beneficiaries under the plan, which is otherwise available under the terms of such plan, to direct or diversify assets credited to their accounts, to obtain loans from the plan, or to obtain distributions from the plan is temporarily suspended, limited, or restricted, if such suspension, limitation, or restriction is for any period of more than three consecutive business days.

"(B) Exclusions — The term 'blackout period' does not include a suspension, limitation, or restriction —

"(i) which occurs by reason of the application of the securities laws (as defined in Section 3(a)(47) of the Securities Exchange Act of 1934),

"(ii) which is a change to the plan which provides for a regularly scheduled suspension, limitation, or restriction which is disclosed to participants or beneficiaries through any summary of material modifications, any materials describing specific investment alternatives under the plan, or any changes thereto, or

"(iii) which applies only to one or more individuals, each of whom is the participant, an alternate payee (as defined in Section 206(d)(3)(K)), or any other beneficiary pursuant to a qualified domestic relations order (as defined in Section 206(d)(3)(B)(i)).

"(8) Individual account plan —

"(A) In general — For purposes of this subsection, the term 'individual account plan' shall have the meaning provided such term in Section 3(34), except that such term shall not include a one participant retirement plan.

"(B) One-participant retirement plan — For purposes of subparagraph (A), the term 'one-participant retirement plan' means a retirement plan that —

"(i) on the first day of the plan year —

"(I) covered only the employer (and the employer's spouse) and the employer owned the entire business (whether or not incorporated), or

"(II) covered only one or more partners (and their spouses) in a business partnership (including partners in an S or C corporation (as defined in Section 1361(a) of the Internal Revenue Code of 1986)),

"(ii) meets the minimum coverage requirements of Section 410(b) of the Internal Revenue Code of 1986 (as in effect on the date of the enactment of this paragraph) without being combined with any other plan of the business that covers the employees of the business,

"(iii) does not provide benefits to anyone except the employer (and the employer's spouse) or the partners (and their spouses),

"(iv) does not cover a business that is a member of an affiliated service group, a controlled group of corporations, or a group of businesses under common control, and

"(v) does not cover a business that leases employees."

(2) Issuance of initial guidance and model notice — The Secretary of Labor shall issue initial guidance and a model notice pursuant to

Section 101(i)(6) of the Employee Retirement Income Security Act of 1974 (as added by this subsection) not later than January 1, 2003. Not later than 75 days after the date of the enactment of this Act, the Secretary shall promulgate interim final rules necessary to carry out the amendments made by this subsection.

(3) Civil penalties for failure to provide notice — Section 502 of such Act (29 U.S.C. 1132) is amended —

> (A) in Subsection (a)(6), by striking "(5), or (6)" and inserting "(5), (6), or (7)";
> (B) by redesignating paragraph (7) of subsection (c) as paragraph (8); and
> (C) by inserting after paragraph (6) of subsection (c) the following new paragraph:

"(7) The Secretary may assess a civil penalty against a plan administrator of up to US$100 a day from the date of the plan administrator's failure or refusal to provide notice to participants and beneficiaries in accordance with section 101(i). For purposes of this paragraph, each violation with respect to any single participant or beneficiary shall be treated as a separate violation."

(3) Plan amendments — If any amendment made by this subsection requires an amendment to any plan, such plan amendment shall not be required to be made before the first plan year beginning on or after the effective date of this section, if —

> (A) during the period after such amendment made by this subsection takes effect and before such first plan year, the plan is operated in good faith compliance with the requirements of such amendment made by this sub-section, and
> (B) such plan amendment applies retroactively to the period after such amendment made by this subsection takes effect and before such first plan year.

(c) Effective date — The provisions of this section (including the amendments made thereby) shall take effect 180 days after the date of the enactment of this Act. Good faith compliance with the requirements of such provisions in advance of the issuance of applicable regulations thereunder shall be treated as compliance with such provisions.

Sec. 307. Rules of professional responsibility for attorneys

Not later than 180 days after the date of enactment of this Act, the Commission shall issue rules, in the public interest and for the protection of investors, setting forth minimum standards of professional conduct for attorneys appearing and practicing before the Commission in any way in the representation of issuers, including a rule —

> (1) requiring an attorney to report evidence of a material violation of securities law or breach of fiduciary duty or similar violation by the company or any agent thereof, to the chief legal counsel or the chief executive officer of the company (or the equivalent thereof); and
>
> (2) if the counsel or officer does not appropriately respond to the evidence (adopting, as necessary, appropriate remedial measures or sanctions with respect to the violation), requiring the attorney to report the evidence to the audit committee of the board of directors of the issuer or to another committee of the board of directors comprised solely of directors not employed directly or indirectly by the issuer, or to the board of directors.

Sec. 308. Fair funds for investors

(a) Civil penalties added to disgorgement funds for the relief of victims — If in any judicial or administrative action brought by the Commission under the securities laws (as such term is defined in Section 3(a)(47) of the Securities Exchange Act of 1934 (15 U.S.C. 78c(a)(47)) the Commission obtains an order requiring disgorgement against any person for a violation of such laws or the rules or regulations thereunder, or such person agrees in settlement of any such action to such disgorgement, and the Commission also obtains pursuant to such laws a civil penalty against such person, the amount of such civil penalty shall, on the motion or at the direction of the

Commission, be added to and become part of the disgorgement fund for the benefit of the victims of such violation.

(b) Acceptance of additional donations — The Commission is authorized to accept, hold, administer, and utilize gifts, bequests and devises of property, both real and personal, to the United States for a disgorgement fund described in subsection (a). Such gifts, bequests, and devises of money and proceeds from sales of other property received as gifts, bequests, or devises shall be deposited in the disgorgement fund and shall be available for allocation in accordance with subsection (a).

(c) Study required —

(1) Subject of study — The Commission shall review and analyze —

(A) enforcement actions by the Commission over the five years preceding the date of the enactment of this Act that have included proceedings to obtain civil penalties or disgorgements to identify areas where such proceedings may be utilized to efficiently, effectively, and fairly provide restitution for injured investors; and

(B) other methods to more efficiently, effectively, and fairly provide restitution to injured investors, including methods to improve the collection rates for civil penalties and disgorgements.

(2) Report required — The Commission shall report its findings to the Committee on Financial Services of the House of Representatives and the Committee on Banking, Housing, and Urban Affairs of the Senate within 180 days after of the date of the enactment of this Act, and shall use such findings to revise its rules and regulations as necessary. The report shall include a discussion of regulatory or legislative actions that are recommended or that may be necessary to address concerns identified in the study.

(d) Conforming amendments — Each of the following provisions is amended by inserting, "except as otherwise provided in Section 308

0

of the Sarbanes-Oxley Act of 2002" after "Treasury of the United States":

> (1) Section 21(d)(3)(C)(i) of the Securities Exchange Act of 1934 (15 U.S.C. 78u(d)(3)(C)(i)).
> (2) Section 21A(d)(1) of such Act (15 U.S.C. 78u-1(d)(1)).
> (3) Section 20(d)(3)(A) of the Securities Act of 1933 (15 U.S.C. 77t(d)(3)(A)).
> (4) Section 42(e)(3)(A) of the Investment Company Act of 1940 (15 U.S.C. 80a–41(e)(3)(A)).
> (5) Section 209(e)(3)(A) of the Investment Advisers Act of 1940 (15 U.S.C. 80b–9(e)(3)(A)).

(e) Definition — As used in this section, the term "disgorgement fund" means a fund established in any administrative or judicial proceeding described in Subsection (a).

Title IV — Enhanced financial disclosures

Sec. 401. Disclosures in periodic reports

(a) Disclosures required — Section 13 of the Securities Exchange Act of 1934 (15 U.S.C. 78m) is amended by adding at the end the following:

> "(i) Accuracy of financial reports — Each financial report that contains financial statements, and that is required to be prepared in accordance with (or reconciled to) generally accepted accounting principles under this title and filed with the Commission shall reflect all material correcting adjustments that have been identified by a registered public accounting firm in accordance with generally accepted accounting principles and the rules and regulations of the Commission.
>
> "(j) Off-balance sheet transactions — Not later than 180 days after the date of enactment of the Sarbanes-Oxley Act of 2002, the Commission shall issue final rules providing that each annual and quarterly financial report required to be filed with

the Commission shall disclose all material off-balance sheet trans-actions, arrangements, obligations (including contingent obligations), and other relationships of the issuer with uncon-solidated entities or other persons, that may have a material current or future effect on financial condition, changes in finan-cial condition, results of operations, liquidity, capital expendi-tures, capital resources, or significant components of revenues or expenses."

(b) Commission rules on proforma figures — Not later than 180 days after the date of enactment of the Sarbanes-Oxley Act of 2002, the Commission shall issue final rules providing that proforma financial information included in any periodic or other report filed with the Commission pursuant to the securities laws, or in any public disclo-sure or press or other release, shall be presented in a manner that —

(1) does not contain an untrue statement of a material fact or omit to state a material fact necessary in order to make the proforma financial information, in light of the circumstances under which it is presented, not misleading; and
(2) reconciles it with the financial condition and results of operations of the issuer under generally accepted accounting principles.

(c) Study and report on special purpose entities —

(1) Study required — The Commission shall, not later than 1 year after the effective date of adoption of off-balance sheet disclo-sure rules required by Section 13(j) of the Securities Exchange Act of 1934, as added by this section, complete a study of filings by issuers and their disclosures to determine —

(A) the extent of off-balance sheet transactions, including assets, liabilities, leases, losses, and the use of special purpose entities; and
(B) whether generally accepted accounting rules result in financial statements of issuers reflecting the economics of such off-balance sheet transactions to investors in a trans-parent fashion.

(2) Report and recommendations — Not later than 6 months after the date of completion of the study required by paragraph (1), the Commission shall submit a report to the President, the Committee on Banking, Housing, and Urban Affairs of the Senate, and the Committee on Financial Services of the House of Representatives, setting forth —

> (A) the amount or an estimate of the amount of off-balance sheet transactions, including assets, liabilities, leases, and losses of, and the use of special purpose entities by, issuers filing periodic reports pursuant to Section 13 or 15 of the Securities Exchange Act of 1934;
>
> (B) the extent to which special purpose entities are used to facilitate off-balance sheet transactions;
>
> (C) whether generally accepted accounting principles or the rules of the Commission result in financial statements of issuers reflecting the economics of such transactions to investors in a transparent fashion;
>
> (D) whether generally accepted accounting principles specifically result in the consolidation of special purpose entities sponsored by an issuer in cases in which the issuer has the majority of the risks and rewards of the special purpose entity; and
>
> (E) any recommendations of the Commission for improving the transparency and quality of reporting off-balance sheet transactions in the financial statements and disclosures required to be filed by an issuer with the Commission.

Sec. 402. Enhanced conflict of interest provisions.

(a) Prohibition on personal loans to executives — Section 13 of the Securities Exchange Act of 1934 (15 U.S.C. 78 m), as amended by this Act, is amended by adding at the end the following:

> "(k) Prohibition on personal loans to executives —
>
> > "(1) In general — It will be unlawful for any issuer (as defined in Section 2 of the Sarbanes-Oxley Act of 2002), directly or

indirectly, including through any subsidiary, to extend or maintain credit, to arrange for the extension of credit, or to renew an extension of credit, in the form of a personal loan to or for any director or executive officer (or equivalent thereof) of that issuer. An extension of credit maintained by the issuer on the date of enactment of this subsection shall not be subject to the provisions of this subsection, provided that there is no material modification to any term of any such extension of credit or any renewal of any such extension of credit on or after that date of enactment.

"(2) Limitation — Paragraph (1) does not preclude any home improvement and manufactured home loans (as that term is defined in Section 5 of the Home Owners' Loan Act (12U.S.C. 1464)), consumer credit (as defined in Section 103 of the Truth in Lending Act (15 U.S.C. 1602)), or any extension of credit under an open end credit plan (as defined in Section103 of the Truth in Lending Act (15 U.S.C. 1602)), or a charge card (as defined in Section 127(c)(4)(e) of the Truth in Lending Act (15 U.S.C. 1637(c)(4)(e))), or any extension of credit by a broker or dealer registered under Section 15 of this title to an employee of that broker or dealer to buy, trade, or carry securities, that is permitted under rules or regulations of the Board of Governors of the Federal Reserve System pursuant to Section 7 of this title (other than an extension of credit that would be used to purchase the stock of that issuer), that is —

"(A) made or provided in the ordinary course of the consumer credit business of such issuer;

"(B) of a type that is generally made available by such issuer to the public; and

"(C) made by such issuer on market terms, or terms that are no more favorable than those offered by the issuer to the general public for such extensions of credit.

"(3) Rule of construction for certain loans — Paragraph (1) does not apply to any loan made or maintained by an insured depository institution (as defined in Section 3 of the Federal Deposit Insurance Act (12 U.S.C. 1813)), if the loan is subject to the insider lending restrictions of section 22(h) of the Federal Reserve Act (12 U.S.C. 375b)."

Sec. 403. Disclosures of transactions involving managementand principal stockholders.

(a) Amendment — Section 16 of the Securities Exchange Act of 1934 (15 U.S.C. 78p) is amended by striking the heading of such section and Subsection (a) and inserting the following:

"Sec. 16. Directors, officers, and principal stockholders

"(a) Disclosures required —

"(1) Directors, officers, and principal stockholders required to file — Every person who is directly or indirectly the beneficial owner of more than 10% of any class of any equity security (other than an exempted security) which is registered pursuant to Section 12, or who is a director or an officer of the issuer of such security, shall file the statements required by this subsection with the Commission (and, if such security is registered on a national securities exchange, also with the exchange).

"(2) Time of filing — The statements required by this subsection shall be filed —

"(A) at the time of the registration of such security on a national securities exchange or by the effective date of a registration statement filed pursuant to Section 12(g);

"(B) within 10 days after he or she becomes such beneficial owner, director, or officer;

"(C) if there has been a change in such ownership, or if such person shall have purchased or sold a security-based swap agreement (as defined in Section 206(b) of the Gramm-Leach-Bliley Act (15 U.S.C. 78c note)) involving such equity security, before the end of the second business day following the day on which the subject transaction has been executed, or at such other time as the Commission shall establish, by rule, in any case in which the Commission determines that such 2-day period is not feasible.

"(3) Contents of statements — A statement filed —

"(A) under subparagraph (A) or (B) of paragraph (2) shall contain a statement of the amount of all equity securities of such issuer of which the filing person is the beneficial owner; and
"(B) under subparagraph (C) of such paragraph shall indicate ownership by the filing person at the date of filing, any such changes in such ownership, and such purchases and sales of the security-based swap agreements as have occurred since the most recent such filing under such subparagraph.
"(4) Electronic filing and availability — Beginning not later than 1 year after the date of enactment of the Sarbanes-Oxley Act of 2002 —

"(A) a statement filed under subparagraph (C) of paragraph (2) shall be filed electronically;
"(B) the Commission shall provide each such statement on a publicly accessible Internet site not later than the end of the business day following that filing; and
"(C) the issuer (if the issuer maintains a corporate website) shall provide that statement on that corporate website, not later than the end of the business day following that filing."

(b) Effective date — The amendment made by this section shall be effective 30 days after the date of the enactment of this Act.

Sec. 404. Management assessment of internal controls

(a) Rules required — The Commission shall prescribe rules requiring each annual report required by Section 13(a) or 15(d) of the

Securities Exchange Act of 1934 (15 U.S.C. 78m or 78o(d)) to contain an internal control report, which shall —

> (1) state the responsibility of management for establishing and maintaining an adequate internal control structure and procedures for financial reporting; and
> (2) contain an assessment, as of the end of the most recent fiscal year of the issuer, of the effectiveness of the internal control structure and procedures of the issuer for financial reporting.

(b) Internal control evaluation and reporting — With respect to the internal control assessment required by Subsection (a), each registered public accounting firm that prepares or issues the audit report for the issuer shall attest to, and report on, the assessment made by the management of the issuer. An attestation made under this subsection shall be made in accordance with standards for attestation engagements issued or adopted by the Board. Any such attestation shall not be the subject of a separate engagement.

Sec. 405. Exemption.

> Nothing in Section 401, 402, or 404, the amendments made by those sections, or the rules of the Commission under those sections shall apply to any investment company registered under Section 8 of the Investment Company Act of 1940 (15 U.S.C. 80a–8).

Sec. 406. Code of ethics for senior financial officers

> (a) Code of ethics disclosure — The Commission shall issue rules to require each issuer, together with periodic reports required pursuant to Section 13(a) or 15(d) of the Securities Exchange Act of 1934, to disclose whether or not, and if not, the reason therefor, such issuer has adopted a code of ethics for senior financial officers, applicable to its principal financial officer and comptroller or principal accounting officer, or persons performing similar functions.

(b) Changes in codes of ethics — The Commission shall revise its regulations concerning matters requiring prompt disclosure on Form 8–K (or any successor thereto) to require the immediate disclosure, by means of the filing of such form, dissemination by the Internet or by other electronic means, by any issuer of any change in or waiver of the code of ethics for senior financial officers.

(c) Definition — In this section, the term "code of ethics" means such standards as are reasonably necessary to promote —

(1) honest and ethical conduct, including the ethical handling of actual or apparent conflicts of interest between personal and professional relationships;

(2) full, fair, accurate, timely, and understandable disclosure in the periodic reports required to be filed by the issuer; and

(3) compliance with applicable governmental rules and regulations.

(d) Deadline for rulemaking — The Commission shall —

(1) propose rules to implement this section, not later than 90 days after the date of enactment of this Act; and

(2) issue final rules to implement this section, not later than 180 days after that date of enactment.

Sec. 407. Disclosure of audit committee financial expert

(a) Rules defining "financial expert" — The Commission shall issue rules, as necessary or appropriate in the public interest and consistent with the protection of investors, to require each issuer, together with periodic reports required pursuant to Sections 13(a) and 15(d) of the Securities Exchange Act of 1934, to disclose whether or not, and if not, the reasons therefore, the audit committee of that issuer is comprised of at least 1 member who is a financial expert, as such term is defined by the Commission.

(b) Considerations — In defining the term "financial expert" for purposes of Subsection (a), the Commission shall consider whether a person has, through education and experience as a public accountant or auditor or a principal financial officer, comptroller, or principal accounting officer of an issuer, or from a position involving the performance of similar functions —

(1) an understanding of generally accepted accounting principles and financial statements;

(2) experience in —

(A) the preparation or auditing of financial statements of generally comparable issuers; and

(B) the application of such principles in connection with the accounting for estimates, accruals, and reserves;

(3) experience with internal accounting controls; and

(4) an understanding of audit committee functions.

(c) Deadline for rulemaking — The Commission shall —

(1) propose rules to implement this section, not later than 90 days after the date of enactment of this Act; and

(2) issue final rules to implement this section, not later than 180 days after that date of enactment.

Sec. 408. Enhanced review of periodic disclosures by issuers

(a) Regular and systematic review — The Commission shall review disclosures made by issuers reporting under Section 13(a) of the Securities Exchange Act of 1934 (including reports filed on Form 10–K), and which have a class of securities listed on a national securities exchange or traded on an automated quotation facility of a national securities association, on a regular and systematic basis for the protection of investors. Such review shall include a review of an issuer's financial statement.

(b) Review criteria — For purposes of scheduling the reviews required by Subsection (a), the Commission shall consider, among other factors —

(1) issuers that have issued material restatements of financial results;

(2) issuers that experience significant volatility in their stock price as compared to other issuers;

(3) issuers with the largest market capitalization;

(4) emerging companies with disparities in price to earning ratios;

(5) issuers whose operations significantly affect any material sector of the economy; and

(6) any other factors that the Commission may consider relevant.

(c) Minimum review period — In no event shall an issuer required to file reports under section 13(a) or 15(d) of the Securities Exchange Act of 1934 be reviewed under this section less frequently than once every 3 years.

Sec. 409. Real time issuer disclosures

Section 13 of the Securities Exchange Act of 1934 (15 U.S.C.78m), as amended by this Act, is amended by adding at the end the following:

"(l) Real time issuer disclosures — Each issuer reporting under Section 13(a) or 15(d) shall disclose to the public on a rapid and current basis such additional information concerning material changes in the financial condition or operations of the issuer, in plain English, which may include trend and qualitative information and graphic presentations, as the Commission determines, by rule, is necessary or useful for the protection of investors and in the public interest."

[Titles x – xi are omitted in this abstract]

Index